I Fort The Lore

The
SHRINE
of The Saint
MARGARET CLITHEROW

✝

AN ANTHOLOGY OF WRITINGS BY
PAUL SCREETON

Typeset by Jonathan Downes,
Edited by Corinna Downes
Cover and Layout by SPiderKaT for CFZ Communications
Using Microsoft Word 2000, Microsoft , Publisher 2000, Adobe Photoshop CS.

First published in Great Britain by CFZ Press

CFZ Press
Myrtle Cottage
Woolsery
Bideford
North Devon
EX39 5QR

© CFZ MMXI

ISBN: 978-1-905723-68-3

Andy Roberts had a picture of himself and his mum on the cover of *Strangely Strange*. I can trump his as I'm sitting on a markstone beside my mother. Was this the source of my megalithomania? It is Wensleydale in 1951. (Gordon Screeton)

The author (right) at Long Meg and Her Daughters stone circle. John Watson set the timer
for this shot on 24 August 1979. (John Watson)

The author about to squeeze through the 18-inch diameter hole in the centre of what is known as the Kelpie Stone, near Pannanich, Aberdeenshire. Legend avers that a woman seeking to become pregnant should pass through the stone in the direction of the River Dee's flow. Maybe our daughter Kathryn was so conceived..... (Pauline Screeton)

To mark the 50th anniversary of Alfred Watkins' rediscovery of the ley system, a celebration described as the 'Mystics' picnic' took place in Herefordshire in 1971. In the forefront of the picture are (left to right): Philip Heselton, Paul Screeton, Jimmy Goddard and John Michell. (Pauline Screeton)

CONTENTS

BOOKS BY THE SAME AUTHOR

Quicksilver Heritage: The Mystic Leys – Their legacy of ancient wisdom, Thorsons, 1974;
Abacus, 1977
The Lambton Worm and other Northumbrian Dragon Legends, Zodiac House, 1978
Tales of the Hexham Heads, private, 1980
Who Hung the Monkey? (A Hartlepool Legend), Printability Publishing, 1991
Seekers of the Linear Vision, Stonehenge Viewpoint, 1994
Whisht Lads and Haad Yor Gobs, Northeast Press, 1998
The Man Who Ate a Domino, private, 2002
Crossing the Line: Trespassing on railway weirdness, Heart of Albion Press, 2006
Mars Bar & Mushy Peas: Urban legend and the cult of celebrity, Heart of Albion Press, 2008
John Michell: From Atlantis to Avalon, Alternative Albion (Heart of Albion), 2010

INTRODUCTION

I think that is a jolly good idea,' was the succinct and enthusiastic response by publisher Jonathan Downes to my inquiry whether CFZ Press would be interested in a volume of my scribblings. 'Start compiling Paul.' So, here is the result. I guess I have Andy Roberts to thank for pioneering this approach to disseminating forteana and it was through reading his *Strangely Strange, but Oddly Normal* which spurred me to contact Jon. Andy has written quite widely within the fortean sphere and my scope has been even broader. Publishing my own magazines since 1969 has allowed me a limitless canvas upon which to indulge my interests and speculations; with the added luxury of having no outside editorial interference. In fact, I was also indulged by a series of editors at the *Hartlepool Mail* over the years who also allowed me privileged status in choosing what subjects I wished – however arcane or unfamiliar – to impose upon a doubtless largely bemused readership. As could be said, I was like a pig in shit. Though I suspect there was an unspoken understanding that articles on morris dancing and incest were taboo.

Where Andy's selection of material resembles a compilation for a 'Greatest Hits...' or 'Best of...' record album, this release is more in the form of one of those selections of 'A' and 'B' sides, plus out-takes. I have studiously refrained from the temptation to reproduce what I regard as the crown jewels from my last three books for another publisher, simply because they are very much still in print and still selling and I wish to direct the reader to those as well. In contrast, I doubt if much of the content here will be familiar to the reader, particularly as I cover such a wide spectrum and draw from a multitude of sources. But let any potential buyer be assured, nothing here would look amiss in an issue of *Fortean Times*. Also, despite many obscure sources, I guarantee a high level of erudition and entertainment value: the serious and the sublime; intellectual rigour with humour.

My anthology also deviates from Andy's in that I have chosen to place my selections into eight parts. As an avowed fortean I am all too aware everything is interlinked and categorisation has its drawbacks. However, this format collects articles with broad similarities and so allows continuity rather than resembling some rag-bag thrown together higgledy-piggledy without giving the reader some signage about the nature of the contents and has its own inner logic of coherent content. The sequence of eight parts – cryptozoology and evolution; forteana; shamanism; alternative local history; speculative archaeology; UFOs, rock 'n' roll and more leys; folklife; urban myths – should form a smooth passage through what in Dylan-speak might be called 'my back pages.'

Pigeon-holing in any form is anathema to any fortean and strangers still try to categorise me: a fortean, so you are uncritical and believe everything you hear and read; a folklorist, you must collect old tales of fairies and witches; paranormalist, so you believe any ghost story; ufologist, so you must believe aliens are visiting us; naturalist, so believe in evolution theory; elderly trainspotter, so you must decry modern traction; wrote the Pub Spy column, so must prefer real ale; wrote a column on the environment, so my Green credentials must be impeccable and stretch to campaigning against man-made global warming ... and so it goes on. As I write this, earlier today an acquaintance stopped me to mention some item he had read but I had not seen, to which he apologised and said: "No, you wouldn't read that sort of paper," followed by, "ask your wife, she'll have seen it." Tommy, and readers, I am not snobbish as regards 'red tops' but as I will demonstrate, you get a better class of urban myth in the broadsheets. Also as a former editor of *The Ley Hunter* and author of *Quicksilver Heritage*, I am expected to endorse whatever crank earth mysteries ideology is fashionable and all too often am assumed to be a pagan. When I reveal I am a Christian, and so as not to appear dull, happy-clappy or born-again, I add Gnostic, which equally has them confused, but we'll also come to that later. And as for being a cryptozoologist, perhaps I might be expected from the name to have sex underground with corpses.

Similarly, the education system attempted to cement me as another brick in the corporate wall. Before I even had an inkling there were better things to learn than what I was being taught, I sussed out that teachers were usually morons who did their best to humiliate pupils whenever possible in order to mask their own inadequacies and immaturity (at grammar school, 'Wild Bill' would pick his nose, line up globs of snot and see how far into the class he could flick them). Consequently, I regard myself as self-educated. I was reading Jack Kerouac's road trip rather than Bunyan's pilgrims' progress; Edgar Rice Burroughs's Mars instead of Jane Austen's country houses; Alan V. Insole's view that Rome's imposition of 'peace' in Britain was more akin to genocide in preference to the standard texts glorifying the civilising butchers; rather than explore Shakespeare beyond the syllabus, there was the excitement of John Osborne. Later came the Mersey Poets as more relevant than John Dryden and J.G. Ballard's surrealist landscapes eclipsed Thomas Hardy's Wessex.

On the fictional front I devoured all the Ray Bradbury, Arthur Machen, H.P. Lovecraft and Dennis Wheatley I could borrow or buy, but my real education began with non-fiction UFO shock-horror paperbacks and then the truly mind-blowing *Dawn of Magic* by Louis Pauwels and Jacques Bergier. This brought a seismic shift to my consciousness. They knew all that stuff taught in school was claptrap and hid the real world. My education had – as I already suspected – been an illusion, a pack of lies, propaganda and all schoolchildren were unwittingly brainwashed as pliable Manchurian 'O' and 'A' level candidates. P&B's endorsement of Charles Fort led me to his books, while I was also devouring all the varied oeuvre of Colin Wilson. Then came an article in *International Times* by John Michell which turned me on to Alfred Watkins and a new perspective on archaeology, history and geography, followed by John Keel and Jacques Vallee disposing of the extraterrestrial theory in ufology. My landscapes became enchanted and my skies took on a different hue. Oh, almost forgot, I'd discovered a new species – girls.

Maybe a little more autobiographical detail might help the reader understand my philosophy, development and wide scope of interests – particularly those showcased here. Like the best of Best Man's speeches I'll keep it brief. Born in West Hartlepool on 10 December 1945, to Gordon Edward and Elizabeth Screeton, I went on to be (mis)educated at West Hartlepool Grammar School and left with three 'A' levels for a career in journalism. Along the way, as a child I was a prodigy in nature study and kept tropical fish, amphibians and tortoises, then took up my lifelong enthusiasm for railways and with an inquiring mind read voraciously and rather indiscriminately all manner of books; fiction and non-fiction. With a good grasp of writing composition, an unbounded curiosity, thirst for knowledge and essential for my chosen trade, already a thirst and capacity for copious amounts of alcohol, I ignored my parents' ambition for me going to university and career in art or zoology for Grub Street and the University of Life. Here I learned camaraderie and guile, and furthermore honed my skills in interviewing, reporting and writing succinctly and accurately. And learned the importance of checking facts and not jumping to conclusions, never accepting anything at face value, never trusting those who approached you, developed bullshit detection and other skills which have stood me in good stead ever since and some of the results are here in your hands. Along the way I acquired a wife, Yorkshire-born lass Pauline, and together we have 'added to stock,' as we locospotters jokingly say; Kathryn and Ian.

I spent more than four years as an indentured junior reporter with the Billingham and Stockton Expresses, tried my hand woefully at freelancing, joined the *Hull Daily Mail* as a trainee sub-editor and made a final move to the *Hartlepool Mail*, where various posts and tasks included feature writing and being deputy chief sub-editor. On a less mundane level, in an act of neurological 'zapping' I had a quasi-mystical experience of sorts, where a visual image of English martyr St Margaret Clitherow of York instructed me to 'be yourself,' which I interpreted as meaning I should quit my job, where I had become very unhappy, and follow my ambition to write full-time. Having had all manner of fortean experiences, this was neither isolated nor unique. The past 13 years have proven far from lucrative, but the freedom has made me tremendously happier, generally more healthy, industrious and I get enormous satisfaction out of my literary output, whether it be books, journalism or contributions to small magazines.

The collection here requires little introduction as my chosen format has been to create a commentary throughout, placing the articles both in the context of their original publication, giving any extra information which has come to light and link them up. Although each selection stands alone – and indeed the book can be dipped into wherever the reader fancies - I hope the continuity is seen within that fortean milieu where nothing can be seen in isolation. Think of the clientele in a pub: all having their own complex lives and interacting socially, each taking that day's conversations home, telling their families and its members, who in turn inform their neighbours and colleagues. What wondrous webs we weave. And at root there's now't so queer as folk. Here are a great many tales about people and extraordinary events and beliefs. So, now enjoy.

Almost finished, but not quite. Just need to mention some technical points. Back to the selection. I was very tempted to take the 'Greatest hits...' option, but at the back of my mind was an anthology, *The Essential Colin Wilson*, which, as I recall, was what he or the publisher's compiler seemed to regard as core material to best introduce newcomers to his ideas and philosophy. I hope this anthology does precisely that and leads the reader to seek out my other books and articles. Lastly, the pieces here are largely as published, apart from some minor tweaking, such as making my meaning clearer. Again, enjoy.

PART ONE
CRYPTOZOOLOGY AND EVOLUTIONISM

CURSE OF THE HEXHAM HEADS

(The Unexplained, No. 117, 1982)

O ne afternoon in February 1972, 11-year-old Colin Robson was weeding the garden of his family's council house in Rede Avenue, Hexham, when he uncovered what appeared to be a lump of stone about the size of a tennis ball, with an odd conical protrusion on one side. Clearing the earth from the object, he found that it was roughly carved with human features, and that the conical protrusion was actually the neck. Excited by the find, he called to his younger brother Leslie, who was watching from an upstairs window. Together they continued the weeding and soon Leslie had uncovered a second carved head. The artefacts, which quickly became known as the Hexham Heads, were claimed by experts to be representatives of two distinct types of Celtic manufacture. One had a skull-like face and seemed to everyone who saw it to be masculine; it was regarded as the 'boy.' It was of a greenish-grey hue and glistened with crystals of quartz. It was very heavy – heavier than cement or concrete. The hair appeared to be in stripes running from the front to the back of the head. The other head – the 'girl' – resembled a witch, with wild bulging eyes and hair that was combed backwards off the forehead in what was almost a bun. There were traces of a yellow or red pigment in her hair.

Having removed the worst of the soil from the carved figures, the boys took them into the house. It was from then on that strange happenings began. The heads would turn around spontaneously, objects were broken for no apparent reason – and when the mattress of the bed of one of the Robson daughters was showered with glass, both girls moved out of the room. Meanwhile, at the spot at which the heads had been found, a strange flower bloomed at Christmas and an eerie light glowed.

It could be argued that the events in the Robson household had nothing to do with the appearance of the heads – that they were, instead, poltergeist phenomena triggered by the adolescent children of the Robson family. But the Robsons's next door neighbour, a Mrs Ellen Dodd, underwent a truly unnerving experience that could clearly not be so easily explained away:

> "I had gone into the children's bedroom to sleep with one of them, who was ill. My ten-year-old son Brian kept telling me he felt something touching him. I told him not to be so silly. Then I saw this shape. It came towards me and I definitely felt it touch me on the legs. Then, on all fours, it moved out of the room."

Mrs Dodd later described the creature that had touched her as 'half-human, half-sheeplike.' Mrs Robson recalled that she had heard a sound like a crash and screams next door on the night in question. Her neighbour told her that the creature that she saw was like a werewolf. And when Mrs Dodd went downstairs, she found - disconcertingly - that the front door was open. Whatever caused the phenomenon, Mrs Dodd was terrified, and was re-housed by the local council after she had told them of her experience. Eventually the heads were removed from the Robsons' home, the house itself was exorcised, and all became quiet in Rede Avenue.

Meanwhile, a distinguished Celtic scholar, Dr Anne Ross, had become interested in the artefacts. In the introduction to *Folklore, myths and legends of Britain*, a book published by Reader's Digest, Dr Ross was quoted as claiming that the Hexham Heads were around 1,800 years old and had been designed to play a part in Celtic head cult rituals. And, after the heads were removed from the Robsons' house by a journalist, and via a museum, they eventually ended up in the charge of Dr Ross. She recalled what happened next:

> "I didn't connect it with the heads then. We always kept the hall light on and the doors kept open because our small son is a bit frightened of the dark, so there's always a certain amount of light coming into our room, and I woke up and felt extremely frightened. In fact, panic-stricken and terribly, terribly cold. There was a sort of dreadful atmosphere of icy coldness all around me. Something made me look towards the door, and as I looked, I saw this thing going out of it. It was about six feet [two metres] high, slightly stooping, and it was black against the white door. It was half-animal and half-man. The upper part I would have said was wolf and the lower part was human. It was covered with a kind of black, very dark fur. It went out and I just saw it clearly and then it disappeared and something made me run after it – a thing I wouldn't normally have done, but I felt compelled to run after it. I got out of bed and I ran and I could hear it going down the stairs. Then it disappeared toward the back of the house. When I got to the bottom of the stairs I was terrified."

That, however, was not the end of the story. A few days later, Dr Ross and her husband arrived home from London to find their teenage daughter in a state of shock. Dr Ross described her daughter's experience:

> "She had opened the front door and a black thing, which she described

as near a werewolf as anything, jumped over the banister and landed with a kind of plop. It padded with heavy animal feet, and it rushed toward the back of the house and she felt compelled to follow it. It disappeared in the music-room, right at the end of the corridor, and when she got there it had gone. Suddenly she was terrified. The day the heads were removed from the house everybody, including my husband, said it's as if a cloud has been lifted; and since then there hasn't been, really, a trace of it" [the paranormal activity].

Paul Screeton holds two pseudo-Celtic heads: one made by Des Craigie (left) and the other by Colin Robson. The photograph dates from 1982, during Paul's pseudo-werewolf phase.

Presence of evil leads to exorcism

Before the heads were removed, however, there were a number of manifestations of the un-welcome 'lodger.' During those frightening months, Dr Ross insisted, the creature appeared to be very real. It was not something shadowy, or only glimpsed out of the corner of the eye. It was noisy, and everyone who came into the house commented on a definite presence of evil. While he never observed it directly, Dr Ross's archaeologist husband was fully aware of the presence of his unwelcome 'guest,' although he is not usually sensitive to psychic phenomena. The weirdness ceased after Dr Ross had the house exorcised and disposed of her entire collection of Celtic heads.

So, what was the origin of the Hexham Heads? Were they, as Dr Ross believed, Celtic – and somehow imbued with an ancient curse? The story took on a new twist when Desmond Craigie – then a truck driver – announced that the 'Celtic' heads were actually a mere 16 years old. They had not been fashioned as votive offerings by a head-hunting Celt – for, Mr Craigie claimed, he himself had made them as 'toys' for his daughter Nancy. He explained that he had lived in the house in Rede Avenue that was now the Robsons' home for around 30 years; indeed, his father had remained a tenant there until the previous year. One day his daughter Nancy had asked him what he did for a living. At that time Mr Craigie worked with artificial cast stone, manufacturing products such as concrete pillars. To explain to his daughter what he did at work, he made three heads for her in his lunch break, and took them home for her to play with. He recalled:

> "Nancy played with them as dolls. She would use the silver paper from Penguin chocolate biscuits as eyes. One got broken and I threw it in the bin. The others just got kicked around and must have landed where the lads found them."

Embarrassed by the publicity that his own handiwork had attracted, Desmond Craigie said he was concerned merely to set the record straight. Speaking of the heads, he said, "To say that they were old would be conning people." But Anne Ross was not entirely convinced. "Mr Craigie's claim is an interesting story ... Unless Mr Craigie was familiar with genuine Celtic stone heads it would be extraordinary for him to make them like this. They are not crude by any means." Scientific analysis has, surprisingly, been unable to determine the age of the heads.

Bearers of an ancient curse?

If the heads are indeed Celtic it is easy to imagine that they may be the carriers of some ancient curse. But if they are not, why is it that they appear to provoke paranormal phenomena? The evidence that they do so is strengthened by the testimony of another scientist, an inorganic chemist named Don Robins. Dr Robins was exploring the idea that mineral artefacts can store visual images of the people who made them.

He suggests that places and objects can store information that causes specific phenomena – an idea similar to Tom Lethbridge's notion that events can be 'tape-recorded' into the surrounding in which they take place. Robins believes, too, that certain minerals have a natural capacity to store information in the form of electrical energy encoded in the lattice structure of their crystals. Summing up the argument, Dr Robins states:

> 'The structure of a mineral can be seen as a fluctuating energy network with infinite possibilities of storage and transformation of electronic information. These new dimensions in physical structure may well point the way, eventually, to an understanding of kinetic imagery encoded in stone.'

Dr Robins drew a tentative parallel with a creature from Norse mythology called the wulver, powerful and dangerous, but well disposed towards mankind unless provoked. There are several reports of sightings of this creature in the Shetlands during the 20th century. It was his interest in the heads that prompted him to take charge of them. As he put them in his car to take them home, however, and turned on the ignition, all the dashboard electrics went dead. He looked at the heads, told them firmly to 'Stop it!' – and the car started! Back at his own home, Dr Robins in *his* turn began to find the presence of the heads disquieting. He described his reactions:

> 'There was no doubt that any influence that the heads possessed came from the girl. I felt most uncomfortable sitting there with them looking at me and eventually we turned them round. As we did so, I had the distinct impression that the girl's eyes "slid round" watching me.'

Perhaps disappointingly however, Dr Robins did not witness any paranormal events that might be caused by the heads. Yet there were some disquieting moments. One day upon leaving the house, he muttered to the heads, "Let's see something when I get back!" Moments later, he re-entered the house to collect a book he had forgotten. Outside it was fresh and blustery, but in his study the atmosphere seemed 'almost electric with a stifling, breathless quality.' Attributing the effect to the 'girl' head, he left hurriedly. He found nothing amiss on his return home.

The present whereabouts of the Hexham Heads is unknown. Whatever, there seems little reason to doubt that they really did produce phenomena similar to those classically attributed to poltergeists – that, somehow they acted as epicentres. But why? There remains the mystery of their age and origin – are they Celtic, as Dr Ross maintains, or were they really made in 1956 by a Hexham man for his daughter? Dr Robins' theory is that the power of an artefact to produce poltergeist phenomena depends, not on the maker, but upon <u>where</u> it was made. This may eventually throw some light upon the Hexham Heads; but clearly, there remain many questions to be answered.

Intrigued by the multifarious aspects of the Hexham Heads mystery, I spent a day in Tynedale doing primary research in 1977 and wrote a monograph on the subject, *Tales of the Hexham Heads*, which although run off a primitive printing press proved extremely popular. I condensed the material for this article in the Orbis partwork *The Unexplained*, masterminded by Peter Brookesmith and which may also have been reprinted in one or more

spin-off compilations from this best-selling project. What is not mentioned in the piece is that my investigative journalism rode on the back of an invitation to meet the prominent exorcist Dom Robert Petitpierre at a hotel in Wall, near Hexham, who pronounced an 'antiseptic' exorcism on the head created by Colin Robson. Over the subsequent years many articles have appeared on this topic with a distressing accumulation and repetition and exaggeration of plagiarised inaccuracies. Editor of *Fortean Times* David Sutton invited me in 2008 to write a two-part resume on the subject, but try as I could there was no way I could satisfactorily condense my greatly extended file on the matter. Hence I have simply bowed to logic and decided to write as definitive an account as I can, which hopefully will be published some time in the future.

A PERSONAL BLACK PANTHER SIGHTING IN NORTHUMBERLAND, 1983

(*The Shaman*, No. 10, 1985; *N-MAG RAG*, Vol.1, No.2, 1997)

I have written hundreds of articles during the past twenty years. This one has given me the least pleasure. If it had not been for the fact that its contents may be useful to help others, I would have declined Andy Collins' request for what you are about to read (written originally for *Earthquest*). This may sound melodramatic, but I have reason to feel this way.

A lengthier 'colourful' article has appeared elsewhere covering the events in a wider context of that day's happenings [1], but I want here to concentrate on a personal big cat sighting. I think that by revealing something of myself I may induce others to share similar feelings. What I will reveal may be crucial to our understanding of such fortean events. As for the sighting, it was 8 May 1983, a damp, foggy, inhospitable day. I was front seat passenger with John Watson. There was no one else. We were driving from Rosden standing stone in Northumberland when an all-black cat of panther form crossed the road 100 or so yards ahead of us from right to left and disappeared into the undergrowth. There was fencing with openings and it would have been easy for it to vanish into vegetation, but I do not recall it passing through the fencing – only its presence on the road. It appeared as high as an adult Doberman pinscher, twice the length and lower slung, moving with a powerful, quick feline gait. Afterwards John felt it moved slower and was greyish. Why I blurted out after the sighting, "Was that a deer!?" is a mystery also, as in no way did it resemble such an animal.

Despite the high strangeness, John neither stopped nor even braked. I had a loaded camera in my pocket and it never crossed my mind to attempt to take a photograph. In fact, our whole lack of real co-ordination and inability to have a common perception of the event is odd. John has since told me that he cannot but wonder why he did not stop. It is all as embarrassing to him as me, he having been a Northern UFO Investigations Network officer. Of course, May 1983 was the height of the Devon operation to find a marauding big cat. Three days before 8

May a large ABC had been sighted at Wendover, Bucks. As for Northumberland, a paragraph headlined PUMA HUNT recorded that 'Armed police and farmers in Bettyhill, North Sunderland, Northumberland, were hunting yesterday for a sheep-killer believed to be a puma'. But there were no details of the sighting to explain the instigation of such a search. [2]

Anyway, we were about 20 miles away. So what did we see? Was it real? It is, perhaps, not widely recognised that the black panther (*Panthera pardus*) is nothing but a melanistic leopard. Melanism is found frequently in some species of wild cats, where individuals have almost uniformly dark fur. Hence the so-called black panther. According to one author: 'Melanistic types are by no means rare in Asia, these animals having dark coats with barely distinguishable rosette-like markings. In other words they are the famous black panthers, which are found in some numbers on many of the islands of Indonesia.' [3]

As for the significance of the event. Well, it happened at NU084204 on the map, below Harehope Hill. Ley hunters may find some significance.

Without being drawn into the debate as to whether such creatures are, as Di Francis argues a truly physical but secretive species, or on the other hand animals on 'the outer edge' and paraphysical, I will make a few comments. Previous to this encounter, during what might be called anxiety dreams, I had a dread of being attacked by dogs. I was once bitten by an Airedale terrier. I have always liked cats but a few years ago I picked up a black one infected with ringworm and it bit me – causing my hand to blow up like a football and requiring tetanus jab treatment. Immediately after the 'panther' sighting the dog dreams ceased and occasional big cat ones replaced them. On 3 May 1984 it peaked with a leopard gently biting me and when I urged it to stop, it spoke to me! Shades of the leopard men of the Mau-Mau. This was a dream, of course. Andy asked me for some extra information on my sighting and experience – make of it what you will. I really think there could be a psychic dimension to these sightings which cause only certain people to see these anomalous big cats.

References:

1. Paul Screeton, 'Wild in the Country (Northumberland Deliverance),' *Northern Earth Mysteries*, No. 24, 1983
2. The Sun, 15/12/77
3. Guido Badino, *Big Cats of the World*, Orbis, 1975.

Despite what to all intents and purposes appeared to be a very large flesh and blood melanistic leopard and able to make a direct comparison from a black panther at Paignton Zoo that summer, my opinion now is that we witnessed a creature from daimonic reality, as author Patrick Harpur defines this fortean realm. I subsequently helped Patrick's talented illustrator sister Merrily with her book *Mystery Big Cats* by donating my anomalous big cat files to her, and my sighting is mentioned in her book. I don't dream of big cats these days.

SHIELSIAN SHAMANISM

By Doc Shiels and Paul Screeton

(*The Shaman*, No. 5, 1984)

Well, what do you do if you're a journalist offered a world exclusive? Adjust that jaunty, weather-beaten hat with a battered piece of card announcing PRESS in the brim and rasp "get me all the Fleet Street tabloids" to a minion. Drama and exaggeration aside, there are those who have the capacity to either put a convincing case for a fortean event to a hardened and dubious newsdesk of a popular daily or present to readers of *The Shaman* what amounts to a 'world exclusive.'

Basically, Doc Shiels has offered his account of an extraordinary series of monster sightings in letter form in response to my request for an article. Written in the same style as his 'Words from the Wizard' pieces for *Fortean Times*, after no little thought I have decided to – with a modicum of editing – present his account as the central part of this article. I have credited this piece under a joint authorship because I feel it benefits from perspective and also because I have been researching Tony Shiels for mention in a book on modern shamanism. So before we get to the nitty-gritty bones ('real,' etheric or otherwise) of the aquatic monster phenomenon, let's look at Tony 'Doc' Shiels. He's been featured in *The Sun*, so *The Shaman* spotlight should not be too embarrassing, though *The Sun*'s Argie jingoism may have – as he suspects – caused mindless violence to him from Task Force supporters. It might not have been a comfort to him at the time or afterwards in hospital, but there again the shaman has been called the wounded healer. 'Patriotic *Sun* readers' – as he puts it – beset upon Doc near Falmouth's waterfront and the results were a fractured skull, badly bruised ribs and a crushed right hand to Doc. There was a subsequent encounter with the bulldog breed. He then chose a period in Erin. However, it is a later visit to the Emerald Isle which particularly concerns us, but...

So, just who is this Doc Shiels character? What claim has he to be a celebrity? Columnist! Cartoonist! Monster invoker! Lexilinker! Showman! Er, golfer and Guinness drinker. Well, for fuller details read on.

Those who were lucky enough to be reshaped by the psychedelic era and the peak experience year of 1967 may have received illumination from the flower children's adult comic-cum-revolutionary vanguard publication *International Times* – better known as *IT*. Cartoon strips appeared within its anarchistically august pages, the 'Astounding Adventures of Ron

Wetlegge' being by Tony Shiels. In fact, a wide spectrum of people from the counterculture have contributed to IT and those from the magical/megalithophile camps have included John Michell, Anthony Roberts, myself and Doc. In those heady days of hippiedom, Doc not only contributed cartoons to *IT* but the 30 June 1967 edition had a strange collage of print on Page 2 about him. The cuttings appeared mainly from, it seems, the sensational Sundays with references to him having four children (?) since his marriage, claiming to rule various covens, detectives examining pictures in his home but there being nothing to implicate him in black magic, if asked to state his current occupation he replies 'demonologist, self-employed,' and mentions the publication *Jinx*, a magazine or play called *Jabberwocky* and *Thirteen....A Devil's Dozen of Macabre Happenings.'*

He was then misnamed 'Shields' by the less radical *The Guardian* (24 July, 1978) featuring his Punch and Judy busking activities in Falmouth under the headline 'Buskers pull no punches.' Ouch! But his Tom Fool's Theatre of Tomfoolery had received even greater publicity in the reactionary *The Sun*. Headlined 'The Weirdest Family in the Land!,' the page lead (28 April 1978) reported how the South-West Arts Council had backed a show with £1,000 which Doc admitted was "very rude and vulgar." He added: "I don't believe it is unsuitable for children. It is naive to think that kids don't have swearing and violence in their ordinary lives." The play called *Gallavant* was his own tongue-in-cheek poke at TV's sex and violence. In it daughter Kate, then 16, appeared topless and 14-year-old Lucy swore throughout the two-hour performance. Son Ewan, 18, wore a pink towelling 'nude' costume sporting three artificial breasts. Kate's twin Meg and 19-year-old Gareth also performed and inspired their 40-year-old dad. Good old Doc!

As for his Doc nickname, Tony is obviously a shaman-witchdoctor in the true sense with a strong rapport with nature and by his experiences with lake and sea serpents patently able to manipulate borderline wildlife. The use specifically by shamans of the term 'doctor' by Paviosto Indians of Nevada is interesting in the context of Doc Shiels, and Rosie Plummer told an interviewer: "Big serpents live in the lake ... these serpents have strong power. They give power to some shamans." So, no doubt, the interface between a wizard and monsters – reacting no doubt as a two-way phenomenon – is highly-attuned regarding a man of Doc's sensibilities. For not only previous to the 1983 account did he see and photograph his 'neighbour' Morgawr in Falmouth Bay, but is credited with having taken pictures which show detail of structure and colour of the Loch Ness Monster never before achieved in a picture of the lake denizen previously. For a full colour view of the beastie see *Fortean Times*, No. 29. The extraordinary photographic opportunity occurred around 4pm on 21 May 1977. The pictures became something of a sensation and I recall one national tabloid, the *Daily Mirror*, having a reproduction filling the whole of its front page of the edition I saw.

Back to Morgawr, witches in Cornwall had swum skyclad on several occasions in 1976/77 to invoke the sea serpent successfully. Not only was this the vicinity of the sea monster but what became known as the Owlman appeared around Mawnan Church. Now then, the bird-shaman was around at least as long ago as the Old Stone Age, and in the famed caves at Lascaux is - among various beasts - the figure of a crudely drawn man wearing a bird mask, having claws for hands and having the erect penis so often an indicator of dream or trance states. His spirit is undoubtedly in mystical flight. But tempting though it is to pursue this avenue of thought, we'll wing back to serpent forms. We've already mentioned the ill-fate encountered by Doc and he has written previously of a 'psychic backlash' he and others invoking monsters have experienced. Several members of his 'Monstermind' team have been caused illness and Doc diagnoses monster raising as the cause. Further discussion of all these matters can be found in various issues of *Fortean Times* and also the admirable *Alien Animals* by Janet and Colin Bord (Paul Elek /Granada, 1980).

However, the events of the Seventies have been matched to some extent by those of 1983. But let Doc take up the story...

Ponsanooth, Truro, Cornwall.
September 29,
1983

Dear Paul,

How are you? We're fairly wrecked, having just crawled back into Cornwall after an exhausting, exciting, boozy, adventurous, mad, wild and very weird couple of months in Mother Ireland. My Monstermind '83 invocations seem to have been incredibly successful (after a depressingly slow and fruitless start). Here's the news:

As you probably gathered, from the publicity, early in August I succeeded in raising Nessie ... a long distance invocation, as I was doing my shamanic stuff on the shores of a Kerry lake. American monster hunter Erik Beckjord then managed to capture the Loch Ness beastie(s) on video tape. Beckjord, I'm pleased to say, formally acknowledged my role in the affair and sent a message, via R.T.E., at the time. He was then very keen to fly me, and some of my witches, over to Scotland, but we had our own plans for the Irish lakes. Lough Leane, near Killarney, is a monster-haunted lake, according to local legends, but is currently badly polluted by the overflowing sewage of that tourist town. As one local jarvy said to me, "Sure tis full of the remains of continental breakfasts"! I've spent many hours, over many years, camping by Lough Leane, but the stink of it, now, is bloody awful and I'm sure no self-respecting payshta, organic or tulpoid, would stick to it for long. Anyway a few weeks back we decided to leave Kerry and head up the coast to explore the wild west. Eventually we arrived in the quite mysterious 'monster country' of Connemara, Co. Galway, which Ted Holiday used to find so disturbing. It was there, in Lough Inagh, that I saw my first Connemara beastie ... a dark hump rose up, just long enough to be photographed, then sank smoothly down. It was very strange ... as if the 'thing' had known I was there and had allowed me just enough time to take its picture! I was delighted, of course, with my good luck ... but that was just the start. A few hours later, we decided to stop by Maumeen Lough. 'We' by the way means Chris, Kate, Kate's boyfriend Charlie Nolan and meself. Again, a dark hump came up to have its picture taken, just as before. It was quite incredible, an exact repeat of the situation at Lough Inagh. Full of confidence, we applied our Sheilesian shamanism to other loughs ... some of which have been written about by Holiday and others ... but nothing else came up that day. All the same, two monsters in one day was really hitting the jackpot, and the photographs meant that I'd scored a hat-trick and got a bonus too (Morgawr, Nessie and a pair of Connemara 'worms'). But this was <u>still</u> just the beginning.

Continuing our exploration of the coast, northwards, we soon found ourselves on Achill Island, Co. Mayo. Now Mayo is my father's family county and Achill is known for its water dragons. Straheens Lough is where the Achill beasts are supposed to reside, but we didn't see a thing there. It's a beautiful island with an amazing variety of landscape. Now, here comes the golf connection ... I decided to take a look at the golf links at Keel, which happens to be beside Keel Lough (which is much bigger than Straheens). From the golf course I prepared to take a picture of the lough and it happened again ... another bloody hump! Much bigger than its Connemara cousins, about ten feet long and glossy, grey in colour, it moved through the water very slowly, then stopped ... as if to have its picture taken --- then slipped below the surface. I laughed out loud, the whole thing seemed utterly crazy, too good to be true, quite impossible. That's the problem, of course, it <u>does</u> seem too good to be true, so no one is going to believe us in spite of the photographic evidence. And it still hadn't finished.

We visited Foxford, home town of several generations of the Shiels family (our branch of the clan), which is very close to two of the biggest loughs in Mayo, Lough Conn and Lough Cullin, both of which have 'monster' reputations. I was keen to invoke something in what I regarded as our 'home' waters, but all we saw were a few odd wakes and ripples, caused I suppose by big salmon. These lakes are great favourites with anglers ... supposed to be one of the best fishing areas in Europe. We really pulled the stops out, in terms of wizardry thought (as far as we could), but the beasties kept out of sight. Later, down on Co. Clare, we saw our fourth monster ... a sea serpent this time, and with golfing connections. I was taking a look at the links at Leinch, overlooking Liscannor Bay, and talking to two elderly golfers from Chicago. We stood for awhile on O'Brien's Bridge facing the mouth of the Dealagh River, and up it came, a classic long neck and small head ... just like Morgawr ... and just long enough to oblige me with a picture. "What kind of animal is that?" asked the golfers. "I think it's a marine payshta," said I, with confidence. "Is that an Irish animal?" they asked. "It is," I replied, "they're quite common in the west"!!! The Americans accepted this information quite casually, as if it was the most natural thing in the world. They were golfers, you see, so they

Appropriate surrealist collage from Doc which is 'a snapshot which sort of illustrates raising a dragon in a glass of Guinness (or, rather, IN NESS)' with himself, a daughter and beasties.
(Illustration Tony 'Doc' Shiels)

would ... and one of them was called Murphy, his father came from Ennis, we talked about golf for quite a while.

So ... there we are. The impossible has happened again as it so often seems to do. My two rolls of film are now being developed and the negatives will soon be with the [Janet and Colin] Bords and the Fortean Picture Library. If, as a journalist, you'd like to do something with the story, go ahead ... it deserves to be published some-where. As I said earlier, I don't expect the monster-hunting 'establishment' to accept the tale of the pix, but that's their problem. I've done it ... in front of witnesses ... and I have the films to prove it. The negs will be available for any kind of scientific examination, and that's that. They contain (or should contain ... I hope nothing nasty happens in the labs!) clear background detail to establish the authenticity of the locale, etc. The only thing I regret is that I didn't have a telephoto lens, but blow-ups should reveal some detail.

I'm continuing Monstermind '83 until Hallowe'en and hope to get movie footage of Morgawr within the next few weeks. I don't really expect any results, I'm already well ahead with these four Irish critters ... FOUR of the buggers, begob! It must be some kind of world record ... should be in the GUIN-NESSIE book of something or other. I can hardly believe my luck; the luck of the Irish I suppose. I know that in some peculiar way golf is con-nected with this ... it really is a most fortean game (you can kill a pike with a gold ball). Oh yes, Loren Coleman has just sent me a clipping about a lynx on the links ... as if I invoked that, too, in New Hampshire!

Well, that's the latest news.
Hope you can use some of it.

What a stunning tale! There's not much to add. Doc included a postscript stressing Beckjord is not a pal of his, nor is Doc involved with Erik's hotel-based expeditions. However, I rang Janet Bord regarding the photographs and she relayed bad news. The monsters appeared, she said, as 'specks' and were particularly disappointing after the Nessie marvels. She kindly al-lowed me to see copies of two of the prints. The 'Moby Mick' of Keel Lough, Achill Island, Co. Mayo, resembles a white wedge shape in the water. 'Lissie' is rather more impressive as a long neck sticking out of the Delagh River estuary, Liscannor Bay, Co. Clare. Nonetheless interesting but such a disappointment. As Janet wrote in an accompanying letter – 'potentially exciting.'

Without using a telephoto lens I doubt if they could have been greatly improved, so for once that 'negativity' jinx so common in the paranormal field, or where the photographer really is desperate for the picture, cannot have been causing mischief. You win some, you lose some. It is all part of the frustrations which conspire to challenge the will of the shaman. But without loss, success can never be sweet.

Ponsanooth,
Truro,
Cornwall.
November 17,
1983

Dear Paul,

The enclosed bits and pieces may amuse you ... or more than amuse you? Yesterday, I received the photo blow-up from Erik Beckjord, taken from my original colour neg of what I regarded, simply, as a rather interesting dark hump in Maumeen Lough. As you can see from my (very rough) sketches ... and from the photograph [unfortunately beyond the scope of any reproduction here – editor] itself ... it could be something else. The blow-up is fairly 'massive' and very grainy, but the 'grain gremlin' revealed by this process appears to have 'ears,' 'eyes' and 'nose,' plus a bulky body area. The pointed ears and the prominent eyes are the most interesting features, from a fortean viewpoint. We seem to have a very 'alien' animal ... either a phantom lynx, or an aquatic 'Owlman' in my opinion ... right in the middle of a Connemara lough!!!

The coloured picture impressed me. I saw the face immediately, the ears and eyes being unmistakeable. The face not only is somewhat lynx-like but also slightly terrier-like. The extent to which my wife's simulacra spotting extended was to suspect two human babies' faces behind the beastie. Doc wondered if I thought his interpretive sketches [reproduced here] were not too far fetched when compared with the original photograph. Can it have been a spooky 'big cat' reclining on the surface of the water or an 'Owlman' type of entity rising from the lough? I remain impressed and baffled.

As I explained in the introduction to Doc's Irish antics here is the Wizard of the West in full flow. For more of the same I recommend his book *Monstrum* (Fortean Tomes, 1990, republished by CFZ Press, 2011), columns in *Fortean Times* and occasional articles in *Folklore Frontiers* where subjects included golf and shamanism, whales, Guinness and Punch & Judy plus his brief dropping of the 'Doc' honorary title. Tony Shiels has been accused of being a total charlatan; his most vocal and vitriolic critic being the late Mark Chorvinsky, who used his *Strange Magazine* to an almost manic level to demonise Doc as a liar. Mark at least published my defence of Doc, but failed miserably with his inability to either understand Shielsian humour or the trickster aspect of shamanism. Or have I been fooled? Whatever, the head of the 'weirdest family in the land' has kept us entertained and informed for many decades – long may he continue his profound tomfoolery.

Two sketches of a creature drawn by Doc Shiels which he witnessed rise from a Connemara lough and photographed.

FREAKS OF NATURE

(*The Mail*, Hartlepool, 9 March 1989)

Heard the one about the rabbit with one ear? No need to pin back your lug 'oles, just read on. When born in 1982 with one ear, sitting squarely in the middle of her fluffy head, the giant Flemish in the Trimdons became quite a celebrity. So odd was the appendage that the rabbit became known as Unicorn. Unlike recently-publicised freaks, the rabbit would seem to have no mysterious origin for its strange appearance. There was no Chernobyl-style disaster in South-East Durham to account for the freakish single ear. Unicorn was bred by James Lister, of Berry Avenue, Trimdon Grange, who had kept rabbits for more than 35 years and competed in shows. Unicorn was the first freak he had bred and he had never come across such a prodigy before. He commented:

> "I was told that millions of years ago rabbits had only one ear. Probably it was one of the many wonders of evolution that Mother Nature decided to equip it with two ears to make its hearing more acute for the purpose of surviving against predatory animals. As far as I can examine there's no evidence of rudimentary formation of normal ears. In fact, I'm not sure if Unicorn can hear."

I sought the opinion of zoologist and science writer Dr Karl Shuker. This is his reply:

> 'A relatively widespread teratological condition exists called cyclopia, in which the organism concerned possesses a single eye, positioned in the centre of the face – hence the Cyclops-derived term for this. I have not, however, previously encountered an auditory equivalent. Instances of one-eared animals are on record, but these refer to animals missing either the left or right ear. ... Certainly radiation can and does produce an exceedingly wide variety of genetic mutations among organisms exposed to this. Nonetheless, it would seem impossible to determine whether this one-eared rabbit is the result of radiation-induced mutation, or whether it was simply a mutant whose origin was totally unrelated to environmental

(epigenetic) effects. Perhaps the Chernobyl disaster was responsible for some/all of this Finnish town's mutated animals, but it may equally be modern-day folklore, comparable to the appearance of teratological freaks in the past being thought of as omens of impending disaster.'

Dr Shuker was referring to a rabbit born in 1986 in the village of Liljendal, where a complication was that Chernobyl is 600 miles away, but only ten miles away at Loviisa is one of Finland's own nuclear power stations containing two Soviet-built reactors. As reported in *The Mail* on 17 February this year, cancer cases have doubled among residents of a Ukrainian farming community contaminated by radioactivity from Chernobyl. The Narodichsky region was 30 miles from the plant and not evacuated after the accident, in which 31 people died. A report stated more than half the local children had thyroid gland illnesses. Moscow News reported there was only one freak birth a year there before the 'meltdown' but almost 80 pigs and 62 calves have been born deformed at one farm. We have enough odd ideas about rabbits from *Watership Down* to Playboy organisation entrepreneur Hugh Hefner transforming the humanised rabbit logo into rabbiipomorphic humans. But will we ever see a sexy, cute Bunny Girl with fluffy tail but only one central floppy ear? I doubt it.

Sources: *The Mail*, Hartlepool, 29/9/82' *Fortean Times*, No. 42, 1984; *The Shaman*, No. 7, 1984; *Daily Mail*, 21/10/86; Dr Kark Shuker, pers. corr., 12/7/88; *The Sun*, 16/12/89; *The Mail*, Hartlepool, 17/2/89

It was good to report some good news following the nuclear contamination and Unicorn's freakish appearance. Dr Karl Shuker kept in touch with the Listers and learned that Unicorn bore a litter of young. It seems this was the result of a liaison with a wild rabbit. Most interestingly, one of the kittens possessed its mother's one-eared trait. But here is the bad news. Apparently they all died shortly afterwards following a thunderstorm (omen?) and Unicorn herself later died, without producing any more offspring. (Paul Screeton, Countryside Concerns column, *The Mail*, 22 April 1989)

(Above and facing) Two views of Unicorn with (on the right) nine-year-old Kathleen Lister, who challenged her father's notion the freak was deaf. She said: "Unicorn turns her head when I call her name."

IMPOSSIBLE TO PICK UP RAQUEL

(Folklore Frontiers, No. 51, 2005)

The actress best remembered for playing a nubile cavegirl in a shrinking fur bikini, became known as the Stone Age stunna in an over-shoulder boulder-holder. Raquel Welch, in the film *One Million Years B.C.* as Loanna, was memorably plucked airborne by a flying reptile. Spoilsport Professor Neil Alexander, of the University of Leeds, an expert in biomechanics, claimed before the British Association in 1987, that calculations showed the pterosaur species called quetzalcoatlus, despite a wingspan of about 40-feet would still not have been sufficiently strong to lift an adult human female. Won't that scientific pedanticism spoil any repeats for all of us?

Naturally with so perfect a body – supposedly in her prime in 1967, Raquel measured 37DD-22-35, stood 5ft 6in (1.68m) and weighed 118lb (54kg), for Alexander and his statistician boffin mates – there were rumours of surgical intervention. For connoisseurs' peace of mind, I can report that former husband Patrick Curtis dismissed all but the possibility of a nose-job, revealing:

> "People have said she had her boobs made bigger, her ribs removed to make her waist so tiny and bits shaved off her thighs. Well, I've seen and kissed every inch of her, and it's all natural. There are no scars. You can't see the joins because there aren't any. In early pictures, Raquel has bumps on her nose, but her story is that an old boyfriend hit her and it was straightened out when she had it re-set in hospital."

Born Jo Raquel Tejada on 5 September 1940 in Chicago, Illinois, her father, Hector Tejada, was Bolivian, and mother Sarah Josephine Hall an American. Neither worked in showbusiness. Raquel has been married four times. The 1966 film *One Million Years B.C.* turned her into a legend, but her personal favourite is the made-for-television movie that she backed, *The Legend of Walks Far Woman* (1979), about a Native American. *The Three Musketeers* (1973) gained her a Golden Globe for Best Actress in a Musical/Comedy. Feuding with Mae West on the execrable *Myra Breckeinridge* (1970) was a distinct low point, but she showed plenty of her chassis in the film *Bedazzled*, which was recently remade starring Liz Hurley, who has the benefit of being three inches taller but deflates to a modest 32-24-30.

A collage from a cartoon strip of the Hammer film *One Million Years B.C.* Script by S. Moore and artwork by J. Bolton. (*House of Hammer*, Vol. 2, No. 2 (No. 19), November 1977 issue) ((c) TopSellers Ltd., 1977)

Yet, inevitably, the Welch image is stuck in the mid-Sixties dinothwoar saga. Having made an impression with Ursula Andress in the film of Rider Haggard's book *She*, Hammer Horror producers got only as far as still photographs of Raquel before deciding to cast her as the seductive heroine in *One Million Years B.C.* Before the film was released, Svengali-like Curtis distributed pictures of that body in a fur bikini costume, and as Welch observed: "That one photo did it all. It was like a tidal wave." And unsurprisingly there's quite a story to the skimpy clothing – longer than her onerous dialogue of "akita" (help!), "Tumak" (her co-star's on-screen name – and who remembers his real name?) and "seron" (pterosaur co-star of this article). On the opening day of filming in the Canary Islands, Raquel's seriousness over her role led director Don Chaffey to brusquely dismiss her with: "You've been thinking about this scene. See that rock over there? You just start from that rock and run across to that other rock. That's all we want from you today." The miffed actress saw an opportunity to steal the show by using her womanly wiles and secretly snipped away at her chamois leather costume, which was to shrink even further with regular immersion in sea water. Upon seeing that iconic publicity photo, one wag observed it was "hardly big enough to wipe a car window." In one year she was on the cover of 95 magazines; the staid *Time* even drooling "Raquel is raw, unconquerable antediluvian woman." Curtis' grooming for stardom had included singing and dancing lessons, and at 46 Raquel embarked on a singing career best forgotten as her voice left more to be desired than her frame. At the time she measured 38-23-36 and explained: "I was given a magnificent body. I've looked after it." Today she lives in Los Angeles and doubtless is still as fit as a butcher's dog.

Indeed, Raquel is still fit and well and the media recently celebrated her 70th birthday with glowing tributes. But back with *One Million Years B.C.*, this and other dinosaur films (although closely related, pterosaurs are not actually dinosaurs but volant ornitodirans) have fuelled Christian Creationists' belief that God populated the Earth with humans at the same time as giant reptiles. Forteans also have to face up to anomalies such as human and dinosaur footprints in the same strata (none of which seem particularly convincing) and artefacts depicting men and monsters together (intriguing for cryptozoologists and the topic features in Part Two). New species of pterodactyl are still being discovered, almost as many in the past 20 years as in the previous 200, from the smallest adults with 30-40cm wingspans, i.e. the size of a thrush, to the largest with 10-11m, a wingspan comparable to a spitfire. So one which could abduct Raquel may be waiting to be discovered. As for the sexy content here, this is explained by this having been extracted as part of the letter 'W' in the actress section of an abortive book project which found no drooling publisher: *Celebrity Tits Out For The Lads*. Shame, as I was enjoying the writing – and the research.

DARWINISM: JUST ANOTHER CREATION MYTH?

(*Foklore Frontiers*, No. 53, 2006)

Perhaps pomposity hides subliminal 'running scared' doubts when Mark Henderson warns 'the creationist movement, and its cloak of "intelligent design" theory' is perceived in the UK as a peculiarly American phenomenon. [1] For if this 'science correspondent' is what he claims to be, I see scant 'science' in his reasoning. The terms 'creationism', 'intelligent design' and 'evolutionism' are mutually exclusive. Creationists believe God created the world literally in six days, intelligent design posits that biological 'irreducible complexity' can only be the work of a designing intelligence and Darwinism relies upon random mutation coupled with natural selection. Henderson's pitiful inability to distinguish between creationism and ID is similar to the public's general lack of differentiating between paganism and Satanism. Henderson goes on to warn of the consequences of evolution denial,' which is an emotive phrase echoing the 'global warming denial' attack upon Bjorn Lomberg (the statistician who believes he has proven greenhouse effect believers to be alarmists), and both of which seek to lump those of opposing camps alongside Holocaust deniers. His paranoia even extends to seeing *The Daily Telegraph* as a propaganda sheet for ID and creationism.

Without any axe to grind, I have, however, long suspected Darwinism to be just another creation myth, little better cognitively acceptable than the Earth being created during a busy schedule during 4004BC. It may not be perfect, but ID is surely the way forward. The fossil record is punctuated by embarrassing gaps; evolution proponents guilty of faked data (melanised peppered moth) and many fraudulent fragments. As for survival of the fittest, the physically-sickly, psychiatrically-ill Darwin (see Prof Anthony Campbell and Stephanie Matthews, *Postgraduate Medical* Journal, 2005; James le Fanu, *The Sunday Telegraph*, 15/5/05) hardly engenders the alpha male model. Also, for a man who was to espouse the cause of evolution, marrying his first cousin, with all the heredity pitfalls that engendered, was hardly a sensible course. As for creationists, to them allegory is a dirty word and the *Bible* a literal record of our beginnings. With so much of interest within the fortean sphere and life in general, the origins of life has been a subject I have hitherto neglected. However, having noted an increased reportage in the media of evolutionary conundrums and refutations, I felt it apposite to take notice. It may of now only be a minor shift, but the evolutionary debate is back on the agenda.

As for scientists themselves, Charles Fort noted perceptively that for every expert there is an equal and opposite expert. I've just read that 'there are more than 90 different scientific theories on how dinosaurs became extinct' and here's me thinking scientists try to boil everything down to one theory rather than expanding options willy-nilly. [2] And here's another. A German team claims dinosaurs did not survive because their sleeping patterns meant their brains did not learn new skills properly. Unlike birds and mammals, reptiles do not experience slow-wave sleep, which helps the memory process needed for learning new tasks. [3] Anyway, evolutionary science would seem to my untutored brain to play some kind of chicken and egg game. Is it me, but do they date rocks by fossils or fossils by rock strata? I ask this, as a previously dated human footprint 40,000 years old left in volcanic rock in central Mexico and believed to belong to the first American immigrants, is now believed to be more than 1.3 million years old, and so, obviously, cannot, scientists say, be human. I ask you, is that logical? Talk about moving the goalposts, even whole playing fields, not to mention open/closed minds... [4]

Red rumpy pumpy
Here are a random selection of recent findings/thoughts/beliefs from the cutting edge of evolutionary science.

- Humans developed colour vision not to help the hunt for food but spot when would-be partners are sexually aroused (blushing primates' reddened bare rumps to human facial blushing). [5]
- A study by the University of London's Queen Mary College showed bees were drawn to the blue in paintings, despite being raised in captivity and never having seen a real flower, a colour associated with high-nectar blooms and which may 'help explain evolution.' [6]
- Ernst Haeckel created his 'tree map' of evolutionary relationships in 1870, but now a computer model has been utilised to fill in the missing gaps. [7] Wishful techno thinking?
- They cannot agree whether we are still evolving; 'proof' being that one in five people today has impacted wisdom teeth, while prehistoric humans appear to have had no such problem accommodating these third molars. So, has increased brain size come at the price of smaller jawbones? Or did genetic mutation 2.5 million years ago lead to smaller jaws and consequently more space for brain growth? [8]
- Just where did humans originate? The discovery of the first-ever chimpanzee fossils close to those of early human species could blow a hole in the theory of human evolution. Anthropologists at the California Academy of Science say it is the first evidence the two co-existed in the same place in the past. It was previously thought evolution occurred when humans moved away from the jungle. But now scientists may have to rethink how humans originated. [9]

- Same day as the above – synchronicity? – Mick Hume cogitated upon 'what makes us human', continuing 'human and chimpanzee lines first separated several million years ago' and because fruit flies share 50% of their genes with humans, should we start treating them as half-cousins too? [10] And they say philosophy is dead.
- A team of Dutch and American scientists believe genetic loneliness stems from prehistoric times when hunter gatherers led a solitary existence so as to avoid sharing food and thus increasing their chances of survival. [11] So much for the generally believed team effort scenario to snare large game.
- Steve Jones, Professor of Genetics at University College London, hailed the bicycle's impact upon human evolution by its ending of the inbreeding that was once endemic in village communities. [12] He has also been quoted as saying a long way back in evolution the male chromosome was big and strong. "Now it's a shagged out version of the X," he confides. [13]

Pissed – hic - as a – hic – newt

- Parisian scientists suggested human hiccups are a hangover from our evolutionary past as amphibians. Although our frog-like breathing abilities have gone, we retain the necessary nerve circuitry and it is this that bursts back into life when we get hiccups. [14] Ever seen a salamander hiccupping?
- Not to forget those diminutive creatures found by fossil-hunters in Indonesia and dubbed 'Hobbit Man.' The bickering among scientists became an unwholesome display akin to football hooligans at their worst, most bloodthirsty and territorial. Professor Maciej Hennenberg, of the University of Adelaide, appeared to be a voice of sanity, pointing out that scientists have around 200 specimens of early man believed to represent ten different species, making 20 specimens per species; with only a single skull for 'Hobbit Man.' "The problem is there are far more palaeontologists than fossil specimens," he noted wryly. [15]
- Lastly, a bizarre one. Maybe, like me, you were unaware that all 3,000 species of centipede have an odd number of leg pairs – 15 to 191 – but an example found in Whitburn, Tyne & Wear, has 48. Chris Kettle's chance discovery means a rewriting of science text books. [16]

The Triple Breasted Whore of Eroticon Six

Recent reading in several scientific fields – not my normal interest, but I like to keep up-to-date – has left me perplexed as to how so often logic is swept metaphorically under the carpet (a magic one perhaps which could lift off at any moment and expose the uncomfortable facts to the delight of forteans and fair play). Therefore I was heartened that no lesser personage than the Astronomer Royal, Professor Sir Martin Rees, has suggested that 'life, the universe and everything' may be no more than a giant computer simulation. Our role being reduced to bits of software. Such a cosmology seems reasonable. It does not prejudice my brand of Christian Gnostic belief. That the world we see and experience is an illusion, as popularised in the film *The Matrix*, I can live with. My preference as a cosmological model is 'steady state' or 'metaverse' as opposed to 'big bang' and the fine tuning (apart from fortean events) and variety of lifeforms and richness of human behaviour must be taken as evidence for some kind of creator at work. Not necessarily the most rational one, but the best we've got. You only have to look at the duck-billed platypus to know that whoever created life on Earth has a sense of humour. But from a Gnostic point of view, I ask you, whatever did <u>his</u> creator think of it?

References:

1.   Mark Henderson, 'How evolution can save lives', *The Times body & soul*, 11/2/06
2.   *Nuts*, February, 2006
3.   *Metro*, 23/3/06
4.   *The Times, Metro*, 1/12/05
5.   *Metro*, 16/2/06
6.   *Metro*, 15/8/05
7.   *Metro*, 6/3/06
8.   *The Sunday Telegraph*, 8/5/05
9.   *Metro*, 2/9/05
10.   *The Times*, 2/9/05
11.   *Metro*, 14/11/05
12.   *The Times*, 27/11/04
13.   *The Times*, 19/3/05
14.   *The Sunday Telegraph*, 13/3/05
15.   *The Sunday Telegraph*, 26/12/04
16.   *Fortean Times*, No 132, 2000

+ Note: *Metro* is quoted so frequently because it has brief extracts supplied by *New Scientist* and is a regular read.

For a fair-minded synthesis of how creationists find the ideas of ID as repugnant to them as evolutionism, I recommend an account of this confrontation in *Fortean Times*, issue 202 by Brian Regal. Evolutionists, on the other hand, often charge ID with being a 'stalking horse' and to use another animalistic metaphor, a sheep in wolf's clothing masquerading as creationism with a pseudoscientific gloss. That's as maybe. My view is that some guiding principle is at work influencing species development; for instance, the *genius loci* of Australia influencing marsupialism in diverse beasts and even an ability to resurrect extinct forms of life. But as a Gnostic and fortean I would say that, wouldn't I?

GULLIBLE'S TRAVELS: RICH-ARD DAWKINS, EVOLUTION, GOD AND GALAPAGOS BOOBY BOOB

(*Folklore Frontiers*, No. 57, 2007)

There are so many ironies surrounding evolutionary biologist Richard Dawkins that we could call him 'Irony Dick.' As Charles Simonyi Professor for the Public Understanding of Science at New College, Oxford, he warns the masses away from quantum mechanics and the uncertainty principle with its pedigree stretching back to the very same post-Copernican Enlightenment he professes to represent; his fanatical intolerance of religion makes his atheism fundamentalist belief; and his monetarist media and publishing earnings on the back of those he derides and despises make him as much of a snake-oil salesman as the alleged fraudsters and the delusional whom he maligns.

Born in 1941 in Nairobi, Kenya, Clinton Richard Dawkins is the son of a farmer and soldier of aristocratic descent. He has had three attempts at finding a suitable mate, his third marriage being to actress Lalla Ward since 1992. Educated at Balliol College, Oxford, he has been a Fellow of New College, Oxford, since 1970 and of the Royal Society. Dawkins made a name for himself with his book *The Selfish Gene*; the notion that evolutionary natural selection equates to the survival of the fittest, while failing to take into account that co-operation is often necessary for survival. His ideology of worshipping at the altar of competitiveness, shows a mind taking Thatcherite economics and applying it to evolution: just as appalling as those who took the crudest ideas of early evolutionists and applied them racially, creating pernicious social Darwinism. Dawkins says that natural selection is the only source of evolutionary change, while even Charles Darwin himself said there were other sources. But here's the rub. Despite another nickname, 'Darwin's Rottweiler,' Dawkins obviously views himself as Darwin's superior, even arguing flamboyantly that 'we can consciously, deliberately and intelligently opt out of Darwinism.' [1]

Dawkins explicitly says that there can be only atheism and creationism – both highly-eccentric positions in themselves – while ignoring the highly-attractive and reasonable option of Intelligent Design (ID). Most of his dire polemic *The God Delusion* is arraigned at U.S. fundamental Christianity, which as Professor Richard Bowen, of the University of Wales, Swansea, notes is 'somewhat like writing a book about gastronomy but focusing on the McDonald's "restaurant." Dawkins' emphasis on what might be termed "McTheology" greatly limits the scope of his analysis.' [2] As many commentators have observed, Dawkins dishonestly packs all religious belief and practice into one crude bag labelled fanaticism. Also denying personal religious experience and serious theology reveals narrow-mindedness and intellectual cowardice.

He makes himself look even more absurd when he says belief in God makes mankind perpetrate appalling acts. Well, so does communism, fascism, monetarism, racism, social Darwinism, dogmatism, and many more isms. Dawkins also gets apoplectic with anyone who says there are mysteries we cannot solve. In actuality, the more scientists learn, the more they should humbly realise the less they know. It's been pejoratively called 'the God of the gaps.' As a fortean I have a sceptical view of science's empiricism and see those gaps forever widening and deepening my faith in ID. Science will never answer many mysteries.

Enigmatic variations
Amidst all this, journalist Cristina Odone, a staunch Roman Catholic, found herself seated beside Dawkins at a country weekend and was berated for her 'belief in the specialness of humanity for its soul. 'In a recent interview (source not specified) Dawkins describes a gigantic intelligence which designs the universe,' she revealed. He acknowledges that there may be an awe-inspiring and uplifting force out there and that he is prepared to encounter it,' Odone commented: 'It sounds suspiciously like God under another name.' [4] Or I might add, more like ID. And if you're like me, a Christian Gnostic creation by The Demiuge. Years ago, Dawkins had a metaphor of a blind watchmaker. Is he consistent? Is he a sinner repenting? Then there's the old adage about there being no atheists in the trenches.

Dawkins certainly doesn't have any love for the paranormal. Using the platform of the 1996 Dimbleby lecture to attack what he assumed to be a constant triumph of the irrational over the logical in popular TV series *The X-Files*, he made the bizarre comparison of 'Imagine a crime series in which, every week the black one turns out to have done it.' Apart from the curious inability to distinguish between imaginative fiction and perceived racism, *The X-Files* was excellently counterpointed by having a believer and a sceptic, or to bring the debate down to a level even Dawkins might understand: good cop, nasty cop. [3] Then in August, 2007, Channel 4 broadcast *The Enemies of Reason*, in which Dawkins attacked all manner of 'New Age' beliefs. One victim was Neil Spencer, *The Observer*'s astrologer, who was given a page to respond. Mischievously giving his detractor yet another nickname, 'The Dawk,' Spencer further took the piss by asking that if Dawkins regards anything pre-Enlightenment as 'primitive,' does that include Gothic cathedrals and Plato's texts; if homoeopathy is merely a placebo effect, how come animals respond to it; and that the world's having 'soul and purpose, that humanity and cosmos are linked, is it to be found not, as he and others claim, in the dogma of religion, but in art and in the depth psychology of Freud and Jung that Dawkins holds in contempt.' [5] In fact, Dawkins's dogmatism is awesome, dismissing every shade of the paranormal as pseudoscientific mumbo-jumbo; so certain doubting, I even guess, that all scientific knowledge is by nature provisional; which leads naturally to forteanism, which has a distinct provisionality clause, but whose stance between belief and scepticism he will never comprehend; and as for urban legends, he prefers to use the catch-all modern term 'meme' and himself fell for a real scientific howler.

What this all means is that however much academic prestige you hold and how high your I.Q, this does not automatically preclude you from appearing as credulous, contrary and confused a buffoon as your targets. Or reviewing his jaundiced programme, heeding the advice of Kathryn Flett: 'Intellectual arrogance is a terribly unattractive quality in a man, particularly one allegedly clever enough to know better.' [6]

Eyeless in Galapagos and cruising for a bruising
Earlier this year Dawkins visited the Galapagos Islands, swimming with marine iguanas, walking among flightless cormorants and watching pelicans and boobies rain down like arrows into the water. In a *My Week* feature, Dawkins recorded:

'Our impressive Ecuadorian guides told us that boobies eventually go blind, the consequence of years of high-velocity impacts of their eyes on the water. As Darwin would have realised (*The Origin of the Species* is rich in such economic insights), this accords with natural selection. Eventually death by blinding is the price paid for successful reproduction in earlier life – successful passing on of the genes that laid down this ultimately suicidal behaviour.' [7]

The only trouble with this is that it is a contemporary legend. Hoist by his own critical petard, Dawkins will have been embarrassed by a letter published subsequently, while I cannot help find the word *schadenfreud* coming to mind. Bryan Nelson corrects Dawkins with:

'More than 40 years ago I spent some time in Oxford University's annex in Bevington Road, where Richard Dawkins (*My week*) was fitting distorting spectacles on to day-old chicks in order to study their pecking response to food particles. At that time I was in the Firth of Forth working on gannets. I extended this to include the blue-footed booby of the Galapagos. The myth that gannets go blind as a consequence of plunge-diving has obviously been extended to boobies and Richard passed it on, though not as a myth. I have concrete evidence from marked individuals that gannets can survive more than 30 years with perfect eyesight. The blindness myth probably arose because gannets and boobies have an opaque 'third eyelid' which they draw across the eye to protect it from the impact of diving.' – Bryan Nelson, Auchencairn, Dumfries & Galloway.

Dawkins boasted of having then been invited to New York - just a dinner to celebrate *Time* magazine's '100 Most Influential People of the Year' and built this diversion into his route to Galapagos. The trip in Darwin's footsteps was something of a 'freebie,' whereby Dawkins had to give only three lectures to other cruisers, who had paid handsomely for this dubious privilege. More of that irony here, too, as his host was the Centre for Inquiry, an American charity devoted to secular humanism and, er, critical thinking. So, next time you see puffed up pontificating 'Irony Dick' – or if you prefer, 'The Dawk' - just think of the booby bird. It would make a suitable motto-cum-metaphor.

References:

1. *The Times*, 31/8/96
2. Letters, *The Independent*, 19/9/02
3. For more background on Dawkins's multitudinous intolerances to a sane world see Richard Whittaker, 'What the Dawkins?.' *Fortean Times*, No. 105, 1997
4. Cristina Odone, 'Let us pray for the soul of Richard Dawkins,' *The Observer*, 13/5/07
5. Neil Spencer, 'The Dawkins Delusion: Science is good, the rest bad,' *The Observer*, 12/8/07
6. Kathryn Flett, *The Observer*, 19/8/07
7. Richard Dawkins, 'My week,' *The Observer*, 27/5/07
8. Bryan Nelson, Letters, *The Observer*, 10/6/07

While researching my homage to John Michell, I discovered Dawkins viewed Cambridge educated Michell as his real nemesis, the mention of whose name was an anathema and would have him spluttering in indignation as his face became purple. This heaps upon him yet more irony via the contemporary legend that John was a Time Lord and the inspiration for TV series *Dr Who*, the TV classic where Dawkins' current wife is a former Time Lord's assistant. Doesn't Dawkins realise everything goes in circles and cycles?

PART TWO
FORTEANA

CHARLES FORT AND HIS PHILOSOPHY

(*The Mail*, Hartlepool, 16 July 1980)

C harles Hoy Fort (1874-1932) is still largely unknown and those with a slight knowledge of his philosophy usually mistakenly think of him as having been the scourge of science. In his own way, Fort was as insistent as scientists upon proper rules of evidence. Yet he was insistent, correctly, that all theories propounded be tentative and temporary.

Often the most successful item in the arsenal against any entrenched body, be it science, a political body, religious bigotry, pressure group such as moral campaigning, or such, is humour. A hand-grenade witticism lobbed correctly can defuse a situation or demolish an argument with hydrogen bomb ferocity. This was Fort's choice of weapon. The lampooning war he waged was not against science as a discipline, but acts of intellectual dishonesty and abused integrity. Scientists as a body have acted to retain a rigidity in science which appalled Fort. Their exclusion of many genuine events and phenomena which conflicted embarrassingly with the comfortable orthodox views they had established was anathema to him. The data he was collating he chose to term 'the damned.' Science, he argued, had taken on a mantle similar to that of dogmatic religion and effectively excommunicated this information.

As we shall see from the cases of frog falls (and in a second article, entombed toads), science has ignored, suppressed, discredited, or explained away in inadequate fashion these phenomena and many others. The inadequacy of the arguments against the chosen two categories (though Fort argued against strict categorisation and posited a continuous universe where all that is reasonable, and also as yet unreasonable, interconnect) are very much a different thing from providing a real explanation. Hence he adopted the policy of inclusionism and railed against the forces which sought to define and divide things, and isolate and categorise them.

An American, Fort spent the last 24 years of his life in the British Museum reading-room and New York Public Library meticulously combing newspapers and journals of all countries and disciplines. He collated his notes on anything mysterious, anomalous or unexplainable. This prodigious feat bore almost forbidden fruit in the form of four books: *The Book of the Damned*, *Wild Talents*, *Lo!* and *New Lands*.

BEER GARDEN UFO PARTY

(Folklore Frontiers, No. 32, 1998)

Forteans must surely live in the hopes that some day they will witness some phenomenological event. A sighting to confirm their belief there is a non-ordinary world out there. One in the eye to sceptics they would give their right arm for. Yet, as readers should realise, life is not so straightforward. Gifts from strange realms are not always appreciated. Even by those most expected to welcome them with open arms – and open minds. "Look, look up there by that plane! It's a UFO." The cry of joy should have brought an amazed, shared reaction from the gathered throng. For this was the 1995 Travel and Earth Mysteries Society annual garden party at Lionel Beer's home, where members were lounging around in the sun, many discussing UFOs. The irony was that most members took no notice and carried on chattering, particularly those with a strong ufological interest. Seemingly others, mostly the women, pointed out to each other a silvery-white disc speeding upwards around a passing aircraft. Their reaction was one of awe and delight. Original UFO-spotter on the day Eileen Roche reported that desultory remarks were uttered by those who had not even looked - "It's not a UFO, of course" – "Rubbish, it must be a balloon" – "It's a joke, it's not true." Eileen summed up sadly: "So, a world in microcosm. Ufologists react like the general public to a report of a sudden sighting of a UFO." [1]

I have sympathy with the hardly-disguised contempt of this lady towards these garden-chair ufologists. A few years ago, walking along a Devon country road, I stopped to ask a woman stranger if she knew when there would be a bus for Tiverton. She found a bus timetable and as she scanned the leaflet I spotted a daylight disc. As it passed behind clouds she began reciting the time of the next bus due and I was too polite (and embarrassed) to interrupt and point out the ufological happening. By the time I had assured her I understood where and when my transport would be, the UFO was gone. Doh!

Similarly, on a foggy Sunday journey by car to visit megalithic monuments in Northumberland with John Watson, we spotted a fully-grown black panther cross the road in front of us. What did we do? Screech to a halt? Get out our cameras? Pursue it? We panicked. I was still shaking as we headed into the first pub we next encountered.

Another tale with irony pertinent to this trail of thought concerns two dozen photographers attending a seminar on wedding photography, during 1995, at the Knockomie Hotel, Forres, Grampian. The words and wisdom of American snapper Heidi Mauracher were interrupted when it was noticed that the Highland cattle in a nearby field were acting strangely. No, not a black helicopter on a mutilation mission, but as participant Les Hester described: "It was about the size of a Labrador but definitely feline. It was dun-coloured and moved just like a big cat." Concentration on the speaker and model bride accompanying them outside now lost, the party saw the beast run beside a fence before darting into the undergrowth. With so many photographers present, surely one was capable of providing incontrovertible evidence of anomalous big cats in our midst. Well, no. Mr Hester admitted: "We were at the seminar to look and listen so we didn't have our cameras with us." [2] Doh!

Then there was a newspaper photographer, camera in hand and ABC... **(see below)**

But all is not lost. More beer. A boozy ufological seminar in a Wigan pub in 1996 was interrupted when one of the students cried out, "Look, look, it's Jesus," and they all witnessed a Shroud of Turin-style face of Christ. At *The Orwell* pub, paranormal investigator Ian Hawthorne had just been discussing the phenomenon where holy images can be seen in everyday things. At this moment someone spotted the bearded face apparent among paint flaking off the side of a canal bridge outside. [3]

Summing up, can there be a reason for some avowed forteans turning away mentally or physically from uncanny events? Or is it just plain human nature? Whatever, it can be bloody embarrassing!

References:

1.   *TEMS Newsletter*, August, 1995
2.   *The Weekend Telegraph*, 25 March 1995
3.   *Folklore Frontiers*, No. 26, 1995
4.   *Daily Star*, 23 August 1996

I have deleted four paragraphs from this article about a newspaper photographer friend of mine as I felt this incident deserved wider dissemination and lengthier exposition here and originally published in a magazine published in North-East England specifically for forteans, cryptozoologists and exotic wildlife aficionados and which fits the theme perfectly.

PHOTOGRAPHIC MEMORY OF BLACK PANTHER

(By Paul Screeton with Dirk van der Werff)

I well recall the day in 1985 when, as deputy chief sub-editor of the *Hartlepool Mail*, I was sitting opposite editor Peter Chislett when a colleague appeared and reported to him an encounter with the 'Durham Puma', as the mystery beast had been dubbed. The irony was that the observer was not an insignificant employee but no less than chief photographer Dirk van der Werff, who, er, had not actually photographed the beast. 'Chisser' and news editor Mark Acheson looked at one another and shook their heads in disbelief. On a national newspaper it would have been a sacking offence.

Eight years later, features editor Bernice Saltzer recalled Dirk's personal experience in an article on anomalous big cats observed in the *Mail*'s circulation area. I was quite proud of the headline I attached to the piece – 'Photographer's Nerve Snapped.' [1] In fact, The *Mail* published numerous pieces about mystery felids, and particularly the stalking of them by wildlife liaison officer PC Eddie Bell, though only one other referred to the negative reaction of Dirk. [2] Actually, having been a car passenger when seeing a black panther cross the road near Wooler, Northumberland, I can well understand Dirk's fear. I was certainly unnerved. [3]

When a Forum piece was agreed - over the phone with *Fortean Times* editor Bob Rickard about those occasions when photographers missed a critical anomalous event, which he failed to publish, but eventually appeared elsewhere [4] – Dirk kindly produced the following account of the incident for me to extract information. Here it is in full:

"I was returning from taking photographs in Trimdon Village and just as I went over the bridge outside Hurworth Burn and approaching the railway bridge, I saw the big cat. The cat was walking quickly across the road and was framed by the bridge as I travelled up an incline. It was perhaps 70-100 yards ahead of me, had a very, very long tail and was completely black. My memory is that as it walked with the tail almost outstretched, its length as a whole stretched across at least half of the road. It took me only 10-15 seconds to reach the spot where the cat had gone across the road into a field at the southern side. I stopped the Mini and grabbed a camera on the back seat which was fitted with a long lens – perhaps a 200mm on a Fuji or Pentax camera. On the other side of the road was a gap in the hawthorn hedge which I presumed the cat had passed through. I walked into the field but could see nothing. I was turning again and again, looking back towards the field as I walked perhaps a couple of yards back to the boundary. I was puzzled as to where the cat had gone. I decided to go back to the car as I had to get back to work quickly with a photograph. As I turned to go back to the car, I caught sight of a large black panther lying lengthways along a ditch in front of the hedge on the roadside. I was perhaps within three feet of the cat and I stood frozen in fear. It was looking directly ahead to the edge of the ditch and didn't seem to see me at first, but then it turned its head and looked up towards me. I immediately started to move very slowly and walked backwards to the car, praying that it wouldn't come for me. When I touched the car I grabbed the handle and quickly opened the door. I jumped into the seat, turned the key and sped straight off along the road. I feel annoyed with myself that I didn't hang about and take photographs, but I was very frightened and wanted to get away as soon as possible."

So there you have it, a black panther witness statement and a confession all in one.

Dirk's just clocked up 20 years at the *Mail*, so it just goes to show all's forgiven, if not quite forgotten.

References:

1.   Bernice Saltzer, 'Photographer's Nerve Snapped,' *The Mail*, Hartlepool, 27 August 1993; *Folklore Frontiers*, No. 20, 1993
2.   Claire Couchman, 'Puma Sightings Have Long History,'*The Mail*, Hartlepool, 26 August 1993
3.   Paul Screeton, 'A Personal Black Panther Sighting in Northumberland 1983,'*The Shaman*, No. 10, 1985; *N-MAG RAG*, Vol. 1, No. 2, 1997
4.   Paul Screeton, *Folklore Frontiers*, No. 32, 1998

This piece appeared in the house magazine of the Northern Mysteries Animal Group, edited by John Tait. Incidentally, as with John Watson and my Northumberland sighting, Dirk was a committed fortean and wrote on early airship scares in *Magonia*, which makes his behaviour more incomprehensible.

THE WYRLEY STONES

(*The Ley Hunter*, No. 87, 1979)

T he 'gee-whiz' brand of lost civilisations and ancient astronaut writing has sought its dubious justification and spurious material in exotic climes. However, the more mundane and less scenic location of Great Wyrley may hold greater mysteries and a more rewarding vein of research ore. For this obscure mining village two miles from Cannock, Staffordshire, and less than a mile from Watling Street, is the focus of an intriguing mystery. The 'Wyrley Stones' have not received the public notice of more celebrated artefacts found at Glozel, France, and featured on television, or the writings about Dr Cabrera's enigmatic findings in Peru, but are equally deserving of attention. However, I will turn first to South America.

Javier Cabrera

A recent book by Rene Noorbergen, trawling the diminishing shoals of fresh ancient civilisation lore, has added to the usual old chestnuts the Cabrera rocks (Noorbergen wrongly calls him Jose Cabrena). I prefer biologist Ryan Drum's less accessible version, which describes Cabrera as a chain-smoking, dashing, qualified surgeon in his early fifties specialising in circulatory ailments, with revolutionary ideas about cancer, genetics, nutrition, mortality and religion. He practises in Ica, Peru, and has built up a staggering collection of petroglyphs depicting amazing scenes. He has been finding these since an earthquake caused a landslide 20 years before. They were discovered in a lens-shaped deposit and he has recovered 20,000!

These show:

a)   Five-fingered (i.e. no thumbs) humanoids with pointed tongues and noses which begin on their foreheads interacting – partially playfully, partially hostilely – with 'dinosaurs' and produced by people living 250,000 to one million years ago.
b)   Mastodon-type elephants, wild pigs and unknown creatures.
c)   Seeming ancient maps of the continents before separation as now located.
d)   Surgery: brain; genitalia; heart, lung, kidney and liver transplants; plus Caesarean birth.

Arguments for and against Cabrera hoaxing his public are:

a)   He produced the stones as the work of frustrated genius. The medical aspect suggesting a surgeon could draw such, but conversely would he do so when such an obvious objection could be raised?
b)   He employed Indians to carve them.
c)   His reluctance to denote his source (arguing that it would be plundered by professional artefact hunters).
d)   Style seemed consistent; a mixture of care with haste.
e)   There are other clay figures from Peru and Mexico owned by Dr A.I. Wiseman, of New York, but not of such elements as liver transplants.

Drum's final comments are worth quoting:

> 'I have examined the rocks at 30 and 60 magnifications in a stereo microscope to study the grooves, and found no obvious grinding or polishing marks or any other evidence of rotary power tool use in making the fine regular grooves. I am not sure how to date the rocks, since they are susceptible to potassium-argon dating only if they are in a volcanic deposit. If Cabrera is right and the rocks are genuine as claimed, they are incredibly valuable and should not only be held in awe, but studied thoroughly as products of human intelligence. If they are a hoax, their existence, number, detail, and bulk represent an enormous input of human resources and should be regarded as a fine combination of intellect and imagination. Anyone who cares to visit Cabrera or myself can examine the rocks.'

Noorbergen's account, as serialised in *The Sunday Express*, reads less impressively than Drum's and has all the 'gosh-wow' of Erich von Daniken's output and its popular appeal. It was suggested by Cabrera that they were scratched in plastic mud and then hardened to become rocks. Similarly some of the Staffordshire artefacts seem to have been drawn in soft clay, too, as will be seen.

William Rigby
Upon retiring from mining, a profession which afforded him the opportunities of building up an impressive collection of fossils, William Rigby opened up a modest museum in a small shed adjoining his home, with the motive of encouraging local youngsters to share his enthusiasm. It must have been a somewhat odd venture, for additional to the fossils and a few curios, soft drinks and primitive fruit machine entertainment was provided. Some of the more observant visitors pointed out that certain 'fossils' were stones carved by human agency, which it appears caused indignation in the curator. Nevertheless, he sold such examples and specimens were offered to the British Museum and other museums' personnel – all it seems to no critical satisfaction or avail.

There were around 100 examples, mostly irregular, but there was always a small flat base on which they could be set. This base was always plain, whereas the remainder was covered with incised lines. They showed occasionally men, a great variety of animals (including one uni-dentifiable by any zoologist) and a few plant forms. Mostly ornamental, there were also a few tools Rigby claimed he found; all these in pits of the Cannock area, and also in the contents of a pit mound levelled and spread over his land. In a slim book on the stones, Helen Travers Sherlock commented:

> 'He was an exceptional discoverer, for he never announced this find, or made any claim with regard to it. It has not been possible to sift the evidence as to the origin for the stones: and we have as yet no proof of the circumstances of their discovery, or perhaps it may be of their manufacture. This however is a secondary consideration. The first question is neither that of their provenance nor even of their authenticity, but of their intrinsic value. If it can be shown that they are of interest for the archaeologist or the student of art, if they should illustrate any problem of anthropology, or even mental science, then it will be worthwhile to find out whether they we found at Wyrley [pronounced wer-lee] or imported from abroad. Then, too, it will be well to ascertain by what kind of tool the iron-stone was graved with marks, some of which seem made in soft clay rather than rock, and to discover whether the actual workmanship is of recent date or of great antiquity.'

She then cautioned:

> 'Nor need the shadow of "an English Glozel" [to be explained later] darken this enquiry, for the circumstances are entirely different. The Glozel finds multiplied in response to a demand. The Wyrley Stones were always of a fixed and limited number. The discoverer at Glozel thought that he had found valuable antiquities, and reported his find. The discoverer of the Wyrley Stones attached comparatively little value to them, neither less nor more than to others of his collection that seemed of equal interest to an undiscriminating eye: and far from maintain that they were antiquities, he even denied that they were carvings, regarding these, together with all his fossils, not merely as works of nature but as the direct manifestations of a divine hand.'

Shades of Joseph Smith and the Mormon tablets! In fact, discussing the Cabrera stones, likewise Drum makes such a comparison.

Emile Fradin

As for Glozel, I was unable to find a more recent work than a translation of a German study of archaeological fakery of 1967, but recall a recent TV programme where the thermoluminescence process was applied to Glozel artefacts, but believe the analysis was inconclusive. [Here editor Paul Devereux interjected: *In fact, TL showed the items to be unquestionably ancient. But archaeologically they are anomalous*]. Certainly this account is biased and yet disturbing in the way eminent scholars became so heated and divided in opinion as to whether farmer Emil Fradin was finding artefacts of the Old Stone Age or manufacturing them for profit.

Whatever the truth, Glozel is part of a repeating scenario of mysterious artefacts. Truth in such cases is generally elusive, however much effort is put into establishing the actuality. In fact, personal involvement with a number of the principal characters in the 'Hexham Heads' case has persuaded me that solutions in such cases are unlikely to be forthcoming if 'rational' logic is applied and invariably the answer lies in some phenomenological dimension of reality.

Helen Travers Sherlock

The major source of information on the Wyrley Stones is taken from Helen Travers Sherlock's book *The Wyrley Stones*. This was published in 1929 as No. 10 in the Caravan Essay series. The slim volumes in this series were written by Sherlock and Dr Rendel Harris (sometimes in collaboration), both of whom became interested in the nature of these anomalous artefacts. In her book, Sherlock describes how Rigby closed his museum in December 1922, and upon selling his exhibits the auctioneer was confronted by a single buyer, who bought the majority (though his name is unrecorded). The remainder not previously purchased were bought shortly before Rigby's death in 1928. Sherlock notes that at least seven people had acquired examples. In fact, the photographs in her book are of examples from several persons' collections. Two of these illustrations are credited to ley discoverer Alfred Watkins and were examples from the collection of Mr Cooper Neal. Another owner of examples, known to Watkins was Mrs Christine Crossland Symms.

At the risk of producing trivia, but in the spirit of ley data inclusionism, I reproduce here a passage from a letter sent by Mrs Crossland Symms to former *TLH* (*The Ley Hunter*) editor Philip Heselton in response to an inquiry, which unfortunately does not record Watkins's thoughts on the stones:

> "... I was a very humble and youngest member. It was through the friendship of my mother with Alfred Watkins that I joined the (Straight Track) Club. It was a privilege to have known him. He was so learned and incidentally a very modest and likeable man. He was deeply religious too, as became his studies of the O.S.T. [old straight track], so I thought anyway. I also met in those days the late Dr Rendel Harris, the noted authority on Egyptian place names and a Hebrew scholar. He was very interested in the O.S.T., and always told us we must bear place names in mind when pursuing our leys. I remember he was somewhat eccentric; always carried an umbrella and made naive remarks about cars, confusing a Ford with the aristocratic Daimler or Rolls-Royce. I have a wonderful collection of ancient carved stones, by the way, which Dr Harris came to study in my mother's time, but that is a long story and much mystery attached thereto. I am writing a paper about them. You shall have it later on, because it rather links up my theories about O.S.T. and origins of the leymen. Now I must go and cook a meal and tear myself away from our O.S.T. It is all so fascinating and opens up such side tracks, but as Major Tyler said, *fieldwork* must be the foundation, after which we may indulge our speculations.'

Philip Heselton visited Mrs Crossland Symms and viewed the stones during the early Sixties and it is possible that she may now be dead for she would now be aged 81. She enclosed to Philip a number of articles, which appeared in *TLH*, but nothing on the Wyrley Stones followed. However, these dispersed artefacts deserve a place in the pantheon of grand stone mysteries alongside the more publically exposed Glozel and Ica remains. Perhaps *TLH* readers can help track down these stones – or even fresh examples in Staffordshire or elsewhere – as we are now acquiring the technology to examine and date them.

By 1976, the magazine I was editing, *The Ley Hunter*, had outgrown my capabilities and capacity to handle the increased subscription list and wished for it to be in the hands of someone with greater resources, more spare time and preferably London-based for ease of distribution. A shocked subscriber, Paul Devereux, was approached and accepted the challenge, taking the magazine to a higher level and greater excellence. For a fuller account of this landmark in earth mysteries affairs, the reader is directed to my 1993 history of ley hunting, *Seekers of the Linear Vision* (available while stocks last at £5 from Paul Screeton, 5 Egton Drive, Seaton Carew, Hartlepool, TS25 2AT). The article here appeared in a series of 43 I wrote as columnist The Long Man of Wilmington, named after the dodman-surveyor hill figure in Sussex. Much of the material here would be unfamiliar to earth mysterians – and indeed forteans and cryptozoologists – and it surprisingly afforded readers a snapshot of ley rediscoverer Alfred Watkins himself. Also, forteans may find the village's name naggingly familiar, for 'The Great Wyrley Outrages' became a Victorian cause celebre when local solicitor George Edalji was convicted of six horse slashings. No lesser figure than Sir Arthur Conan Doyle (creator of Sherlock Holmes, a name chiming pertinently with that of Helen Travers Sherlock) spent eight months proving Edalji's innocence. In 2005, Julian Barnes gave this miscarriage of justice a fictional gloss, and his novel *Arthur & George* was nominated for the Man Booker Prize.

THE FORBIDDEN THEORY OF MOUNTAIN UPLIFT

(*The Mail*, Hartlepool, 21 June, 1980; *Ancient Skills & Wisdom Review*, No. 11, 1980)

When an author entitles his book *A New Explanation of Mountain Uplift*, one would expect a good controversy to emerge among his academic peers. When the title adds the rider *based on Lunar Gravitation and Oceanic Pressure*, one can discern a maverick spirit and expect a fierce ding-dong with Establishment orthodoxy. And when there is a secondary title proclaiming 'the British Association for the Suppression of Science,' one is left in no doubt that the author feels he has been maligned and will attempt at all costs to have his views aired. And costs were indeed met by the author, for he published his views privately (through Ordprint, of Hartlepool), the book in question appearing in 1955 and being the work of Dr Charles Thomas Trechmann.

Theories attacking uniformitarian geology are gaining ground, but it is not my purpose, nor do I feel adequately qualified, to quantify rival geological and astronomical theories. However, I feel that Trechmann may find more allies for his theory if his work were better known. He was in his seventies when he published his book, and has since died. In his controversial work he commented:

> 'A friend of mine at the British Museum after reading one of my papers said he thought in 50 years' time it may come to be the favourite explanation. I said that I will then be 120 years old and may need an ear trumpet to hear the applause."

Trechmann seems to have been snubbed and hence the damning subsidiary title. So, to explain briefly: the book is an extension of a paper submitted to the British Association for the Advancement of Science for the 1953 meeting. He wrote:

> 'It was accepted for reading but I requested that it might not be put on in the afternoon when the delegates were due to go on excursions nor on the last day when they were packing up to leave. I was away in the West Indies

and I was given half-an-hour on the last morning, with delays this meant 20 minutes, time to read about one-third of it and no time for discussion. It was refused publication in the Proceedings with the usual excuse, "The Editor regrets, lack of space."'

Every discipline has its independent scholars and Trechmann did not have to rely on an academic post and the toe-the-line-or-else hierarchy involved. With private means, he spent much time abroad, particularly in the Caribbean, and could indulge his hobby and visit locations of which others of his speciality had no knowledge. From this experience of close observation during 50 years he could state: 'I conclude that the current theories are unable to explain what the rocks have been doing, as we see them actually'.

Basically his theory was that lunar - and possibly solar - attraction draws up the higher and more compact rock masses, with deep columns of oceanic water exerting pressure on the floor or sloping sides to reinforce the upward pull. That is just the basic idea, and - of course - he backed it up with many other observations. His attitude towards orthodoxy was stinging. He remarked that when aged 20 he satisfied the examiners, but at 70 they did not satisfy him. As for the wandering continents viewpoint, he called it a 'hoax.' He also listed publications – like the one in question – published at his own expense because learned journals declined to accept his papers. Maybe he felt something of a scientific martyr; perhaps even being a little paranoid. Whichever way, he is not the first (and many throughout history have died for their beliefs), nor will he be the last.

At one time he was an analytical chemist in his father's cement works in Hartlepool and so was trained to know about stone. But it was more than a job and he built up his knowledge of geology through careful personal observation.

Trechmann was greatly interested in the effects of glaciations and studied the submerged forests of Hartlepool and Roker. Such remains can be seen from the Longscar Rocks off Seaton Carew to the Headland. These beds seem to represent deposits of the post-glacial North Sea as it returned some time after the retreat of the last ice sheet and before it regained its present completely marine character. From beneath this deposit have been found a mammoth's tusk and antlers of red deer and Irish elk. More interesting is the occurrence in the forest bed of chipped flints of the Maglemose culture. Trechmann found several chipped fragments of flint himself of a dull leaden coloured surface embedded in the peat at the junction with clay. He also recorded a chipping site occurring under the sand dunes on an elevated spit of boulders near the south shore of the mouth of Crimdon Dene. His finds can be seen in Hartlepool's Gray Art Gallery and Museum, whereas his butterfly collection was presented to Sunderland Museum.

Irish question
But back with geology, when it comes to hard evidence, Trechmann stated his facts clearly and without any semblance of evasion – though as if there could be no alternative or superior reason for their incidence. Mountains become mountains, he stated, because they continue to rise higher all the time despite the forces of denudation. Without statistics, he claimed Ja-

maica's Blue Mountain Peak may have risen two inches each year since 1865 and Mount Everest 'is said to be rising rapidly' – but by whom? He also took a particular interest in raised beaches and in his book noted that at Shippersea Bay, between Easington Colliery and Hawthorn Dene, such might seem small effects, but pointed to 'some great universal force.' This being gravitational uplift. He also argued that volcanoes fall into line with this process, noting that the eruptions of Vesuvius followed a pattern of the lunar cycle.

Personally I support the view that huge ice sheets caused uplift, but we agree that the notion of drifting continents is implausible. Trechmann remarked that 'professors, like film stars, must do something to get talked about' and attacked the arch-proponent of wandering continents Prof Alfred Wegener, saying his idea was 'enough to make a cat laugh but fortunately the evidence would not suffice to hang that devoted animal.' The problems of Ireland are hardly the subject for humour, but Trechmann wryly surmised what would happen if Wegener's theory was introduced seriously here to show Ireland had drifted away from England, with the consequent propaganda plus for a fully integrated United Kingdom, and recalled a Newcastle lecturer who said the first injustice to Ireland was when its coalfields were almost entirely denuded away and the material used to cover and preserve English coal measures 200 million years ago. He noted that some geologists went further and had not only continents wandering over the sea but one another – 'like the drunkard or the gambler they never know when to stop.'

Astronomers, too, came in for a drubbing, one in particular who claimed the Moon came out of the Pacific, almost taking New Zealand with it. Trechmann dryly asked: 'What would we have done without Canterbury lamb for lunch and stuffed kiwi, poor little things, in our museums beggars description.' He admitted to having sent copies of papers to astronomical societies and received not even the courtesy of an acknowledgement of receipt, believing they 'went straight into their august waste-paper baskets.' But this did not create the disillusionment caused so often by such encounters. Trechmann was made of sterner stuff. So he published privately and damned all. One of the joys of publishing one's own work is the non-interference from outside of tangents, eccentricities and other indulgences which most editors would blue pencil into oblivion. In his book, Trechmann also brings to task a body called The Ray Society, noted he was not among its 'clique' and so having no hope of being published by it, and for his £1 subscription received 'in return books on spiders, water beetles, etc., which lie around the house unread.'

More significantly he attacked a particular contributor on the subject of glaciations and following his castigation challenged: 'I therefore offer to present £50 to the Home for Deserving Inebriates or any worthy charity for any undoubted Scandinavian boulders...' And these boulders – correctly glacial erratics – were another major interest and he listed examples around Hartlepool, including the 'Wishing Stone' by the main road in Hart.

But his greatest contribution seems to be the central thesis of this book. In the epilogue he stated:

> 'This then is my forbidden theory that mountain uplift is due to upward pull of the planets assisted by changes going on below.'

Time will tell whether his theory will be validated. Even if this happens, he seems to have known what would occur:

> 'It is said that when we propound a new theory everyone says it is not true, and when we prove it they say we knew that before.

Dr Trechmann (1884-1964) was one of the great unsung geologists who challenged the current orthodoxy and he had the advantage of solid scientific credentials. This 20th Century gadfly had the same attitude towards academics as Charles Fort and an equally waspish sense of humour, whereas his maverick spirit makes him also resemble a controversial neglected (as in his book title) British Immanuel Velikovsky, of sorts. Of course, freethinking forteana is littered with rival theories which were dismissed or ignored. Tommy, as his biographer (unpublished) Reg Wright, of Blackhall Rocks, called him, suggested to me Trechmann had a lively private life (unelaborated).

Ancient Skills & Wisdom Review (1976-1982) itself sprang to life when I relinquished editorship of *The Ley Hunter* (1969-1976). Rather than lose the welcome stream of review copies from publishing houses, I immediately touted for literature to fill the pages of a new reviews magazine to keep me supplied with up-to-date reading matter on subjects I enjoyed and which were of relevance to my studies. The publication had a loyal readership wishing to hear my recommendations – and caveats. It also developed into *The Shaman* (1982-1985), which incorporated *AS&WR*. I also published *Terrestrial Zodiacs Newsletter* (1977-1981). Lastly has been *Folklore Frontiers* (1985-continuing).

Mail journalist Paul Screeton and the "Wishing Stone" in Hart. C. T. Trechmann suggested this block of Whin Sill granite was moved to Hart by a glacier around 15,000 years ago, from east Northumberland. At one time it was used by horsemen as a mounting block and tradition avers that by spitting upon it and making a wish, that hope will be fulfilled.

TANGOED! 'THE HOLLINWELL INCIDENT' ANNIVERSARY WALTZ

(Folklore Frontiers, No. 51, 2005)

A s an avowed fortean, I love a ding-dong between warring explanationists. In a case whose 25th anniversary it is this year, ranks of mass hysteria supporters were put under pressure by crop-spraying adherents to explain what happened. Yellowed cuttings tell the tale of Sunday, 13 July 1980, and what became in journalese 'The Hollinwell Incident.' In one of the most mysterious happenings in the East Midlands, almost 300 people, mostly children, were taken to hospital as a freak illness struck at a country show. Another 200 children were treated on the spot for fainting, running eyes and sore throats. Initial suspicion was that insecticide fumes had been stirred up by the juvenile marching bands at the Hollinwell Show, held near Kirby-in-Ashfield, Nottinghamshire.

The facts are, that halfway through a pageant of junior marching bands, girls and boys aged between five and fifteen began sweating, trembling and fainting. A fleet of ambulances and buses ferried 290 sufferers to hospital, with seven children detained overnight for observation.

Witness Christine Willetts said: "Some of the kids were catching their friends as they fell and then were falling down themselves. No one could understand what was happening. It looked just like a battlefield, with bodies everywhere." A spokesman at Mansfield General Hospital said: "It took a long time to bring some of the patients round."

Det. Insp. Eric Hogden, heading the investigation, made two points very early on which need to be borne in mind as my inquiry continues:

- "We have interviewed local landowners and officials at the nearby Nottinghamshire Golf Club and are unable to find anyone responsible for any crop spraying recently."

- Also: "Food poisoning and mass hysteria have definitely been ruled out."
  Right: That's mass hysteria, pesticides and food poisoning ruled out.
  Det. Insp. Hogden tellingly observed that a gymkhana went ahead on the field later that day with no problems.

On the medical front, a spokesman at Queen's Medical Centre, Nottingham, said the symptoms tallied with exposure to fumes of some kind, causing nausea, burning eyes and a metallic taste in the mouth. Some of the children discharged later returned to hospital when their symptoms reoccurred. None was said to be in danger. [1] Another newspaper report added that 15 adults and two horses had also collapsed. It also referred to 'another report' that claimed a light plane had sprayed the field two days previously. However, the owner of the field said it had not been sprayed for years. [2]

Two days later Dr Malcolm Lewis, the head of Nottingham public health laboratory, said tests on blood and urine samples from almost 300 children who were taken to hospital showed that possible causes, such as pesticides, food poisoning and water pollution, could not have been responsible. He said tests were undertaken for chemicals such as pesticides, but all proved negative, adding: Nor is the picture right for food poisoning; too many people were taken ill too quickly and there was no common food. Most brought their own sandwiches. In his view, the extraordinary scenes of fainting children were due to fatigue heightened by the excitement of the carnival competitions and the warmth and humidity of the weather. Describing what happened next as a 'domino effect,' Dr Lewis said that when children saw others collapsing, obviously in distress, they began falling down, too. In other words, pesticides were ruled out and mass hysteria the official explanation. [3] After concluding more tests, Stanley Beedham, chief executive to Ashfield District Council, said that chemical spray, weed-killers and all kinds of insecticides and fungicides had definitely been ruled out, but the hysteria theory was still being investigated. [4]

Girls' knickers scrutinised
 Comprehensive coverage was given by Bob Rickard in *Fortean Times*, where in addition to analysing the main explanations, *FT* considered and rapidly dismissed: high-frequency radio waves (gas board transmitter quickly eliminated); plastics factory fumes (six to 12 miles away, wrong wind direction); mystery bug (coxsackie virus epidemic in area discounted). [5]

Almost two weeks after the incident the tally was put at 414 taken to hospital, of which 236 were booked as casualties and nine admitted. There were also claims of a cover-up, which angered doctors. Dr Alan Scott told a press conference: "I find it distasteful that people who cannot even be bothered to come to the meeting can accuse us of a cover-up." He was one of a panel of medical and environmental experts at the conference in Sutton-in-Ashfield which was told that poisoning, chemicals and insecticides had already been ruled out. Dr Scott added: "Chemicals are non-selective agents. They affect everyone. There is no such thing as a jazz band bug.

Dr Michael Lewis – quoted earlier, but as Malcolm – said the experts were sticking to the mass hysteria theory. "The children in the bands had stood to attention for longer than was usual on a hot day. An air of tension and emotion had built up. Some fainted and others who saw them in distress developed similar symptoms. But the symptoms were not fazed. They were a genuine physical condition. It is something which has happened before and can happen again. The natural instinct of any young animal is to freeze in situations of fright. To some extent this was an exaggeration of that reaction. Suggestions will be made to the band organisers to ease tension at future contests." One local newspaper was very critical of the four judges and condemned the long period of standing to attention 'while the judges inspected the children behind the ears and checked each girl's knickers.' [6] If they tried that today they would be on the sex offenders' register. Was that normal and routine then? Or could that have upset the children? I know what I would have done if a stranger had done that to my daughter! So many ifs...

Flying saucer landing

Dr Lewis added: "There has been no cover-up. We have looked at every conceivable possibility. We even sent an officer to investigate when someone reported that a flying saucer had landed in the next field." [7] *Fortean Times* commented: 'They (the police) found no evidence for the landing, but it is interesting as an indication of the desperation or seriousness with which they were looking into every possibility.' A reappraisal of seeming dubious merit was broadcast by BBC East Midlands on 22 September 2003. The internet account doubts the mass hysteria verdict. It added that water companies were quick to check supplies were not contaminated and asked rhetorically if workers seen several weeks earlier near the site were responsible or if it could have been a gas leak, adding 'there was also talk of radio waves and even UFOs being responsible.'

However, BBC East Midlands provided a fresh twist – despite 1980 categorical statements that there was no crop-spraying, and forensic tests ruled out pesticides – by reporting:

> 'We have discovered that the chemicals sprayed on the field which were thought to have been harmless at the time have since been banned by the Government – this being tridemorph, classified by the World Health Organisation as Class II – a "moderately hazardous" pesticide, harmful if swallowed and irritating to eyes and skin. Did it also cause other side-effects such as fainting and malaise?'

Viewers and readers were invited to comment after the internet article: bizarrely the first two of five commentators rambled on about alien big cats without mentioning Hollinwell. Perhaps the programme was not satisfied with the purported UFO connection and introduced scary felids. More prosaically, Kelly Louise Randall, a band member on the day, asked how if it was mass hysteria could it affect babies and adults as well as children. Author David Haslam, who appeared on the programme, questioned the reliability of expert witnesses. If pesticides were the cause, why didn't medical tests on victims reveal this and pondered if medical science failed to find a solution then, what might any long-term damage to those involved be? At this point contributions were closed with undue haste.

The documentary team claimed they had discovered a pesticide, Calixin, which contains tridemorph, was sprayed in the area during the week leading up to the event. But what does 'area' mean anyway. Just how close to the showground? Remember again, officials had failed to locate any evidence of spraying at the time. The TV programme then played on viewers' fears by reporting that tridemorph had not been considered harmful at the time. Tridemorph, formula $C^{19}H^{39}NO$, is a fungicide that first gained commercial clearance in 1969. However, in 1995 it was listed as teratogenic, meaning it could be responsible for birth defects such as cleft palate. By 1999 it was banned by MAFF, yet given two years' grace to dispose of existing stocks in the supply chain. The internet has dozens of sites worldwide advertising tridemorph for sale. False panic? British nanny state mentality?

Back on more solid ground, the documentary makers were told by Ashfield District Council that it had no plans to reopen the inquiry. It commented that the official explanation of 1980 remained mass hysteria (babies, horses, adults notwithstanding), although other causes had been considered.

I personally recall learning from some source the suggestion that a large contingent of people, concentrated in a neighbouring county, transmitted their 'vibes' down a ley (ley-line, to younger readers) and zapped the juvenile jazz band participants, supporters, babies, horses and so on. These people were attending *The Ley Hunter* magazine's Moot '80 who congregated at Arbor Low henge monument in Derbyshire. As moot scribe Philip Heselton was to note:

> 'As more and more entered the circle, it was as if it was responding to our presence there – perhaps the largest gathering since it had been in regular use? The "interaction of the people of the people within the site" was certainly happening.' [8]

In my column in *The Ley Hunter*, I mentioned in passing:

> 'I understand there is now talk that because the great wave of juvenile bands' children collapsed at the same time as the 1980 *The Ley Hunter* mootgoers were at Arbor Low, a rumoured cause and effect has been posited.'

Posited from where, I cannot remember. This guided tour with energy dowsing was attended and greatly enjoyed by this writer. However, sadly for any wilder shores theorists, it was just before midday that the Hollinwell Incident began in earnest, while the mootgoers congregated after lunch in Hartington, the time when the gymkhana was being held without incident. Nevertheless, it makes 13 July 1980 doubly special in its own way.

References:

1. Robert Turner and Donald Young, 'Mystery fumes that hit 500 children,' *Daily Mail*, 14/7/80
2. Tony Birtley, '280 kids in poison riddle,' *Daily Star*, 14/7/80

3.　'Children's illness hysteria,' *The Daily Telegraph*, 16/7/80
4.　'Poison ruled out of jazz festival probe,' *Daily Express*, 24/7/80
5.　*Fortean Times*, No. 33, 1980
6.　*The Mansfield and North Nottinghamshire Chronicle and Advertizer*, 17/7/80
7.　Jazz band illness investigators deny "cover-up" claims,' *The Daily Telegraph*, 26/7/80
8.　Philip Heselton, 'Moot '80 Report,' *The Ley Hunter*, No. 89, 1980
9.　Paul Screeton, 'The Long Man of Wilmington column,' *The Ley Hunter*, No. 91, 1981

Fortean Times founding editor Bob Rickard revisited his original *FT* article in the magazine's September 2010 issue as an extract from a chapter on cases for a proposed book on mass hysteria and social panics in schools around the world, by himself and Dr Bob Bartholomew. In his final analysis, Bob noted no new evidence has resolved the matter conclusively and the pro- and anti-hysteria camps remain at loggerheads. With regard to the 'it was the ley hunters wot don' it' theory,' in the year of the 25th anniversary, The Society of Ley Hunters' moot was again in Derbyshire and guess where mootgoers went on the Sunday? Yes, Arbor Low, and again John Barnatt was the guide. (see Jimmy Goddard, 'Moot at Buxton,' *Touchstone*, No. 71, 2005.

47299
PREDICTING THE FUTURE

(*Traction*, No. 59, 1999)

Destiny seems to have finally caught up with jinxed loco 47299. Prophecy foresaw the Brush Type 4 diesel-electric locomotive heading for an accident as 47216, but even renumbering failed to influence the hand of fate. Now the cursed survivor of so many mishaps and great escapes from withdrawal looks like it has a final date with destiny – even its final demise. Old in tooth and with the track record of a showbooth pugilist, this bewitched loco has been placed in pool WNXX, allocated for stored main line machines. What a shame after it was returned to traffic in mid-January this year.

Originally numbered D1866, the Class 47/0 loco left the Brush company's Loughborough works in May 1965. In February 1974, it was renumbered 47216 on the TOPS computer database. In 1981 it became 47299, the remaining unallocated number before the 47/3 slow-speed control fitted series began. The reason for this latest renumbering has about it something of the magical ritual – a banishing one – for normally fresh numbers are only allocated when a machine has a major modification necessitating the TOPS computer to identify its new sub-classification for allocating its duties commensurate with its re-equipped capabilities, in the case of 47216 there were no mechanical changes; only a psychic component.

As a keen rail enthusiast, I had never understood the reason behind the renumbering. The first inkling came when the loco was involved in a crash, where one magazine reported: 'After predictions of impending doom, BR [British Rail] even renumbered 47216 to 47299 ... but it obviously made little difference.' The brief news item also claimed that 'the jinx that has haunted an Immingham-based Class 47 for over two years followed it to a remarkable crash.' This occurred at Wrawby Junction, a convergence of lines just west of Barnetby, Lincolnshire. At around 18.18 on 9 December 1983, 47299 was hauling the 15.02 Drax power station to Lindsey oil refinery 900-ton empty oil tanks when a set of power points, which had been cranked but not clipped, reset themselves in front of the freight train. A collision then occurred with the 17.32 Cleethorpes to Sheffield two-car diesel multiple unit. Student Rachel Taylor was killed and a dozen other passengers injured. Both cabs of 47299 were stove in and the DMU severely damaged.

The official report stated 'the weather was fine and visibility good,' yet another report claimed 'emergency services were stretched to the limit in appalling weather conditions,' while adding that the renumbering came 'after a soothsayer predicted a crash involving its earlier guise, 47216.' So, who was the psychic with a line to mediumistic ferroequinology? Perhaps we'll never know. The report with greatest detail did not say and even the 1 April dateline should not necessarily concern the reader. Graham Bell's by-lined article in the *Sunday Express* was as accurate a railway news story in a national newspaper as I have ever come across; particularly as in this case an offbeat, human interest story. A clairvoyant had a recurring vision of a train crash involving a big blue engine hauling oil tankers, nothing could stop it and someone would die. She could even decipher the number 47216. She called British Rail and insisted her name be kept secret before revealing the accident in minute detail. Apparently those in authority found her predictions had previously been taken seriously in police investigations.

After the crash, an enthusiast contact of Bell's recalled phoning Immingham depot to ask why 47216 had been renumbered. He was told that staff had been warned of a clairvoyant's predictions, and made a special application to BR headquarters in London to change the number. According to Bell, who checked his story out with BR and confirmed 47299's history, the prediction was not mentioned at the collision inspectorate hearing and the BR spokesman said: "We regard the whole thing as an amazing coincidence."

Does all this give the story credence? The press loves supernatural, human interest stories and with police, BR spokesman and depot officials, you either accept the reporter's investigation was thorough or you cynically mutter about 'authority figures are always used to firm up urban belief tales.' Dave Rapson, in a profile on the loco, focused upon the locospotting fraternity supposedly terming it 'The Demon,' and stating the reason for 'its sudden change of identity had never been revealed, although it is generally believed a visionary foretold of impending doom ... even the depot staff at Immingham had been sworn to secrecy, though the general belief was that, as 47216, the locomotive had been involved in a number of incidents." Yet many locos have had chequered careers without such publicity (Great Train Robbery engine Class 40 D326 being an exception) or renumbering. (*)

As Rapson pointed out, 47299 was condemned on 5 September 1989, only to be reinstated three days later when a replacement wheelset was found. He concluded: "Whether or not this stay of execution is merely temporary, time will tell, and we may never know just how sinister the tale behind 47299 is!" In another magazine, a lengthy caption of the loco as D1866 disputed two earlier points: 'stating BR officials at York' – not London – permitted renumbering and its worn tyres reprieve came after seven – not three – days. Trivialities, perhaps, but accuracy does not equate to being anorakish!

As a writer on contemporary legend, the 47299 saga had always interested me and I got in touch with Immingham depot and have a letter dated 13 February 1992 from S.D. Boner, Area

* A Class 91 electric locomotive was actually renumbered subsequently after being involved in two fatal accidents on the East Coast Main Line.

Fleet Manager. I specifically asked about the clairvoyant, renumbering and any earlier accidents to the loco. The brief reply states:

> 'I refer to your letter dated 5 February and the "folklore" surrounding locomotive 47216/47299 and the Barnetby crash. This is not a matter about which I have any knowledge. I personally have been here since April 1989 and this is the first time it has ever been raised. Renumbering of locomotives occur quite frequently for many varied reasons, all of which are decided at Headquarters level. I am sorry that I cannot be more helpful. Hopefully the foregoing is of some assistance.'

Not really, actually, in fact very disappointing. So what conclusions can be drawn? There are several possibilities: that he was too busy/uninterested to inquire further; that there was no mystery or psychic; or the conspiracy theory that the depot staff had been sworn to secrecy was still active and being enforced. However, the matter does not quite end there. Researchers for TV programmes have twice contacted me regarding 47299; on the second occasion I was told that an exorcism had been carried out at Tinsley depot, although I could neither elicit fur-

A clairvoyant saw a big blue engine hauling oil tankers heading for disaster. Here on such a train, but heading from Humberside is 'jinxed' 47299.

ther details nor confirmation.

Obviously 47299's jinxed reputation had followed it to its new depot on the outskirts of Sheffield, to which it moved on 28 June 1991, where it had an unofficial name applied – *Ariadne*. (**) Whatever, time will tell to see if bell, book and candle were sufficient to have the seemingly doomed 47299 saved. Will the sanctuary of preservation beckon or is 'celebrity' *Ariadne* too spooky to risk with heritage line paying passengers?

As the article implied, chances that 47299 would eventually meets its end in a scrap-yard were high, and indeed it was disposed of with unseemly haste upon eventual withdrawal.

It was dragged to Wigan's Springs Branch depot, where component recovery took place and the carcass totally dismembered by 7 January 2000.

I wrote about the life and times of sheet metal devil 47299 in my hybrid book *Crossing the Line: Trespassing on railway weirdness* (Heart of Albion Press, 2006), a tome whose progress seemed to me equally cursed by its contents, whereby railway publishers were put off by the folklore slant whilst myth and legend publishing houses by the railway element. A chance 'phone call to publisher Bob Trubshaw, on a completely different matter, led to him inquiring whether I was still writing. Yes, and having problems. Like record producer Rick Rubin, who has resurrected so many moribund careers, Bob invited me to submit the synopsis and sample chapter and as they say, the rest's history. More astute than earlier traditionalists who had baulked at my genre-miscegenation mongrel of a proposition, Bob quickly whipped my puppy into shape, and he was publishing-house trained in no time at all, proving popular with the public and profitable for the two of us. Indeed it was pitched to The History Press for republication by Bob as *Mysteries of the Tracks: Weird tales of the railways of Britain*, but did not get the green light to proceed from the acquisitions committee. As for *Traction* magazine, editor David Brown encouraged me to write a couple more articles, failed to publish them, and one on names selected for locos, but never carried in service, ended up appearing in *Folklore Frontiers*.

** Ariadne was the daughter of Minos, King of Crete. She helped Theseus overcome the Minotaur and they married, but he abandoned her on an island where Dionysus found her and made Ariadne his bride.

A TIME-SLIP?
AT 'THORNABY TOR'

(Folklore Frontiers, No. 59, 2007)

My life, on a daily basis, is both enlightened and blighted by what we committed forteans would call 'weird shit.' Perhaps I attract it as some form of minor suburban shaman. Maybe I should share with you some experiences at 'Thornaby Tor'?

I call this mound of earth such, but unlike Glastonbury Tor it is modern, overlooks North-East England's Tees marshalling yard and doomed traction depot - being created when the University of Durham on Teesside campus and main road were being created on the opposite north side. In addition to the land formation climbing to a peak, vaguely resembling Glastonbury Tor, without its ruined church tower, Thornaby Tor shares another earth mysteries aspect, this being the track stretching from near Thornaby railway station to what one of my trainspotting buddies terms Anorak Bridge, where a wide road crosses the huge freight yard, frequented by middle-aged rail enthusiasts. Spotters' boots have created a near-linear path so as to resemble a Watkinsian new straight track, a terrain-oblivious line as modern archaeologists term them or even an echo of a South American ceque.

If, as West Country folk believe, Jesus Christ walked to Glastonbury, on one visit I spotted what at first appeared to be an aged, brown-skinned holy man sitting cross-legged. From a distance, he looked to be meditating or in a trance. As I got closer, he looked up, beamed like the Maharishi Mahesh Yogi and took a can of beer from a large open bag and offered it to me. Never one to refuse a gift, I thanked him, opened it, took a swig and said "cheers." He nodded, grinned, dipped in again, persuading me to take another beer and a Red Bull chaser.

However, this was not the only encounter I have had along that path with Asians; twice in one week I came across a boy and girl engaged in midday copulation. Each time the same pair (as far as I could tell – too early in the day for dogging-style scrutiny), presumably enjoying some light relief and horizontal calisthenics between lectures at the campus below, showed no intention of interrupting their alfresco practical biology trip, if indeed they even noticed my presence passing. In addition to trainspotters, boozers and fornicators, the path is used by dogwalkers and excluded school kids; a pair of whom gave me verbal abuse, while another enthusiast was savagely beaten up on Anorak Bridge a couple of years ago, seemingly purely for being a railfan.

On another occasion, I came across a young man behaving oddly, who admitted he was probably a sadder character than wagonspotters for seeking an object the size of a cigarette packet buried by others, which he explained that by locking on to three orbiting satellites, his global positioning system should lead him to his hidden goal. Or so he said. Wildlife is varied, but the only creature worthy of mention here would be a hedgehog I discovered in broad daylight. To put it out of harm's way, I rolled it energetically down the side of the mound, only to find upon my return 20 minutes later, it having climbed back onto the path. Vegetation is lush on either side of the path and affords a haven for partridges, while skylarks and kestrels can be seen overhead. I noted that on 17 October 2005, with no-one around, I was nonchalantly relieving myself when I casually had the thought, "Hope I'm not pissing on a four-leaf clover," and when I looked down I'd just missed watering such a plant. I had never previously found such a rarity at Thornaby, nor since. Telling such a tale and ascribing some small importance to it sounds like some parody of psychic phenomena; trivial it may be, but true.

Jeff McBride, a talented and respected stage magician who also blends performance magic with alchemical 'magick' and traditional shamanic rituals, has stated in conversation:

> "The major thing that happens in ritual space is synchronicity. You notice the synchronicity. For me, yes, I could name instances for you that, in recounting, might seem minor but that had thunderous impact internally. You know, you can never really measure interior depth by recounting the surfaces." [1]

Equally trivial is a recollection that one morning I realised I had travelled without a pen to take the numbers of the locomotives on the depot and in Tees Yard. After cursing my misfortune, I offered a silent Manichaen prayer to my good guardian angel, walked on for awhile and then my eyes alighted upon a scruffy, partially-broken Century Radio pen which luckily was still functional. And as this fortean weird shit mounts up, back with bodily functions and loco numbers, on another occasion I felt the urgent needs of nature and made an Olympic dash along the path and into *The Dubliners* pub, committing a medal-winning No. 2 to the toilet before discovering there was no paper. Bad guardian angel (or just incompetent staff). I had no choice but to use the sheets of paper carrying my day's sightings before realising I should have copied them on to the back of my hand. My incompetence. Also, unfortunate shit happens.

Retracing one's steps from that superb little pub, [2] the first object along the path is a spot where spotters congregate, mentioned on the enthusiasts' internet bush telegraph as 'The Rock' by railway photographer Andrew Pearson; it being a large, dolmen-like bricks and concrete slab. Another internet item claimed that the area was to be enclosed by spiked metal palisade fencing, but after much forum agitation the originator admitted it had all been a jape.

However, the weirdest occurrence was on 9 March 2006. Thornaby Traction Maintenance Depot, a state-of-the-art steam centre when new in 1958, went on to become one of the ten largest diesel servicing depots. It is memorable for its allocation of Class 37 locomotive No. 37069 and named *Thornaby T.M.D.*, whose spooky reputation has been written up by one of the depot's fitters and also yours truly. [3] Its closure by English, Welsh and Scottish Railway (EWS) in 2007 sent shockwaves through the freight industry. [4] A fuelling facility remains. Platform end rumour has suggested that another operator will take over the depot, whereas more mundane speculation suggests that the university wants the land to expand its campus.

The March day I watched EWS Class 66 locomotive No. 66191 through binoculars, I saw it power off the depot and head eastwards towards the steelmaking complex at Lackenby. Yet a couple of minutes later it passed on the northern single track avoiding the yard sidings immediately below me, again heading east. There was no way it could have got to this second position so quickly nor without me seeing it go westwards and then return east. I am equally certain I correctly identified loco 66191 leaving the depot and have photographic evidence of its second appearance. Nor could there be two engines carrying the same number. The network's TOPS system is configured to disallow such, or as the unhelpful operator in *Little Britain*

Has EWS loco 66191 ever bilocated? Here it is seen at Eaglescliffe on a train loaded with coal on 7 September 2006. (Paul Screeton).

would say: "Computer says 'no'." In fact, a print-off for the TOPS computer at that time showed no other Class 66 loco in the vicinity of Thornaby at that time with a number which I could have mistaken for a second '66191,' nor any which could have been working on the south bank of the Tees at the time of my sightings. I am not suggesting that I had one of those hypothetical 'missing time' experiences or that an EWS Class 66 loco was being used in some latterday Philadelphia Experiment, where 66191 took the role of warship *USS Eldridge*. Yet it suggests something odd. Maybe time is not necessarily linear. Perhaps as quantum physics suggests, an object can be in two places at once.

To close, I found a comment from that extraordinary US anomalist John A. Keel which might shed (unintentional pun, but Class 66s are nicknamed 'sheds') some light on the seeming bilocation of 66191. In conversation with the then editor of *Fortean Times* Bob Rickard, Keel controversially ventured:

> "I have a theory about all this. Most anomalous phenomena are in fact demonstrations of Black Magic powers or something intended for just one or two people. It doesn't make any sense to the rest of us." [5]

Which certainly resonates with Jeff McBride's comment.

References:

1. David Jay Brown, *Conversations on the Edge of the Apocalypse*, Palgrave Macmillan, 2005
2. Paul Screeton (as Pub Spy), 'It's definitely on the right track,' *The Hartlepool Mail*, 9/9/00; Paul Screeton (as Pub Spy), 'Variations on an Irish theme,' Hartlepool Mail, 115/12/01
3. Hugh Watson, 'Old 69 – Thornaby T.M.D. – "The Ghost",' *Folklore Frontiers*, No. 15, 1992; Paul Screeton, *Crossing the Line: Trespassing on railway weirdness*, Heart of Albion Press, 2006
4. *The Railway Magazine*, June, 2007; *Steam Railway*, issue 339, 2007
5. *Fortean Times*, No. 65, 1992

Since writing this piece, Thornaby depot has fallen into dereliction and the yard is a shadow of its former self since the mothballing of the blast furnace at Lackenby and subsequent downturn in metals traffic. Hence I have no reason to go there these days. As for the mystery of bilocating loco 66191, 2010 saw the unveiling of Stephen Hawking's M-theory, with its 11 dimensions. Could 66191 have separate realities in other spheres of existence whereby I stumbled between parallel universes? Was the guy using satellite triangulation really seeking some 'stargate' portal? Were the copulatory couple indulging in 'magick' and was the silent distributor of gifts a time traveller? As they say, weird shit...

FAIRIES' REVENGE?

(*Folklore Frontiers*, No. 10, 1990)

One day in June 1692, the Rev Robert Kirk (1644-1692) was walking upon a fairy hill at Aberfoyle, where he was minister. Here he collapsed and died. But Kirk, however, was no ordinary mortal. He was the seventh son of the Rev James Kirk, also an earlier incumbent of this parish in the foothills of the Scottish Trossachs. In 1691, Robert Kirk had written a book called (in shortened form) *The Secret Commonwealth of Elves, Fauns and Fairies*, in which he made plain his belief in the reality of fairyfolk as a separate set of races to mankind. In the eyes of the superstitious, this Gaelic scholar perpetrated the cardinal sin of taking too close an interest in the elemental stratum of life. Probing into the supernatural was regarded unwise and the inquirer could disappear; if not bodily, at least in spirit.

Did this happen to Kirk? For according to Sir Walter Scott, the form of Kirk appeared to a relation after the ceremony of his seeming funeral and commanded him to go to his successor, the Rev Dr Grahame of Duchray, and tell him he was not dead but a captive in fairyland. Before his abduction, the spectral minister had apparently left his wife pregnant and he told his relation that when the child was brought for baptism he would again appear, and a knife should be thrown over his head, which would break the spell and restore him to society. However, he warned, "If this is neglected, I am lost forever." On the appointed day all was going well, but when Kirk made his spectral appearance his cousin Grahame of Duchray was so dumbfounded that he failed to throw the knife, and as the inscription on his tomb mourns, *and to society, Rev Kirk has not yet been restored.* Kirk's book, which was published posthumously, was revived after the interest shown in it by Sir Walter Scott, who wrote in his *Demonology and Witchcraft* that Kirk's tomb could still be found at the east end of Aberfoyle church.

London-born Anthony Roberts, the self-appointed guru geomant and guardian of Glastonbury, wrote about Kirk and at great length about the ultraterrestrial strain of fairyfolk (he swore he saw one in his own house). I understand he was planning a trip with others to magically invoke Kirk and hopefully rescue him from bondage within the fairy hill, Sith Branch, which was still regarded as a dangerous site, and as Scott put it, 'the joyless Elfin bower.' Elemental dwellers there supposedly still hold feasts and mysterious lights have been seen hovering over it. Roberts had also written a fiery pamphlet entitled *The Fairies' Revenge* a few years ago.

Tony and Janet Roberts in the orchard at Croft Ambury during the 50th anniversary celebration of Alfred Watkins's rediscovery of leys. (Paul Screeton)

On 9 February this year, Tony Roberts climbed Glastonbury Tor. For the last time. A major lunar eclipse was due. During this significant event Tony collapsed. His son Michael ran for help, but to no avail.

That Tony died on his beloved Tor would seem poetical; that this site, a geological anomaly of geomythical psychogeography was choice may be both appropriate yet sinister. It may have been where Tony would have chosen to die, but this is where the Welsh saint Collen had his cell on the lower slopes, just as Tony had his home (not the 'Dunrovin' of settled retirement, but the 'Gondolin' of a wry-humoured recipient of the Welfare State). Collen told two peasants he heard discussing Gwyn, the king of the fairies, that such elementals were in reality demons and for doing so was summoned to the top of the Tor. When he finally ventured into the palace there, he declined the traditional hospitality which would have trapped him, scattered holy water and created mayhem before the company of Fairyland vanished. Gwyn was also Lord of Annwn, a marshalling yard for departed souls related to Avalon; what Tony called 'the metaphysical balance of Celtic mythology.'

Tony has also been quoted as saying/writing:

> 'I represent the elemental forces that structure the Avalonian Spiritual Matrix, and as such I am alchemically bonded to the power of the Tor.'

That quote was selected for a denigratory and ill-natured rant from Valerie Remy (*Pipes of Pan*, No. 24, 1986). Its focus was Tony's proud anti-matriarchal feminist viewpoint and that unintentionally-hilarious, pathetic diatribe which ended the lengthy attack (upon others also, including myself) ended ominously:

> 'The Goddess will not be mocked! Unless they wake up soon to the folly of their ways then Roberts & Co., who are sowing the seeds of such a lot of negative karma, will reap a bitter harvest.'

Tony Roberts, R.I.P. Prophecy fulfilled? Moon as Harsh Mistress? Adam's rib bone pointing? Fairies' revenge? Or simply cardiac arrest? He'd suddenly swooned in a bookshop recently and his youngest son thought he had simply fainted on his way up the Tor. He was walking up a steep hill and carried between 18 and 20 stone in weight. Perhaps also his enjoyment of food in bulk and consumption of alcohol had not always been too wise. He looked a good candidate for British Heart Foundation concern.

Equally, any portrait of Tony cannot fail, in all fairness, to mention the swings suggestive of some instability. As one of those ostracised by him once over a Glastonbury debate and his failure to see I was trying to remain impartial, I found he had a dark side. Others suffered vitriolic letters. Shortly before his death, he seemed to mellow and sought to rebuild bridges with those with whom he had been crossing swords.

Yet he could be a charming companion, particularly propping up the bar, and when in flow – words tripping over one another - he was a great convivial conversationalist. I first met Tony and his charming and supportive wife Janet at the first *The Ley Hunter* magazine moot at Hereford in 1971. He subsequently published my book *The Lambton Worm and Other Northumbrian Dragon Legends* in 1978 and we kept in regular touch. In fact, he took a keen interest in nurturing talent within the geomantic fraternity. As a writer himself he was widely published in such journals at *IT*, *Frendz*, *Arcana*, *The Ley Hunter*, *Torc* and *Mantra*. After much self-publication, under his Zodiac House imprint, his breakthrough came with Unicorn's publication of *Atlantean Traditions in Ancient Britain*. He edited an anthology of articles on Glastonbury which was published in 1976; being republished by international house Rider in 1978. This company also published Tony's book on giants, *Sowers of Thunder*, and his collaboration with Geoff Gilbertson, *The Dark Gods*, which drew heavily upon John Keel's approach to ufology.

In earth mysteries, Tony created the useful portmanteau word 'geomythics,' meaning Earthmyths or myths in relation to our planet's metaphysical concepts – its topography, history and sociology, dimensions of cosmic time and space. Man, myth and magic seem cyclically fashioned rather than in a deterministic linear way. In this sense, Tony found himself very much at odds with a neo-Darwinian archaeological establishment.

Sadly his earlier work – and large-scale work-in-progress – may have been eclipsed (no pun intended) by the anti-matriarchal papers and *The Fairies' Revenge*, an obvious candidate for canonisation by conspiratorialists of various hues. Tony liked to see himself as a mystical anarchist in the Blakean tradition. Unfortunately history is more likely to view him as a proud male bigot who lost his way. I don't know at what stage the manuscript now stands, but some time ago Tony wrote to me saying 'my magnum opus *The Secret Commonwealth Revisited: A Geomythic look at Fairies* is now being finally "polished" and it has a promised introduction from John Michell to help it on its admittedly thorny way.'

Were those Dark Gods influencing publishers' editors and have the fairies again taken their revenge?

But let Tony himself close this tribute; he always like to have the last word! When Valerie Remy said his body would return to the earth from which he was allegedly estranged, Tony replied:

> 'My body may return to earth, but my immortal soul is *free* and
> will go where it fucking well wishes in accordance with my own
> true will under God.'

Selected bibliography:

Atlantean Traditions in Ancient Britain, Unicorn, 1974
Glastonbury: Ancient Avalon: New Jerusalem, Zodiac House, 1976; Rider, 1978
Sowers of Thunder, Rider, 1978
Geomancy: A Synthonal Reappraisal, Zodiac House, 1981
Sacred Glastonbury: A Defennce of Myth Defiled, Zodiac House, 1984
The Fairies' Revenge, Zodiac House, 1985

* An encyclopaedic bibliography is available at: thehobgoblin.blogspot.com/2009/01/anthony-roberts-bibliog...

This obituary/tribute to Anthony Frederick Roberts is an amalgam of separate pieces for *The Ley Hunter* and *Folklore Frontiers*, sharing a central core, but more EM in the former and extra Kirk context in the latter. The connection with Tony continues in that I have recently been contacted by his son Simon, a tour manager for bands (as a friend of *The Stranglers*, Tony would have surely approved), and widow Jan, recently retired from running a Montessori school. Through Simon I learned that – as I originally thought – Gondolin had a Tolkien connection, being the city of the Elves, mentioned in *The Silmarillion* (Tony received a handsome redundancy payment from *The Times*, where he was a librarian, so he probably never signed on to the dole).

It all seems so long ago when Tony published the first of two dragonlore books I wrote, when in lieu of payment or royalties he lumbered me with 36 copies for me to sell for myself and I struggled all the way back from London's Festival of Mind, Body and Spirit (or as someone called it, Mind, Body and Money) in 1978. Another time I met him was to introduce him to Paul Devereux in 1976 and Jan drove us to a pub, Tony drinking whiskey in the car and continuing from the bottle in our first tavern, wherefrom the landlady ejected us. Jan republished my obituary from *TLH* in her tribute to Tony: *From Atlantis to Avalon and Beyond* (Zodiac House, 1995).

John Michell gave a eulogy at the funeral, but his most telling comment after Tony's death was that "a mighty oak has fallen."

OPPOSITE:This extraordinary illustration appears almost at the end of *The Fairies' Revenge*. Leering elementals ogle a girl, while one of them's implement lies pointedly upon her private parts. Uncomfortable for her; perhaps also for the reader. Those who thought Tony a misogynist would draw their own conclusions. And what of the crow, symbol of death? Some shadow of prophecy?

DAIMONIC REALITY: A FIELD GUIDE TO THE OTHERWORLD by PATRICK HARPUR

(*Folklore Frontiers*, No. 23, 1994)

I have seen a daylight disc and craft like zeppelins; a black panther in Northumberland; a wood gnome and under sleep deprivation the tooth fairy; a half-human, half-zebra entity enter the office toilet during a mycological flashback; a woman medium's face turn into that of a Chinaman; a bird give its life to save mine. This book is about this sort of anomalous phenomena and the author suggests that 'if these strange visitations have any purpose at all, it is to subvert the same modern worldview which discredits them.' Luckily I need no convincing, nor have done since adolescence.

Patrick Harpur, too, approached the subject as a believer, but wanted to examine the data within a framework; to present it to himself as much as to others. He notes that this worldview with its comprehension of the importance of dreams, contents of the unconscious, soul-images, existence of apparitions, and so on, exists unofficially and instinctively among groups and individuals in our own monotheistic culture against all the odds. He notes that such people largely lack a sense of precedent for their view, a historical context for their own eyes and senses; and this is partly what his book aims to provide.

Which brings us to the book's title. The daimons here, for the sake of convenience, embrace all apparitional figures, including fairies, angels, souls and aliens; flexibly changing form to suit their times, i.e. cultural tracking, as abstractions or preferably remaining personified. Archetypal personages going back from Jung to the Gnostic/Hermetic/Neoplatonic tradition of philosophy. The Neoplatonists described the world of gods and daimons as Anima Mundi (Soul of the World) and Harpur reckons this has the advantage over the collective unconscious as a root metaphor because it returns us to the idea of soul instead of psyche; reintroducing the idea of an objective ensouled world 'out there.' Particular places are where we are more likely to encounter the unseen order of things. Lights hang over prehistoric sites while military bases, power stations and reservoirs attract hovering UFOs because these are the shrines of our modern secular culture, becoming a shadow display of hi-tech alien 'spacecraft' to mirror our technological preoccupations. At such places the laws of time and space, matter and causality seem attenuated: caravan sites and trailer parks being in that liminal area between town and countryside are specially prey to UFOs or strange creatures which particularly favour boundaries. The greater transparency at certain sacred sites has led to the ufological – and broader – term 'window areas.' Paradoxically they straddle many borders, such as that between fact and fiction.

Patrick Harpur concludes the section with a discussion of urban myths, seeing them as also spanning the gap between fact and fiction; ambiguous and using the friend-of-a-friend convention to distance us from the alleged event. After the collective unconscious and anima mundi, he constructs a third model, that of imagination, for making intelligible the nature of daimonic reality. Primary imagination is here defined as encountering the sacred; secondary imagination is recreative and evaluating, making from the human condition art or at a personal level being therapeutic. Not only is a rather complex theory of models made to make sense (he could have included other models such as Mercurius or faery), but as all forteans will understand, daimonic phenomena cannot, by definition, be explained (for explanations are images and myths anyway). Daimonic is a self-coined metaphor to emphasise the power of the models examined. However, after taking the reader through such topics as missing time, scars, strokes, near-death experiences, stigmata, changelings, midwifery, alien sex, Bigfoot, supernatural food, satanic child abuse and bogus social workers, shamanism with Shiels and Shuttlewood, John Keel's quest, soul and body, he ends the book with two instructive examples of successful descents into the Underworld – 'now more than ever the most appropriate spatial metaphor for daimonic reality.' These visits involve ufology's notorious greys and C.G. Jung.

For a book that is arguing that its subject matter cannot be explained and that soul resists spirit's wish to find single underlying principles, Harpur has come as close as anyone so far to producing a unifying theory for the great diversity of subject matter loosely labelled paranormal/supernatural/occult mythological, fortean and folkloric. Naturally the author recognises the paradox, aware that the book's perspective is partial and incomplete. Nevertheless it is a remarkable *tour de force.*   (Published by Viking, £18)

In response to my review, Patrick Harpur sent me a letter, the relevant parts of which read:
'Dear Paul – Many thanks for the handsome review: you're the only reviewer (incl. *Sunday Times, Literary Review, Independent*, etc,) who seems (a) to have actually read the book I wrote rather than one they imagined I wrote! and (b) to have grasped what I was driving at so that's encouraging at least, I've entered the book for the Folklore Society prize ... I hope you'll give us another quick plug when the paperback comes out next year! [1995] Good luck!

PART THREE
SHAMANISM & ESOTERIC CHRISTIANITY

ALAN GARNER AND THE SHAMANISTIC PROCESS

(Common Ground, No. 6, 1982)

When writer Alan Garner made a move to kill an actor it was a dramatic form of neo-dissociation, or as Garner intellectualised it, "a Western European's experience of a primitive catastrophic process." Its cause and resolution sheds much light on shamanism, a subject with which Garner is familiar. In fact, when sketching the framework for a book, I had decided Garner already fulfilled certain criteria for being a 'suburban shaman.' He wrote books for children to read in their homes and mixed the everyday world with the realm of myth. In particular, *The Guizer* revealed a sympathy with the Trickster archetype, though its mode of presentation was a dubious enterprise. A gallant failure, I guess. I had also read of strange events surrounding a production of his book *The Owl Service* for television and a later TV play. So when I came across the transcript of a talk he had given, full of self-revelation and mental turmoil, I felt doubly justified in choosing him as a topic.

Inner Time is a lucid account of a psychological phenomenon associated with the shamanistic process. It was delivered as one of a series of lectures by writers at the Institute of Contemporary Arts in London in early 1975.

Perhaps, like me, you saw and enjoyed the television adaptation by Garner of his novel *The Owl Service*. He began work on transferring the words into pictures in the autumn of 1968. The process produced an unexpected malaise. Eventually the script was completed and filming began in April the next year. He found filming on location equally unpleasant. He felt 'pain, a threat from no direction, and a threat with no shape.' Garner began arriving late for shooting, experienced nausea and then was regularly physically sick. It developed into a threat of paralysis and rage against the actors. The symptoms combined in one moment of blind fury. A particular actor was incompetent in Garner's opinion and when it came to filming a delicate climax he was clowning about, antagonising everyone and lacking any emotion for the sensitive scene to be shot. Garner recalled daylight blanking out except for a clear line around the actor's head. A cry from some primeval bestiality broke through and he moved to attack. But the sound engineer inserted his microphone boom between Garner's legs and gave him a flick into a puddle. Lifting Garner to his feet, he observed, "I know, but wait till next week, we still need him"

From then until filming was completed Garner kept a low profile. It was all over on 21 June; summer solstice. Garner's psychological health deteriorated further. He slept, he became like a zombie, then went seemingly mad. With sufficient nous to diagnose that he needed help badly, he sought a psychiatrist. Here it is preferable not to paraphrase, but tell it in Garner's own words:

> 'What happened to me was something normal; yet it was superficially so close to the esoteric and occult that it could easily be misinterpreted and misunderstood. And if "normal" should be thought too imprecise a word, let me define it as "that which is found to be common among a group or species".'

What Garner precipitated would be familiar to Australian Aborigines. They would say he entered 'Dreamtime.' Not insanity, but the conscious awareness of another dimension. The veil of illusion had been rent. A psychotherapist performs a shamanistic function in our disordered society, and it was to an experienced practitioner that Garner went. With clinical precision 'Mr Smith' needed to ask only one question: in what tense and singular or plural was *The Owl Service* written? It being in the past tense and the third person. When filming, that distancing dissolved, and two times were present at once. The time bomb ceased its ticking and exploded.

Scientology aside, and in strictly clinical terms, 'Mr Smith' simply removed an engram. An engram being, in neuro-physiology, the term for a hypothetical change in the protoplasm of the neural tissue. It has been posited as accounting for memory. Some experience or stimulus creates it. The brain files away all our experiences; pleasant or hurtful. A smell, a sound and our other senses can reactivate an engram or it can surface through a dream, drugs, or hypnosis. We may wish baleful engrams stay forgotten, but once imprinted they live on in inner time. This inner time creates illusions. Pleasantly memorable encounters from times widely separate in calendar time can be recalled simultaneously. Similarly the starry sky we see is composed of bodies existing at different times, with many of those flickering lights having been extinguished aeons ago. Engrams are, however infinite. Put out the candle and tomorrow it burns bright again.

Lord of the Underworld

The psychologist C.G. Jung would have known equally how to deal with Garner. 'When I see a man in a savage rage,' he noted, 'I know that he is, in reality, wanting to be savage towards his own unconscious self.' That is the engram store from which occasional attack is normal. It is the unconscious where during childhood and adolescence in particular we store our fears and aspirations, likes and dislikes. What we prefer not to face or cannot comprehend we force into forgetfulness. But maturity brings with it memories, nagging prejudices and elements of passion which retain the same vitality as at the moments of repression. Their hidden nature creates the illusion that they play no part in our lives, but they can be dominating the conscious mind, causing confusion, depression and generally upsetting the physical and mental health of the individual. They must be faced, be challenged, be overcome, be exorcised. There is a strong case to be argued that engrams can be transmitted genetically. That is beyond the scope of this article, but an inherited inner time could explain Jung's collective unconscious and psyche of a given race.

Garner concluded that writers unconsciously plant encapsulated engrams in their characters. When an engram is manifested simultaneously in inner and outer time, and as when Garner moved to assault the actor, the disorientation can lead in the direction of madness. A memory trace of Garner as character from some place in 1950 met himself as in the actor on a Welsh mountain in 1969. From a one-dimensional engram was created a fourth dimension scenario as the inner-time co-ordinates were identical, but had externalised to the present. 'Mr Smith' explained in simple terms to Garner that energy holding an engram can be released, one's co-ordinates can be recast, and not to be afraid. Leaving Garner as someone to walk in 'Dreamtime,' and 'to be with the vehicle of myth, to go voluntarily (and now knowingly) to inner time, and to come back increased instead of diminished . . .' Sensibly Garner also warns that 'no one should be seduced into foolhardy experiments by any superficial lure in the experiences I relate.'

We now come to the crux of the matter. Is Garner a *bona fide* shaman, or at least partially one? He comments: 'For what I am, and what Mr Smith does, in other societies is seen quite differently. To the shamans of Turukhansk I should not fulfil their recruiting standards.'

In a scene from *The Owl Service* are
(left to right) Francis Wallis, Gillian Hills and Michael Holden.

I feel Garner, despite his subsequent argument to the contrary and sympathetic portrait of the traditional shaman, is too modest. He allowed himself to become a keen and willing channel for mythology, chose to live on a site dating back to Neolithic usage and below the brooding Alderley Edge, opened doors of perception which all writers of any worth cannot fail to do, and was spiritually reborn. Certain commentators have noted the relationship between mystical vocation and nervous instability, but it would be wrong to assume a shaman must be a neuropath. In fact, the receipt of shamanistic gifts presupposes the resolution of a psychic crisis; an integration bringing about initiation, which one must assume occurred in Garner's case. An illness or epileptic attack can reveal the vocation, and initiation becomes the cure. Hence the argument that shamanism is a mental ailment is clearly absurd, for they succeed in getting well. In fact, when choosing Garner as a subject, I recalled that I had read somewhere that he had been seriously ill as a child. This suggested another clue to his special capacities. In his self-revelatory address he reported a second trauma and revisiting 'Mr Smith.' This was triggered when his opera *Potter Thompson* was about to go into rehearsal and malaise returned. His analyst took him back to the engram and it led him to visualise himself, aged six, vomiting after eating the top half of a teacake covered with blackcurrant jam. He then developed the first symptoms of what was later diagnosed as spinal and cerebral meningitis.

'Wounded healer'
Garner did indeed spend most of his early life ill in bed, and the wartime blackouts may equally have formed a mental stimulus to create his worlds of mystery and fantasy. He says he was 'thrown back on myself,' won a scholarship to Manchester Grammar School and, after National Service, to Oxford University. Endurance plays a major role in shamanism and despite his early bedridden past, amazingly drove himself to become Northern Counties Sprint Champion. Talk about the 'wounded healer.'

That early solitude and precarious balance between life and death may well have manifested itself on the psychic plane as a parallel to the torture and abandonment of initiation, only to be another factor in the arsenal accumulated awaiting triggering. He found, following his mental maelstrom, an explosion of literary projects and 'I am told my work is richer now, less diffused.'

For those unfamiliar with the literary output of Alan Garner, a brief resume seems in order. The earliest novels were *The Weirdstone of Brisingamen* and *The Moon of Gomrath*. Garner's preoccupation with myth saw even more powerful expression in the following three novels, pitched each time at children but with their ages rising through puberty and equally enjoyed by adults: *Elidor*, *The Owl Service* and *Red Shift*. His method was to take a traditional ballad or other encapsulation of myth and bring it to life again in a fresh context. Accusations of opportunism or shallow imaginative capacity are groundless, for any writer of fiction will tell you elements will conform to an objective pattern with the author's subjectivity merely the icing on the cake. The inability to come to terms with this process whereby a myth can select its teller, and rather than he tell it in his own way and have it told as living myth demands, is what Garner believes caused him to appear to go mad.

In addition to the traumas experienced by Garner on the set of the making of *The Owl Service*, others found it a 'jinx,' as journalists love to describe any series of mishaps. Rosalie Horner explored this for *Daily Express* readers. *The Owl Service* was based on a Welsh legend about a woman transformed into an owl and a strong strand was provided by Garner's mother-in-law, who rescued a dinner service with a strange aura from a barn attached to a Somerset family home. This was owl-patterned and guests said they got indigestion when they ate off it and found the birds staring uncomfortably at them as they ate. "The plates seemed a perfect kind of battery waiting to be switched on," observed Garner.

The author spent a holiday at Bryn Hall, in North Wales, and realised this was just the sort of place he had been trying to visualise for the book. Long after publication, he learned that a film crew had been in the attic there and found a brass knocker in the form of an owl. Equally strangely, one character's mother is called Nancy and in the gardener's house on the estate the name 'Nancy' was discovered on a beam. Chance? Occult intervention? Who knows?

Owner of Toad Hall

But it was the real-life tragedies to follow which are even creepier. The memorable photography was by David Wood, who died at the age of 44. The character Gwyn was played by Michael Holden, brutally murdered in an unprovoked attack in a Mayfair bar in 1977. Gwyn's step-sister was played by Gillian Hills, who had strange experiences while filming and chose to opt out of acting, as apparently did another performer in the series, Francis Wallis; at least in 1978, when the original black and white showing (due to a technicians' strike apparently) was rebroadcast by Granada in colour. Then in 1980, Garner's television play *To Kill a King* was screened. It was about a writer who wakes up in the middle of the night to face a nightmare that ends his career as a wordsmith. It was filmed in his 15th Century home, Toad Hall, bought for £500 when he graduated from Magdalen College, Oxford, which has what he called a 'presence.' In an earlier article it was described as a long-dormant poltergeist. "An old woman who lived here when it was two tied cottages told me she had seen a picture float from the wall into the middle of her room. I asked her what she did and she said, 'I put it back'."

Red Shift, also filmed for a one-part television drama, was a post-breakdown, multi-layered novel and despite what others may say, I feel his work since has become too abstruse for me – never mind the children at whom it is aimed. Recently I saw a huge stack of his £4 published price *The Guizer* reduced to 75p in a Leeds remainderer's (*CG* even introduces you to new words!) bookshop. This work was trumpeted by Hamish Hamilton and is a diligent, crafted, but exceedingly boring book. Slimmer volumes have also appeared and they, too, leave me cold. No doubt there is a 'message' but it eludes me. Nevertheless, although his work is not easy, he seems to find particular nerve points to write upon, and his output never fails to leave me intrigued, if not puzzled.

This abstruseness is apparent in a reply to journalist Michael Moynihan, regarding the then forthcoming *Red Shift*, when Garner commented on one passage that:

> "The two young people meet once in a church and quarrel. It is a church near here, where there was a massacre during the Civil War. They do not know about the massacre and the reader will not know. But it will be in the writing. I often go to the church and sit there, hearing the screams."

Unless he is spinning a yarn, which I doubt, this suggests shamanistic contact with the departed.

Anyway, writing is a funny old business. Garner suggests its motivation could be the discharge of engrams. I wrote four novels during puberty and early adulthood, partly to gain a better understanding of myself and my situation. Not that they were embarrassingly puerile – though they hardly had the publishing world agog, but coming from a very personal period of my life were no doubt too egocentric and lacking a critical perspective; cathartic but immature. Perhaps the pen is mightier than the sword and a re-reading would only open old wounds and create a plethora of stigmata of self-consciousness and regret for some perceived golden age of adolescence. If I didn't exorcise the engrams then, I'm not risking confronting them now!

Suppressed engrams, developed prejudices, these conspire to make us old before our time. We miss opportunities. The shaman catches the energy released at puberty and holds on to it for his and the community's benefit. Adolescence is where we choose between the world of security and engrams or the wider vistas of danger, facing our fears and finding the light. This is free will and our Western education has no place in its curriculum for it. Not so, primitive tribes. Our survival pattern is geared to the monopolistic, capitalist slave economy and Garner's analogy of the Aborigine applying 'Dreamtime' techniques to crossing an arid desert naked and yet being unable to cross Sydney alone is apposite. As Garner says, the Australian Pitjantjatra exist simultaneously with 20th Century city dwellers, but our cultures are essentially 20,000 years apart. Along the way of so-called civilisation, the dominant breed of supposedly enlightened minds created ever more sophisticated technologies at the expense of the numinous. The complexes, neuroses, hang-ups, engrams, call them what you will, they remain. Few remain humble.

Garner does have that quality, at least with regard to his own work. He calls himself a survivor, better equipped to work following his traumas. He understands it 'comes through me, not from me,' yet he can retain a proper pride in his craft of what could be called translation. He closed his I.C.A. talk by stating:

> 'Perhaps the artist's job is to act as a cartographer for all navigators, and I simply plot the maps of inner stars.'

Bibliography:

'Deadly Bird of Prey...,' by Rosalie Horner, *Daily Express*, 1/7/78
'Dark Dreams at Toad Hall,' by Michael Moynihan, *Sunday Times*, 22/12/80
Science Fiction at Large, edited by Peter Nicholls, Victor Gollancz, 1976; as *Explorations of the Marvellous*, Fontana, 1978

Common Ground magazine acted as journal of record for the Association for the Scientific Study of Anomalous Phenomena and blazed a trail briefly while under the inspired tutelage of editor Kevin McClure. The content of my piece seemed to baffle Kevin and he admitted difficulty in placing it 'in context,' whereas I thought it fitted perfectly this mature magazine's high standard of thought-provoking contributions. *Common Ground* only ran to six issues but ASSAP is still going strong. As for the article, as so often annoyingly occurs in this anthology, it had its genesis in a project aborted through publishers' reticence to accept such a work in progress from yours truly; in this case analyses of such famed or unknown characters as Garner, Doc Shiels, Tom Cole, John Keel and J.G. Ballard, to be entitled *Suburban Shamans*. This article is your gain and their loss.

With regard to following up the material in this article, in an attempt to fathom out why Gillian Hills quit acting and whether it was due to her experience filming *The Owl Service*, an internet search directed me to *The Indigo Fleapit* blog. Interesting observations include how (as a 'running joke' – really?) the three main characters wore outfits throughout of predominantly red, black and green; colours of electric plug wiring at the time, as if to show their vulnerability as individuals, but strength when they teamed together. As for Gillian Hills quitting acting – I watched the series in colour in 1978 but cannot recall the salacious scenes – her role was rather risqué for a children's drama and a 5.45pm slot, appearing 'in a skimpy bikini, in the bath, writhing in a bikini on a bed and in the last scene as she deals with possession writhes orgasmically as the camera pans on her legs and crotch.' I doubted this took her thespian aspirations a step too far as she had already appeared naked in *Blow-Up* and despite the intended exploration of teenage hormonal angst, she was actually aged 25 and had enjoyed success as a singer in France. She later appeared in the equally disturbing *A Clockwork Orange*. In fact, when I rechecked Rosalie Horner's article focussing on the 'jinx' she attributed to the series, I found she had conceded that Hills quit acting because she never enjoyed it.

MYSTERY HILL

From the outside it looks like the last place you would expect to find treasure. For relics in an archaeological sense lie within an old barn in South-East Durham. The dark interior of an outbuilding overlooking the North Sea contains mysterious carvings of baffling antiquity and purpose. There are strangely-shaped human heads, a scene of someone bathing and one which is robustly sexual in nature. How they came to be carved, by whom, at what age and why they have been affixed to the walls are all puzzles. Being hidden and so little known has meant no professional or academic opinion has been sought. A dozen possibilities for their presence and meaning could be given. Superlatives fail to capture the magical quality, sheer oddness and captivating quaintness of these carvings plastered into the weatherworn walls of this humble cattle barn.

The archwayed building adjoins Mickle Hill Farm, a homestead overlooking Blackhall Rocks [at grid reference NZ456387]. Amateur historian Reg Wright mentions the carvings in his book *Blackhall Rocks in the Parish of Monk Hesleden*, published in 1985. There is a picture taken outside the barn in 1984 [depicted here] and another of some of the carvings [one from his collection also appears here]. Reg surmised they could be scenes from Norse mythology, fertility scenes, Christian or more probably mediaeval. All he seemed sure of was that there were 19. And well worth seeing. Indeed! I had to squeeze past a large item of mechanical farm machinery to enter the otherwise empty barn. Even with the aid of a lamp, not all the carvings could be made out with clarity, several being very high up on the walls out of safe distance of reaching them.

I was shown them through the kind hospitality of Tom and Jenny. They expressed bafflement at the identity of the carvings, their purpose and age, just stating that they had been there for as long as anyone could remember.

The large number of human heads cut off at the neck is suggestive of Celtic influence. The head cult was central to the fierce warrior Celts' worldview and there is evidence that it still exerts a baleful influence in certain areas of the Pennines and perhaps also the Tyne Valley. A particularly large head has a Norse look to it, though it also could be said to resemble the contemporary pop idol George Michael! (By coincidence Mickle seems a derivation from Michael, a dragon-slaying saint of somewhat pagan origins, perhaps? Mickle – Michael – George

Michael?) Below this is what could be a Christian design. It looks like a broken representation of the Crucifixion. Another block shows what appears to be someone washing, kneeling before a dish. Reg thought this to be a Greek-style motif. Too high for me to see it, was what Reg says is a crudely pornographic depiction. There are also people's initials which are probably recent additions. There is this puzzling seeming mixture of paganism and Christianity, perhaps a Gnostic strain of the latter. Was the barn used at some period as a place of worship by some sect difficult to identify?

Also where did the stones come from? One clue is that they all seem to be made from the same grey stone. My geological knowledge does not stretch to identification of composition, but I have seen two boulders of the same type along the Hart Station to Haswell walkway. They are quite probably a type of glacial erratic detritus and not native to the region. But I doubt there is so mundane an explanation for these strange figures, for no single aspect seems to be simple. Mickle Hill really is mystery hill.

(Long Man of Wilmington column, *The Ley Hunter*, No. 107, 1988; *The Mail* (Hartlepool), 17/12/88; *Folklore Frontiers*, No. 10, 1990)

Jenny Smithson by the entrance to the outbuilding containing carvings. (Reg Wright)

This article was very slightly changed for the readership of *The Mail* and illustrated with three photographs by Reg Wright. I subsequently revisited Mickle Hill Farm with a friend while seeking corn circles. This time Tom Smithson speculated that the carvings could have been the work of a Polish farmworker employed during the Second World War.

'Crucifixion' scene with 'Norse god?' above it. (Reg Wright)

Paul Devereux, who published the original version, drew my attention to a sacred place known as a *Hof*, an otherwise ordinary farm building in which sacerdotal feasts were observed, such as belonging to farms of varying importance but serving entire communities. These existed long ago and belonged to the Northern Tradition (Celtic/Germanic/Baltic/ Norse). Mickle Hill has a crucifixion depiction and perhaps the heathen god Odin above (Greek ancestry of George Michael aside). Rival faiths together may trouble religious purists, but as a Gnostic myself, with its pick 'n' mix flexibility that allows, plus how the well-known carvings at Royston divide scholars, I would simply like to have the full 19 works examined in detail before anyone comes to any conclusion. *Hofs* left little trace and excavation of ancient versions finds it almost impossible to distinguish between a non-liturgical farm building and a *Hof*. [1] The modern mystery of an extant building in South-East Durham should offer a better chance of a solution, but being a fortean and knowing experts' propensity to argue, who knows?

Reference: (1) Nigel Pennick & Paul Devereux,
Lines on the Landscape: Leys and Other Linear Enigmas, Robert Hale, 1989

THE WIZARD OF STANLEY

(The Shaman, No. 8, 1984, and No. 9, 1985)

The stroke of midnight on New Year's Eve, 1969, became a life-changing moment in Tom Cole's life. Seated at home with his wife Sharon and two friends, he was busily working on an astrological chart, attempting to discover the cause of climate effects. It was a beautiful clear night. His wife and friends were discussing the celebratory mood. Tom left the table to sit on an old sea chest near the window to listen, being a little prejudiced against what he regarded as 'introduced' festivities. During this time he became aware of his attention being drawn out of the window. Someone mentioned that it was almost midnight and the radio was switched on to hear the celebrations being broadcast from Trafalgar Square. Just after midnight on New Year's Eve it is customary in North-East England to go first-footing; a ritual of shared hospitality with neighbours and other friends, the first-foot traditionally being male, a non-member of the household and bearing a piece of coal. They were expecting to greet one or more first-foots.

On the stroke of midnight it was to be no hand-shaking, back-slapping, merry-making jingling Geordie ushering in 1970 and good fortune. Instead, right on cue, from the south-western horizon appeared a large ball of fire, appearing to head directly towards Tom. He called to Sharon and his friends to witness it, too, while mentally noting its position in the landscape. It reached the place marked on the map as The Middles and departed over Taylors Hill. Realising this occurrence of an aerial phenomena to be significant, Tom cursed that he had no map of that area of County Durham around Stanley, but was able to use a celestial chart as a substitute. He knew from where it came, the point where it paused and where it went. The result was an incredible angle of 30 degrees. Knowing the area intimately, he calculated it had appeared to land at Langley Castle. There was even the coincidental – or was it? – similarity between Langley and 'Old Lang Syne.' Next morning Tom walked along the apparent path of the fireball but discovered nothing of significance. Following the festivities an Ordnance Survey map was purchased. Then the real revelation struck home.

The Stanley Zodiac

What the down-to-earth astrologer of the decaying industrial community of Stanley was still to discover was the 'as above, so below' link decreed by Hermes Trismegistus. With a map laid corresponding with the celestial north of his charts, the cosmic exploration was on to link the heavens and the landscape. Tom observed that the guiding light moved along Aquarius to the centre and then along the winter solstice line. Using The Middles as his celestial pole, Tom plotted a map of the heavens on the Ordnance Survey map. The result was that on each star of a constellation there corresponded a special landscape feature such as mound, spring, pit, waste ground and so on. Significant to him at least. Even more confirmatory were names of communities and public houses. Seeking further corroborative evidence, Tom decided that each zodiacal month he would visit the relevant sector and examine the species present to see if they corresponded with those expected to be particularly prevalent. This they proved to be so. Also it became readily apparent that the footpaths had developed to fit the design of the celestial chart. As Tom continued to map out the shapes, lo and behold, a terrestrial zodiac began to emerge as a tapestry in the landscape, with other constellations becoming delineated in their appropriate places.

To both believer and sceptic alike, his advice was simple: 'Set your points or compass to four and a half inches radius for a one-inch map. Use The Middles as your centre, Iveston as the vernal equinox and begin as for a celestial chart. It would be helpful to note that the lamb's tail begins at Lope Hill (to frisk), Taurus is White-le-Head and Tanfield, Virgo is Vigo, Libra is Chester-le-Street and Lumley, and Scorpio the Lambton Worm.'

Tom deduced that the zodiac around Stanley was not unique. He believed there were many, but it was a while before there was positive evidence of this. At the time of his revelation a few other examples had been fully charted; at least to their discoverers' satisfaction. Katharine Maltwood even today towers monumentally over the chequered history of terrestrial zodiac hunting; and earth mysteries study seemingly born under a bad sign. It is certainly currently in eclipse, and despite continuing sterling work by Mary Caine to interest people in her adjustments to the Maltwood figures depicted in the Somerset countryside around Glastonbury, and her own Kingston-upon-Thames Zodiac, the subject has entered a state of limbo. I edited *Terrestrial Zodiacs Newsletter* and kept researchers in touch with developments, but there came a sudden lack of interest. Perhaps this will revive, maybe in slightly altered form.

The Fleet Shot Hill Zodiac

With words something like, "Hi, I've found a zodiac," Tom Cole stood in the rain on my doorstep. There are times when you are bursting to tell someone of a great revelation, sometimes a great notion, earthquaking discovery and no-one wants to know or even has the faintest idea what you're talking about. Who would understand? Terrestrial zodiacs laid across the landscape may not enthuse many people, but Tom had been informed I'd definitely be infected by his enthusiasm for his revelation. His contact with me had been through doyen of earth mysteries John Michell. Sharon Cole, a secretary for The Law Society, had visited a library and chanced fortuitously upon a copy of Michell's *The View Over Atlantis* and noted the reference to Mrs Maltwood's contentious claim to having seen the shape of a lion's back in a Somerset waterway and eventually mapped all the other figures of the zodiac, plus the Girt Dog of Langport guarding this 'Temple of the Stars.' Tom had written to Michell, via his publishers, to share his vision, and Michell suggested that - both as a fellow researcher living in the region and editor of *The Ley Hunter* magazine - I would be equally enthusiastic about Tom's discovery.

Portentously, Michell's reply arrived at the Coles' end-of-terrace house on my day off and Tom had driven directly to Seaton Carew from North-West Durham in the hopes I would be at home. The spaghetti meal I was preparing for a friend of my wife's staying as a guest and myself was split three ways and we discussed the landscape zodiac and other esoterica. With wiry build, swarthy outdoors complexion, unruly hair, lively eyes and moustache falling in narrow bands to his chin, Tom looked as though a good meal would not go amiss. Imagine if you will an underfed Peter Wyngarde in his *Jason King* role, but without being dandified or the posh voice. Then with the rain having abated, the three of us got into his Land-Rover, along with Tom's friendly wolfhound Avalon, as I wanted to show him the Saxon church at nearby Hart. When we arrived it was not only open – rare in itself – but the rector was present and offered a guided tour. Tom made a move to take his dog outside to be tethered, but Canon D.T. Eastwood made some remark about all animals being welcome in God's church, so Avalon had a new haunt to sniff about in.

Inside and out, the 1,300-year-old edifice is a gem and one hardly appreciated even locally. Additions since Saxon times have given the church a jumbled austerity; the decoration being functional and the interior squat and just right for the size of congregation a small village generates. Generations have worshipped here and the church is more than traditionally the hub of communal life, for gates and stiles at each corner of its charming churchyard of crumbling headstones give access to footpaths radiating in several directions. The path between two high walls leading from the south, reaches a gate - under which, and right in the middle of the path - lies buried Ellen Thomson. Her wickedness was so great that she had been excommunicated and was buried there outside consecrated ground so the pious churchgoers would press down the earth and ensure she remained underground. Within there is a 15th Century font, richly carved with figures of angels, apostles and northern kings. An earlier Norman example also draws admiration for its uncommon form and here also are displayed early Anglo-Saxon shafts. The parish records are revealing, too, preserved since 1567 and recalling the plague years, local witches such as the aforementioned Ellen Thompson, Old Mother Midnight, Alison Lowe and Helen de Inferno, and a scurrilous and rude commentary upon Oliver Cromwell.

However, almost as if he psychically recognised the bond between Tom and I forged only a couple of hours earlier, Canon Eastwood's opening remarks of his tour were directed towards astrology. He pointed to ten corbels around the roof and two lying on the ground, adding words, with some emphasis, to the effect that if we thought the 12 would represent zodiacal figures we were in for a disappointment, as only one fitted the celestial scheme. We both found that a stunning commentary in the context of our visit. After we left, Tom assured me that there was an inner circle of Anglican clergymen with occult knowledge who were entrusted with especially potent churches. This was my first taste of his brand of conspiracy theorising, of which more shortly.

However, before venturing within the church, I had pointed out to Tom what I considered special. This was a carving on the south wall of St George and the Dragon, believed to date from around 1500. Of this, too, more shortly. It certainly intrigued Tom that day. As we returned towards Hartlepool, Tom reflected that the trees and plants in the churchyard were those associated with Scorpio. Here, too, he considered there might be yet another terrestrial zodiac. Fired by Tom's enthusiasm, I spent that evening pouring over the one-inch and six-inch maps of the area. Sure enough, working from a centre at Fleet Shot Hill and Hart as Scorpio, there seemed some substance in the notion. Where the Libran dove could be expected was a dovecote and Leo's front feet lay at Pawton Hill and Crookfoot.

A prediction of my death abroad, aged 53

Tom certainly took his astrology seriously. He spent a long time casting my horoscope one afternoon and if I die abroad when I'm 53 he'll be vindicated. When a man he would meet on street corners who knew of his reputation would ask which horse to back, Tom would give a cryptic reply and he claimed that invariably the punter would read into it a coded message and relieve the turf account of his ill-gotten cash. As with many people having real (or no) knowledge, Tom was often evasive or oblique in expressing his learning. The heady mixed brew of verbal boasting and buffoonery, anarchy and allegory, the fantastic and fantasy, exaggeration and bullshit, liberally leavened with urban belief tales, rumours and conspiracy, only now takes on the full weight of positive value. The negativity nobbled my naïveté. No wonder Carlos Castaneda was able to commit his hoax so plausibly. My Stanley sorcerer similarly exasperated me and lessons are still being learnt. But he overstepped the mark on one occasion, maybe deliberately, by feeding me a stunning example of double apocrypha by claiming Jewish mystical rock singer Bob Dylan faked his motor-cycle accident so he could probe the death of two friends in a South American flying saucer encounter. Sceptical – as Dylan fanatic and ufologist – I spent a couple of hours going through UFO magazines and books to locate the familiar event in question and found its timing did not correlate with the equally shrouded-in-mystery Dylan tumble. When I pointed out the disparity in dates, Tom just laughed.

It was more or less a teacher and pupil, sorcerer and apprentice, guru and little grasshopper relationship. Tom was about ten years my senior and kept his age a secret, yet I had much to offer in the way of information on leys and prehistoric technological material surfacing in the early Seventies and many personal psychic experiences to share. These wider points of counter-cultural reference were a useful and welcomed addition to his instinctive survivalist savvy. Yet I feel I gained immeasurably more from the friendship. And to stretch the Carlos Castaneda and Don Juan Matus analogy a little further, aficionados of the academic allegorist will recall that the greenhorn ethnographer attached himself like a groupie to the magician he was first introduced to at a bus station in Yuma, Arizona, and subsequently they would rendezvous at those liminal places, bus stations.

On my visits to Tom (including once with my wife and on another with author John Michell), he would pick me up at Durham City bus station. Then we would perambulate the Stanley Zodiac as if symbolically beating the bounds. In fact, he imagined himself to be the guardian of this special circle with its 12 holy hills bordering it all around, each with some form of edifice or aerial mast atop, which he argued to have a sinister presence. Within his sanctuary Tom expounded that weather patterns would change relative to the region outside. It could be wet within, dry without. It is worth recalling that it was a weather chart he was working upon when the zodiac fireball made its first-foot.

This identification with the Stanley Zodiac was extremely strong. He told me a tale of how within the sign of Aries he came across a public house which had a ram's skull. Tom paid the landlord a token sum of money for it to be left *in situ,* and for him to feel a bond of ownership and the symbolism so alive as part of the psychogeograhy. In fact, the end of terrace house he lived in lay in a special position with regard to the zodiac.

Tom also had an affinity with animals. Even his pet Avalon hardly resembled your average dog, except naturally when it was nosing around our lounge sniffing for chocolate, but had a poignant facial wisdom which spoke volumes and seemed to span the ages. Avalon died after a skirmish with a large black Labrador which was taken in after its owner mistreated it. Also there was always at least one black cat around and on one occasion I mistook the coal scuttle being full of coal when it was actually alive with all-black kittens.

Visits to Stanley would include a sampling of wine appropriate for the astrological month. The bottles of home-made fruit wine were kept in the sea-chest from which Tom had viewed the fireball. Also, there were rows of herbs in bottles on shelves; a particular interest of

I was surprised to see this picture in *The Northern Echo* of 21 March 1990 depicting Tom Cole and his lurcher Mushi, a cross between a Scottish deerhound and a Persian saluki. Master and dog had passed gruelling tests for Mushi to become one of only 37 dogs to be registered nationally by the Search and Rescue Dog Association, and he was the only lurcher.

Sharon's. She offered a titbit of mycological advice one day as we crossed Seaton Carew Common; that the psychedelic effect on any mushroom would be in proportion to its location – lush pasture, good 'trip'; derelict bomb site, watch out!

Rock on Tommy

Tom's interests were wide, ranging from pop music (identifying with the title character in The Who's rock opera *Tommy* and referring to Mick Jagger, evading tax in France, as 'the king in exile'), through the visionary writings and art of William Blake, theorising on the whereabouts of the allegedly still sleeping King Arthur and secret hiding place of the bones of Saint Cuthbert, to a cautious fascination with New Age cults (visiting the Findhorn Community, while in the chapel, where it had become known it was his birthday, Tom was asked to choose a hymn and as it was the only one he could recall, the congregation sang *All Things Bright and Beautiful*).

Tom lived each day as it came. He occasionally painted signs for the likes of farmers and ran a delivery service of groceries and household items from Durham City to outlying areas of North-West Durham a couple of days a week. This gave him the financial security to spend the remaining time on personal projects. He had abandoned full-time employment in 1966 with the reclassification of nature to the 'zodiac rule' as his primary aim. He had served his time as an aeronautical engineer but had no wish to return. He applied for the job of Northumberland footpaths officer, for which he would have been admirably suited. Never idle, yet never hasty. Tom's way of life followed a path of spontaneity and the zodiacal year.

As far as his personal history went, it was largely erased for my benefit. He claimed genuine gypsy pedigree for himself and tinker roots for his wife. He did have a gaily-coloured traditional wooden caravan parked at the back of the house and told me his taking it to Appleby Fair behind his Land-Rover caused some raised eyebrows among hereditary travelling folk. He shunned the commercial world, yet carried a chequebook and his evasive smokescreen about his past rolled away somewhat the day he got out his scrapbook of personal cuttings.

There was a story about how he protested about the proposed felling of a tree by sitting in its branches, which conjures up the shamanistic motif of the World Tree and the magician in its boughs. There was also another news item about him barricading himself in his house, though I cannot recall the circumstances.

There was also an account of his terrestrial zodiac discovery from his local newspaper. Following this, he claimed a car outside his house was vandalised and Tom believed it was retribution for his revealing the whereabouts of this geophysical wonder in the landscape. However, the attacker lacked the elementary psychic skill to realise the car was not Tom's or even known to him. Though he hardly gave the impression of wanting to court publicity, he did write two articles for *The Ley Hunter*. But pride of place went to an old Sunday newspaper piece with a picture of himself and friends being deported from one of the Channel Islands. They looked like beatniks and this had outraged the sensibilities of the cultured natives of whatever community and island it was.

Shamanistic initiation and astral travel

It was while sleeping rough in the Channel Islands that Tom experienced the phenomenon which is generally seen as a major aspect of shamanistic initiation. He and his friends were dossing in an abandoned World War II defensive bunker. In the darkness Tom noted a light which raced towards him from the sky with blinding brilliance. He held this experience in high regard. Later, of course, was to appear the zodiac-message fireball. Subsequently, when my wife and I were being driven home one night by the Coles, we all watched a huge globe of light for about fifteen minutes as we descended the South-Durham Plateau. It was bobbing above the south works of British Steel's Hartlepool plant. It would be easy to dismiss this latter sighting as a reflection of some steel-making process on low-lying clouds, but there were none, and others have reported weird phenomena over the pipe mills, including a retired Royal Air Force group captain of my acquaintance who told me that in all his service days he had never seen a craft like it. In those days I was keenly interested in ufology and could not understand why Tom was so decisive in not reading any ufological import into any of these occurrences. Incidentally, when we arrived home that night we found the fuses in the house had blown in our absence, and so in one respect we were definitely not in the light. I wondered if the light/UFO was to blame; Tom thought it more like to be a burglar disabling the electrics, and so joined me in a thorough search of the house.

As for UFOs, there has been some speculation to link sightings and persons travelling out-of-the-body. Tom boldly claimed that he had visited all the planets in our solar system, and found them to be nothing like astronomers' predictions. He also insisted he had travelled in his transparent 'astral egg' to torment a vicar for whom he delivered supplies.

The shaman's gift of healing and psychism join in the occasion one Sunday when I had felt ill all day and was laid on the settee when Tom arrived with a friend. They had been up ladders all day painting and it had been very windy. His friend actually looked worse than I felt, but Tom said he felt an urgency that they had to come. By the time they left and hour or so later I felt on top of the world. Tom also claimed he had cured a boy of asthma by placing him on a specific stone at the Derbyshire henge monument Arbor Low.

On another occasion this walking contradiction may even have saved my life. He once told me a curious tale involving seeing a black-robed figure carrying a huge silvery scythe in broad daylight; this being the guise of the Grim Reaper. Whilst driving later that day, he struck a bird and upon stopping found it to be dead and about to have laid eggs. Upon driving on, he narrowly avoided a fatal smash himself and concluded the sighting of the hooded figure carrying a scythe and the bird's death, which he formulated to have been a sacrifice on his behalf, were part of a cosmic scheme and one of life's lessons.

For no obvious reason this particular tale surfaced in my mind as I was cycling between Sedgefield and Wynyard on the A689. I was at a particularly narrow stretch of the road when a small car overtook a petrol tanker at speed. The car pulled right over to my side of the road, causing me to swerve on to the verge and into a hedge. Upon disentangling myself, I noticed a sparrow lying by the roadside. One wing was missing, and it was bleeding and stunned, so I crushed the body as quickly and humanely as I could. The role Tom's tale had played in the event must remain imponderable. Did some 'guardian angel' process select it to resurface in my consciousness at that instant as a warning signal? Was it a lesson that such 'coincidences' occur and are meaningful? Could the tale have even been an invention of Tom's, knowing prophetically that it would one day have substance and relevance for me?

What compounds, intensifies and extends the significance is the fact that a chillingly similar incident occurs in *Miracle Visitors*, a science-fiction novel by Ian Watson. This, incidentally, is the most thought-provoking and intellectually absorbing fictional account of the UFO enigma and more believable than 90% of the non-fiction books on the flying saucer enigma. Here, one of the key characters, Michael, is cycling at a point where he always freewheels at speed, but is stopped by two strangers and bundled into their car. From inside one man points to where Michael would have reached, travelling very fast, when suddenly a petrol tanker takes the bend in the opposite direction, hitting the far verge, skidding out of control, overturning and exploding. That's how the alien describes it and Michael believes it. Until, that is, the tanker heads up the hill past them, with its driver looking as if he's just seen a ghost. Nevertheless, Michael has been saved by two Men in Black parked in this antiquated yet seemingly brand-new car.

To me this fictional reflection of a quite similar experience made the book especially intriguing for me personally. As a means of recommending the book, I'll digress here a short while and stress its relevance to those interested in the paranormal and ask what this has to do with earth mysteries.

Not simply that the character Michael learns about 'ley lines' and is led to plant biosensors as ley/UFO linkage. It is because this aspect must be considered in the context that virtually all elements of the UFO mystery are woven with considerable skill into the narrative. Ufology is a reef around reality, encrusted with coral mythology of ancient archetypes forever taking on new form, but retaining a base and building forever to keep out all but the shrewdest investigator and ready to deceive and ensnare the unwary and unworthy. Watson shows a clear grasp of the complexity of ufology and comes closest to forwarding an answer through the character Deacon, who observes: "UFOs can't yield to our science, because they're part of a higher psychic pattern" and "...the Saucer People - who are only us, of course - part of our collective psychic life."

Watson's book may be science-fiction but its intellectual astringency is so effective and stimulating that it makes most serious 'factual' ufology writers seem like banal charlatans or gullible geeks, rewriting one another's books *ad nauseum* and nauseatingly being patronising to one another as they plagiarise so thoroughly that each 'new' work's only shock factor is one of terminal déjà vu. Watson expresses much of the UFO mythos in terms of psychosociological interaction and this, I believe, is the most promising route to a solution. With an abductee in the recent Aveley case talking about ley information being given by aliens, it now seems timely for this tenuous ley/UFO link to be reappraised. Is it all coincidence? Or like the accidents involving Tom, myself and Watson's ley activator Michael, are we dealing with a psychical survival system stretching from the individual to the Gaian lifeform's nervous network and on to cosmic consciousness?

The experience of death and resurrection

The primary goal of a shaman is the experience of death and rebirth. Tom claimed he came through this ordeal. Tom had felt there was something significant about the position of the St George and the Dragon effigy on the wall of Hart's St Mary Magdalen Church. After we had visited for a second time and had a drink in the *White Hart* pub, Tom returned home and began an attempt to learn what, if anything was significant at Hart. From mulling over white hart myths, to meditation also to no avail, and magical practices, Tom came to the conclusion there was either a very well kept secret at Hart, or none at all. He then resolved to take a drastic course.

He would 'enter the underworld,' a domain previously unexplored. After several days of venturing he returned and told me he felt little benefit apart from the experience of death. Tom said his body stank of death. His hair was like electricity. His skin itched; perhaps from a 'death mite.' His breath was horrible. So after a shower he headed for a particular hill, not even feeling hungry.

One other positive aspect, however, emerged. He believed St George's lance was pointing to something of importance. At the time the ground immediately below the Hart effigy was railed off and overgrown with red roses. Tom surmised someone of stature could have been buried there. The railings have now gone, the roses are pruned and I was told that a previous incumbent had been laid to rest beneath the dragon-slayer. But why just there?

Hart does have claims to fame, for here Robert the Bruce of spider fame was born, as was Derby winner Voltigeur, and by the main street stands a glacial erratic of Whin Sill granite, which could well be a markstone in the ley system. It occasionally gives off a voltage ranging from a 'pins and needles' sensation, to an unpleasant electric shock. Here one evening with Sharon Cole and my wife, Tom 'baptised' me with rainwater from the dip on the stone as a 'child of Albion,' whatever that meant. We got some odd looks from people heading home from the pub.

Maybe Hart remained elusive then, but at least it led Tom to the experience of death and rebirth. Certainly he managed an extraordinary act of weather manipulation, the authenticity of which I can vouch for, but feel it unwise to enlarge upon.

There are many other aspects of his teaching and personal affairs which are not for sharing. I considered telling the whole story in its full fantastic form and protecting Tom under the cloak of anonymity, but I have always felt that pseudonyms lack authenticity and devalue any statement or claim. I feel it important that there should be public recognition of the fact that there are people like Tom with shamanisitic gifts among us and that each of us can develop toward these, better ourselves and improve the lot of humanity. Tom widened my horizons, made me think for myself and maybe saved my life. Tom was an enigmatic and charismatic character, a mixture of guru and trickster, man of myths, magic and mystery. This is his story: at least partially.

A portrait at least. The last I heard he was down Glastonbury way.

Bibliography:

Tom Cole, 'One of the Durham Zodiacs,' *The Ley Hunter*, No. 14, 1970
Tom Cole (as 'Atun'), 'Gypsy Lore, Zodiacs and Albion,' *The Ley Hunter*, No. 19, 1971
Paul Screeton, 'Stranger Than Fiction,' *The Ley Hunter*, No. 90, 1981
Ian Watson, *Miracle Visitors*, Panther/Granada, 1981

Down Glastonbury way. That was 30 years ago and I was last in touch with him five or so years ago when he telephoned out of the blue from Scarborough, telling me he was work-ing as a palmist. We discussed John Michell meeting him down a drove road in Somerset, his photo in a North-East newspaper with a lurcher and how I had missed my annual holi-day in the Algarve when I was 53 as a precaution that his prophecy that I would die abroad at that age would not come true. He laughed and made some excuse and saying I should not have taken his astrology boasts so seriously. Rather miffed, I then told him I was under-whelmed by his crass gullibility in forwarding to me a chain letter from Glastonbury which threatened dire consequences if I did not pass on ten more copies, to which there was long seemingly embarrassed silence. Of course, I destroyed the letter and broke the chain (despite it probably having some cultural value as another signee was the reclusive singer Vashti Bunyan, who after a 40-year absence from the music business made a surprise comeback and graced mobile phone adverts with her *Diamond Day* in 2006. The purpose of that telephone call to me was to re-establish contact, but I felt it inauspicious and would rather remember the Seventies Tom, not a 21st Century version. Back with Glastonbury, after telling me had discovered Tom down a drove road, John wrote on 14th November 1977 to relate: "I met Gypsy Tom Cole yesterday on the Somerset marshes and heard some good yarns," and again on 1 December 1981, "No sightings or news of Tom Cole lately. When last I saw him he told me a literally incredible story of finding a fairy shoe, distressed fairy, etc."

This piece actually formed Chapter Three of the unfinished manuscript for *Suburban Sha-mans*. The Alan Garner piece would have formed part of Chapter Eleven and Tony 'Doc' Shiels in Chapter Twelve. I was making use of rejected material even before 'recycling' be-came fashionable. The Grim Reaper phenomenon attracted the late Mark Chorvinsky, who wrote about how true-life encounters led him to set up the Reaper Project to investigate the enigma and write a book (*Strange Magazine*, No. 18, 1997). He also touched upon The Azrael Project, still going strong, which collects first-hand accounts of encounters with the anthropomorphised figure of the Angel of Death. Also listen to *(Don't Fear) The Reaper* by *Blue Oyster Cult*.

++ Hart Church seems to have changed from Magdalen to Magdalene at some point during the past 25 years, now finding itself at the end of modern housing in Magdalene Drive, TS27 3AP.

WANDERING CANONS?
(CLOSER TO THE LIGHT, THE
LARGER THE SHADOW)

(Northern Earth Mysteries, No. 40, 1989; *Folklore Frontiers*, No. 55, 2007)

A secret society within the Anglican Church? The notion was put to me 20 years ago and at times since I have pondered the possibility. The notion seemed plausible then when it was put to me as fact. I'd taken a shamanic gypsy who had arrived on our doorstep that day to the ancient church at Hart, near Hartlepool. By a stroke of luck it was open and we were given a guided tour by Canon D.T. Eastwood, whom I knew slightly. As for Tom, he was an astrologer who had called to show me on a map a terrestrial zodiac he'd discovered in North-West Durham. The canon pointed to ten figures along the roof and two others at the back of the church. He pointedly announced that they were <u>not</u> zodiacal figures. Tom told me he reckoned Eastwood was one of a select inner sanctum of clerics chosen as guardians of specially-selected churches.

Then I read in Andy Collins's excellent magazine *Earthquest News* about an ecclesiastical underworld. The Anglicans use the term '*Episcopi Vagantes*,' translated as 'wandering bishops,' for a hierarchy of clergy, being bishops, abbots and other holy men who claimed a direct apostolic succession from obscure Eastern sources. This Masonic-style line of thinking should be referred to by those interested as it is too complicated to follow through here. [1] Collins suggested members of the '*E.V.*' may have felt Runwell, Essex, where one of their high-ups was rector, important geomantically. Would not the same apply to Hart?

Our story now turns to another village on Hartlepool's outskirts, Greatham. Here is the Hospital of God, St Mary and St Cuthbert, founded in 1272. It was opened on the Eve of Epiphany, 6th of January, by Bishop Robert Stichill. It is home and sanctuary for the aged, both clerical and lay brothers. Brothers in alms.

I visited the Hospital of God for a four-page feature on Greatham for the newspaper I work for

[2]. The Master, Canon Clive Wyngard, showed me around, introduced me to lay brethren but when one of those suddenly took ill the visit was curtailed and I did not get to meet the clerics. But one who once lived there whom I knew well was Canon Shepherd, who looked after Seaton Carew parish while the incumbent played soldiers as a Terriers' padre. When he christened my son, Ian, he whispered: "Next time I see you it will be in a better place than this." He was alluding to Seaton Carew Social Club, whose balance sheet was boosted by his awesome rum intake (he had been a parson in the Caribbean). After Ian's confirmation at Greatham, during refreshments in the village hall, I was reacquainted with Canon Eastwood, by then another Hospital of God resident.

Briefly, Dennis Townend Eastwood was born in Manchester to well-off parents. However, he turned his back on a management career in his father's printing business after he saw a little girl, aged four, cradling a baby in her arms, sitting in front of an empty house in the city's slums. Twenty years old, he realised his vocation was to help others and to that end he became a vicar. After serving several Lancashire parishes, he moved to the North-East to become Vicar of Hart and Rector of Elwick Hall. A profile of him noted he spent money on little else but books and was married, with two dogs and a cat. [3] Perhaps the dogs give a clue to his encouraging Tom to take his wolfhound into Hart church.

Another step along this curious trail was a re-reading of Andy Collins's book *The Knights of Danbury*. [4] In it, Collins focuses on the St Clere (Sinclair) family. The Somerset branch was associated with St John's Eve, and Greatham has its week-long feast around St John the Baptist. Collins concluded:

> 'There is simple evidence to support the view that the St Clere family were guardians of an esoteric tradition, a form of Christian mysticism which was fused with elements of ancient sun worship of pre-Christian times'.

Children dance around a maypole at Greatham and I wondered if the village could have a St Clere connection. It does. Apparently, the manor of Greatham belonged to the celebrated Simon de Montfort, slain at the Battle of Evesham. Following this, the estate was forfeited and granted by the king to Thomas de Clare. For reasons I cannot discover, the gift was revoked due to a claim from Bishop Stichill, who founded the hospital.

In conversation with our local vicar, Bill Worley, who has the freehold of Seaton Carew, he mentioned that Canon Wyngard had been his 'boss' when he was a curate in North-West Durham. More coincidences. Would it be sensible to - however cautiously - ask pertinent questions of Canon Wyngard? Not politically sound anyway. My editor happens to be a friend of his.

Pieces for a jigsaw; a geomantic riddle; perhaps pie in the sky. Canon fodder for thought.

References:

1. *Earthquest News*, No. 7, 1983

2. Paul Screeton, 'Village Portrait: Greatham,' *The Mail,* Hartlepool, 20 June 1988
3. 'Friday Profile: Revelation on his doorstep,' *Northern Daily Mail*, circa 1964
4. Andrew Collins, *The Knights of Danbury*, Earthquest Books, 1985

From Andrew Collins, Leigh-on-Sea, Essex, 20 October 1991:

Dear Paul,

Thanks for the article on '*Episcopi Vagantes*.' I now know an awful lot more about the whole set-up and have read extensively of its origins. Most of it concerns orthodox unorthodoxy and Celtic churches. However, of more importance to the Anglican Church was the Tractarian Movement, ritualism and the Oxford Movement. Their main secretive body was, and still is, the Order of the Corporate Union. It strives to reintroduce pre-Reformation ritualism and church services and possesses many secret signs and symbols known only to members. Most high church clerics will belong to it, although few will admit it. A vicar I know who is a member openly supports my work and has listened to psychics on energy patterns in his church. His services are pure occult rituals. He is also into the whole holy blood, holy grail mystery and is psychic himself.

Cheers, Andy.

The original article was published in 1989. Sorting old correspondence and finding Andy Collins's intriguing letter in response to my sending him the article, I decided to reprint the article in 2007. Also, in 2010, while searching the internet I found the Christian faith L'Abri ideas library, begging donations and its UK base is in ... Greatham. As for Canon Eastwood, after he died on 2 May 1995, he left a net estate valued between £40,000 and £70, 000, with typically two £1,000 bequests to children's charities.

AERT DE GELDER'S 'U.F.O.' PAINTING

(With Chris Castle)

(*The Journal of Geomancy*, Vol. 2, No. 2, 1978; abridged in *Fortean Times*, No. 25, 1978)

A whispered 'Paul must see the flying saucer picture' whilst staying in Cambridge alerted me to the contents of the most extraordinary painting that I have ever seen. A hurried viewing of *The Baptism of Christ* at the Fitzwilliam Museum persuaded me that here was a picture of mystical content and that the strange object casting light upon a significant religious occasion could well be placed in the UFO phenomenon context. It did not have to be an exact replica of the archetypal, supposedly extraterrestrial vehicle photographed in dramatic circumstances by the late George Adamski; the similarity to countless reports of alleged interplanetary craft and the curious juxtaposition with a highlighting of an episode in the Christian faith was sufficient. But this was no psychedelic portrayal from the palette of the hip awareness of turned-on, tuned-in, dropped-out consciousness of the 20th Century visionary art. The brushes here were in the hands of Aert de Gelder, born 26 October 1645 and who died on 28 August 1727.

De Gelder (Aert or Arent – both names being commonly attributed to him) is hardly held in high esteem by the art world, but maybe a re-examination of his work for content rather than technical expertise would prove profitable. His work, however, is widely dispersed and seemingly ignored as far as published works are concerned. The only book devoted to him is *Arent de Gelder; Sein Leben Und Seine Kunst*, which was published in Holland in 1914. This work by Karl Lilienfeld does not appear to have been translated into English.

As for his other paintings, he was greatly influenced as a pupil by Rembrandt and continued his teacher's style into the 18th Century, giving it a rococo flavouring by lightening Rembrandt's palette and using violets and pinks. He used oriental costumes in his Old Testament scenes with warm colour. As for the New Testament scenes of around 1715, examples can be found in many galleries, including five in England. He was a pupil of Samuel van Hoogstraten, and between 1665 and 1667 of Rembrandt van Rijn, whose manner he followed closely. He was a portrait painter and also depicted biblical scenes and tableaux showing oriental influence. His art was welded into the flow of the Dutch School and the mystical nature of *The Baptism of Christ* may have been inspired by a special religious outlook. As for his role in Dutch art, he was among many pupils and followers of what the American professor C. Van Dyke called the 'Rembrandt Snowball.' [1] At the time of Rembrandt's ascendancy, court and aristocratic patronage had disappeared and dealers were emerging to cope with the flourishing schools of varied and rich styles. Specific commissions were rarer and works produced spontaneously had a ready market through dealers. Nevertheless there was considerable competition to supply the market which led to a tendency of specialisation. In Rembrandt's later works his technique is free and bold, and suggests an obsession to express a vision. He had lost his former rapport with the public, who found themselves unable to follow him in his 'profound search for the spiritual essence of the biblical subjects which increasingly occupied him.' [2] Rembrandt van Rijn, born 15 July 1606 in Leyden, is regarded by many to be the greatest Dutch master and among the top three greatest painters of the European tradition.

It is a speculative link of religious brotherhood between Rembrandt, van Hoogstraten and de Gelder which concerns us primarily, hence it is reasonable to sketch a few details of the prevailing religious climate within which their work was produced. On breaking bonds in the 17th Century with Spain, Holland became a Calvinist nation, set apart from the Roman Catholic world. Consequently this rupture was decisive for artists. Previously the Church commissioned great numbers of new works covering large-scale treatments of religious motifs. Calvinism, however, deplored the Roman Catholic display of religious paintings in churches, hence such subjects were only commissioned by private individuals for their own homes. Religious art waned.

But for Rembrandt, the Bible continued to be the main inspiration of subject matter for his compositions. And as for Calvinism, following his wife Saskia's death and the entry into an asylum of a woman he took into his service named Geertyhe Dirox, he fell foul of the Calvinist church of Amsterdam regarding his relationship with Hendrieje Stoffels. Their neighbours were upset by his liaison, but the couple failed to answer the summons. The charge was repeated in July 1654, citing only the woman and on a third summons she was admonished. Biographers deduced Rembrandt was not a member of the national church. Furthermore, Filippo Baldinucci related that the artist had joined the Mennonite sect, 'which is possible but not proven.' [3] However, if we consider the Rembrandt and de Gelder link and take into account the latter's *The Baptism of Christ* painting, the Mennonite connection takes on another hue, Mennonites having as a cornerstone the radical belief in adult baptism.

One of Rembrandt's pupils was Samuel van Hoogstraten (1627-1678), who had previously studied under his own father. The Rembrandt influence in his drawings and some of his paintings is obvious, but his lively mind stopped him from being a copyist. A man who travelled widely, his art also covered several territories, such as landscapes, marines, animals and still-life. He caused a scandal in his native Dordrecht when he was expelled in 1656 from the Mennonite community to which he belonged, for marrying without the community's approval and for wearing a sword (they being committed to non-violence). A scientific theoretician, van Hoogstraten had pupils had pupils at various periods, including Aert de Gelder, and in his old

The Baptism of Christ by Aert de Gelder.

age composed for their benefit an elaborate treatise on painting, *Introduction to the High Art School*, illustrated with his own engravings. At one stage his study of optics led to him painting pictures producing uncanny visual effects. [4] Contemporary judgement places Rembrandt on a pinnacle, van Hoogstraten as interesting only for his optical effects work and de Gelder as a minor painter. Indeed, market prices of de Gelder's work reflect this conspicuously. Nevertheless, one commentator has stated: 'He was a fine colourist, fond of picturesque effects and had a broad and masterly touch.' [5]

A characteristic of at least two of Rembrandt's Biblical scenes is that 'aerial' personages occur in the top left hand corner: a winged angel in *The Sacrifice of Abraham* and a floating figure in *The Sacrifice of Manoah*. It may, of course, be pure coincidence that Aert de Gelder placed his aerial object left of centre at the top of his picture.*

The Mennonite and adult baptism metaphysical link between Rembrandt and his pupil de Gelder may actually be tenuous. In his major study of Rembrandt, Joseph-Emile Muller mentions several pupils, but not de Gelder. He notes that up to 1660 around 30 young men had been tutored by Rembrandt, each paying him 100 guilders a year, plus a percentage of the proceeds from their paintings. There is the postulated religious link between Rembrandt and van Hoogstraten through the Mennonites, but that Quaker-style sect seems unlikely to have induced a mystical-type view of religion. Consequently, we are left to examine the painting on its own merits. Physically the canvas is 48.3 x 37.1cm. and the Fitzwilliam Museum catalogue suggests its date as c1710. Marianne, Viscountess Alford (Lady Marian Alford) bequeathed it to Lord Alwyne Compton, Bishop of Ely, who donated it in 1905.

I asked a Cambridge artist, Chris Castle, for his opinion of the work, and this is his critical commentary:

'It is twilight, a hilltop, a landscape stretches away, the slightly glowing outlines of two towns, then mountains beyond. But on <u>this</u> hilltop, a gathering of people in ancient dress gaze motionless, entranced at the scene taking place before them. Two figures, the one knee deep in water, head bowed, hands in attitude of prayer, stoops slightly towards the other who with outstretched arms sprinkles him with water. Something momentous indeed has caught the attention of the surrounding onlookers. The water and the two figures are bathed in a special kind of light, softly glowing. High in the sky above hovers a greenish disk at the centre of which is a tiny dove with outstretched wings. From that disk emanate four narrow rays which seem to travel down to earth penetrating the centre of the place/event below. The rays seem both to support the disk above and to come down as a blessing and completion of the baptism. But the rays themselves are painted in such a way as not to appear as light beams. Perhaps some other kind of 'light' is intended. The peculiar light quality of the scene is enhanced by the glow of the central event; indeed one feels the water to be charged with some spiritual energy.

'The overall harmony of the painting is maintained throughout by de Gelder's strict control of his palette. The rulebook of his master Rembrandt is in the strong evidence in his coloration and his handling of the paint. The painting doesn't break through any revolutionary ground on the technical level. It is basically quite safely in the Rembrandt tradition. But the subject matter and overall atmosphere created is so unusual an interpretation of the Baptism of Christ that the shortcomings of the painting technique are overshadowed and soon forgotten. As Rembrandt's later works were those which influenced de Gelder, the surface of the painting is loose and almost impressionistic in soft smudgy brushmarks. No detail of importance emerges from either the figures looking on or the landscape beyond. Both landscape and people function only as setting for the cosmic fusion of sky and earth spirits.

'There is some doubt about the artist's intentions regarding the distribution of land masses in the painting. The baptism seems to be taking place in water (the Jordan?) on a hilltop (a river on a hilltop?). Maybe a dewpond is intended or maybe this is not the Baptism of Christ at all.'

Assuming that there is a revelatory message in the scene as depicted by de Gelder, we might consider a few aspects which appear to be relevant. Firstly the disk in the sky is so tantalisingly akin to reported UFOs that it could be easily utilised to substantiate the tiresomely tedious welter of paperbacks in the 'Was-God-an-Astronaut?' genre. Uncle Erich von Daniken and a horrendous host of bandwagoners have quarried this strata and their banalities have devalued the mercurial link between the UFO syndrome and mysticism. Central beneath the disk is a dove, and the Gnostics, regarded by Christian orthodoxy as heretical for their numerical interpretations, believed that 'the divine spirit, represented by the dove, entered into Jesus, the man, at his baptism, while the Church held that the spirit and the body of Jesus Christ were indivisible, and looked forward to bodily resurrection.' [6] This prophetic, rather than priestly, notion seems to be specifically pointed at in this painting. It can be added that another disk object, the Holy Grail, is accompanied – as here – with beams of light and sometimes preceded by the flying in of a dove. [7] Altogether hardly a Mennonite Brethren dogma.

In *UFOs from Behind the Iron Curtain*, pictures are reproduced of 'astronauts' on the walls of mediaeval Yugoslavian monasteries, particularly in association with Christ's crucifixion. Also similar pictures have been identified in Russia and Romania. [8]

But our quest has been to delve into the inspiration of a Dutchman; the subject of the piece hanging in a corner of a sedate university city museum. This has been necessarily only a speculative account of one man and an isolated creation of his, but I regard the painting as being an astonishing depiction of the inexplicable.

Notes:

1.   John C. Van Dyke, *Rembrandt and His School*, Charles Scribner's Sons, New York,

1923
2.   A.C. Sewter, *Baroque and Rococo Art*, Thames & Hudson, London, 1972
3.   Joseph-Emile Muller, *Rembrandt*, Thames & Hudson, London, 1968
4.   R.H. Wilenski, *An Introduction to Dutch Art*, Faber & Gwyer, 1924
5.   John Denison Champlin, Jr., (ed.) *Cyclopedia of Painter and Painting*, Vol. 2, 1952
6.   John Michell, *City of Revelation*, Garnstone Press, London, 1972
7.   Dr W.B. Crow, *A History of Magic, Witchcraft and Occultism*, Aquarian Press, 1968
8.   Ion Hobana and Julien Weverbergh, *UFOs from Behind the Iron Curtain*, Souvenir Press, 1974

* Editor's (Nigel Pennick) note: In Hieronymous Bosch's painting *The Ascent into Empyrean*, souls are seen being escorted by angels into a tube of light in the sky. The focus of this tube is on the top left of the panel. This is part of a series of four paintings which probably originated as the wings of two triptychs. For further details see *The Complete Paintings of Bosch* by Gregory Martin and Mia Cinotti, Wiedenfeld & Nicolson, 1969.

**The edited version in *Fortean Times* included a salient postscript by editor Bob Rickard:
'Readers interested in pursuing the psychological interpretations of the UFO, or glowing aerial disc, or numinous hole in the cosmic fabric, are referred to Dr C.G. Jung's *Flying Saucers* (recently reprinted by Routledge & Kegan Paul, London, 1977) which discusses generally the UFO as a symbol of psychic unity, and which has a chapter on the UFO-symbol in art.'
To view de Gelder's painting in colour go to www.thebluntblogger.com//673/ufo-at-baptism-of-christ or www.uforc.com/religion/page1.html (where the painting is perversely reversed!)**

HOW AND WHY GNOSTICISM _LOST_ OUT

Lost Christianities: The Battles for Scripture and the Faiths We Never Knew
by Bart D. Ehrman (Oxford University Press, 2006)

A rriving at an inn late at night, the apostle John is dismayed to find his mattress infested with bedbugs. He orders the loathsome insects remove themselves. The following morning, to his companions' amusement and amazement, the unwanted bedmates are found obediently gathered together in the doorway, patiently awaiting permission to reoccupy their home in the straw. John awakens, grants permission for their return and he and his chums go on their merry way. Such are saints' paranormal abilities and kindness.

This book is full of supernatural intervention, miraculous resurrection, attempted necrophilia, asceticism, liberation for Christian women (until proto-orthodox misogyny snuffed it out until modern times), but is essentially an overview of the prevailing social, political and religious milieu of the time. But what are these 'lost Christianities'? Simply the practices and beliefs of those who called themselves Christians during the first three centuries CE. Not so simply they were even more varied than the differences between 21st Century Christian groups. More controversially these 'lost' Christianities came to be reformed or expunged, their texts proscribed, marginalised, destroyed, forgotten, claimed as forgeries – i.e. 'lost.' Those forgeries were from the early period, but the tern merely applies to their being attributed to some other well-known person; some or all of the New Testament being equally suspect. We're not talking Hitler's fake diaries or Jordan's novel. Forgery here being usually a form of tribute or in some cases financial motive. Apparently most readers, even in those days, would not have been fooled anyway. It was the message not the medium which mattered in this pre-McLuhan era. Lost, yes, but now as in _Amazing Grace_, lost but now found. Discovered either by trained archaeologists seeking them or found by chance by wandering Bedouin.

As a professed Gnostic of many years standing, I applaud Ehrman's conclusion that this is 'arguably the most significant and certainly one of the most fascinating forms of Christianity that came to be 'lost'.'

One of those fascinating brands is the Carpocratians, a sect following a peculiar doctrine of reincarnation, where the trapped soul must experience everything bodily possible, so in order to speed up the process they not only indulged in wife-swapping but every type of profligate activity to ensure quick release. It is a pity the *News of the World* wasn't around then to publicise their wild licentious orgies under the name of religion. This led to a dodgy, and possibly modern 'real' forgery by an academic, a Secret Gospel of Mark, a Carpocratian corruption, with distinctly homoerotic overtones involving Jesus and a young man, stressing his having nothing but a linen cloth over his naked body, both spending the night together. As in the world of forteana, the relevant document's whereabouts are now unknown, and it is a super detective tale involving warring so-called experts taking up opposing positions in an unsavoury academic ding-dong.

Whether real or imagined as a 'dirty tricks' campaign against another Gnostic sect, the Phibionites, they were charged by their proto-orthodox enemies as wife-swappers, where the male would withdraw before climax, gather the semen and share it as 'the boy of Christ'; consume menstrual fluid as 'the blood of Christ'; if a foetus occurred it would be manually aborted, covered with honey and spices, and cannibalistically devoured as a Eucharist meal; for those who had achieved perfection they would indulge in homosexual relations; plus sacred, private masturbation.

On the subject of polemical warfare and falsification, Ehrman goes to great lengths to explain the several factors which have long perplexed scholars as to how, with an early Christianity so diverse, the side which is generally identified as proto-orthodox established itself as dominant. It is likely that the diversity of doctrine with the Gnostics themselves played into the hands of their opponents. For instance Basilides (highly regarded by SF writer Philip K. Dick) claims Jesus transformed himself to look like the carrier of his cross, Simon of Cyrene, and vice versa, leading to the wrong man being crucified and laughing at his subterfuge. Ehrman remarks drily: 'Simon, presumably, did not find it so funny.'

Those who enjoy theological speculation can debate whether Didymus Judas Thomas was Jesus' identical twin; after the Virgin Mary gives birth, a midwife called Salome gives her a postpartum inspection, but as she inserts her finger to see if her patient is still intact, her hand begins to burn as if on fire; call for chastity even within marriage; docetism, where the divine Christ descended from heaven in the form of a dove at Jesus' baptism **(see Aert de Gelder's 'UFO' painting – previous article).**

Regarding folklore previously discussed in *Folklore Frontiers*, we have Pontius Pilate said to have converted to Christianity after Jesus' resurrection – 'This is the stuff of legend, of course, borne out by no non-Christian source.' Probably being American, Ehrman does not discuss the perennial belief that Pilate was born in Scotland at Fortinghall).

Then there is the Apocalypse of Peter in which the eponymous hero is given a guided tour of heaven and hell: similar and more touristically engaging than the 1950s contactees' tours of the solar system's inner planets, but probably a similar psychological scenario. Also we learn, at least to my surprise, the Dead Sea Scrolls never mention John the Baptist, Jesus or any of his followers; not even anything Christian. Neither had I realised that the phrase 'sweat blood' comes from the Gospel of Luke. But I'm straying from the core ...

On the book's minus side, it is massively repetitive. Perhaps this is not shoddy editing but simply to hammer home his points – '(Recall: *gnosis* is ...)' – and possibly sensing many readers are newcomers (via *The Da Vinci Code* and the *Matrix* films) who need to be re-minded of the arguments. Gnosticism, he describes as a 'strange, even inviting, set of religious practices and beliefs,' but I somehow doubt it is his chosen faith. I even suspect he is <u>agnostic</u>. He considers, too briefly, an alternative history for Western civilisation had proto-orthodox Christianity <u>not</u> won the day (but then he did not write *The Man in the High Castle*). What the author fails to acknowledge or realise is that Gnosticism's influence is probably at its most vibrant since those ancient desert days. There again, this has only become possible through the Nag Hammadi discoveries and Sixties onwards religious revivalism, shared all over as in the olden days.

However, as can be guessed from the main thrust of the review, this book has enthused me and should grab any reader willing to absorb a fascinating subject presented cogently and with gentle humour. Already aware of the basics of Gnosticism, Ehrman has opened my eyes wider to its actual roots and early beginnings and trials. It is erudite and intelligible, that is if Gnosti-cism ever can be; blazingly illuminating regarding a dark and mysterious religion of almost lost beliefs. A *tour de force*.

INTERLUDE – ONE
IT TAKES A LOT TO LAUGH,
IT TAKES A TRAIN TO CRY

(Crossing the Line: Trespassing on railway weirdness, Heart of Albion Press, 2006)

Around 6.30p.m. on 2 October 1995, I was travelling second class on a 'High-Speed Train' between London Paddington and Newton Abbot. At some point during the journey an image of a familiar book cover, *Margaret Clitherow* by Mary Claridge (Fordham University Press, USA, 1966), appeared to my right side peripheral vision. Saint Margaret Clitherow was one of the English Martyrs, persecuted and put to death for harbouring recusant Roman Catholic priests. Her shrine is in The Shambles, a narrow mediaeval street in York, and I have held a fascination for her over many years. I had a feeling her appearance – even as a mere book cover portrait – was to give me a message and it was – 'Be yourself.' This instruction just came into my head. Suddenly gripped, a dread feeling overtook me. In a state of utter panic, I dashed down the carriage and locked myself in the toilet. I felt compelled to curl up into a foetal position in a corner on the floor and cried uncontrollably for around fifteen minutes before normality returned and I could return to my seat.

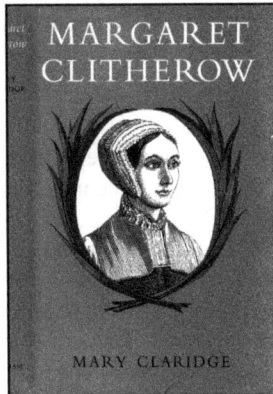

The book cover depiction which delivered a message.

Conclusion: At the time I put this down to being a quasi-mystical experience, though I am not a Roman Catholic nor sympathiser, being Protestant Gnostic.

Upon reading about an aberrant working of the brain known medically as temporal lobe epilepsy or, more appropriately, dissociation, I attributed the episode to the strobe lights above the train aisle flickering on and off and causing my dissociation. I should add that I was not aware of any lighting malfunction at the time, although I have observed this subsequently when travelling on 'HSTs.' I must also stress that I do not take drugs, but would have had several pints before and on the journey. Novelist Will Self (himself self-confessedly no stranger to Class 'A' substances) wrote jokingly in a column: 'Now as any fool knows, the way industrial designers proceed with two-class transit systems is to design the first class and then make the second class worse. This was evident on the old British Rail, where the lighting in first class was just about tolerable and the lighting in the second class modulated so as to provoke an epileptic seizure in every third passenger. ('Self critical' column, *The Times Magazine*, 21 March 1998).

All I really want to do

Also the 'Be yourself' message may have been illusory – the vision was obviously hallucinatory, so perhaps too the auditory adjunct – but quitting my job on its say-so to seek greater fulfilment was tangible enough! Others undergoing alien abduction, near-death experience and so on, often report dramatic changes in personality and lifestyle. I know I am a damn sight poorer financially, but more extrovert, easy-going and enjoying greater quality of life. Some false epiphany, perhaps, though neurologists at the University of California have located an area in the temporal lobe regarded as a spiritual 'hot-spot.' This could also have been a hypnopompic hallucination if I had dozed off and awoken. Also to reach God, so the Gnostic credo goes, is to make a 'call to self.'

I have, over the years, had many other strange experiences. With regard to railways, when young, I could see a steam locomotive approaching in the distance, concentrate and know its number from afar: this scrying would entail a feeling at the lower back of the head and this would confirm I was predicting correctly. More singular and significant transient personal episodes include the following.

Starry-eyed and laughing

During the mid-Sixties I was employed as a junior reporter on the *Billingham and Stockton Expresses*. One day prior to a regular pub lunch, I accompanied colleague Geoff Daniel to the Billingham Synthonia Theatre, where Geoff was to report a performance by one of the foreign dance groups appearing at the annual Billingham Folklore Festival. Seated in the auditorium, I not only found the sight of grown men in *lederhosen* amusing, but when they began a rhythmic dance and banging pieces of wood together, the sight and sound led me to begin laughing uncontrollably. Deeply embarrassed at myself, I pushed my way through the audience, who obviously thought my behaviour even more bizarre than the spectacle on stage. I walked around Mill Lane laughing helplessly, hysterically almost, tears streaming down my face, for fifteen minutes until it subsided.

Conclusion: dancing combined with wood-banging sound as ritual activated the temporal lobes and caused the hysterical behaviour. It may also link with the 'Toronto Blessing' charismatic phenomenon which led to Christian worshippers falling down laughing. Or on a more mundane and secular note, as Groucho Marx once observed: "He who laughs, lasts."

Chimes of freedom (flashing)
One Bank Holiday weekend in the late Seventies I was passing a night-club on Seaton Carew seafront to find for the first time ever its ground-floor bar doors wide open to attract passing custom. It was lunchtime and out of curiosity I ventured in and ordered a pint of bitter. I had only drunk a little when the flashing lights and tempo of the disco music took a hold on me. I realised that if I did not leave quickly I would pass out, so I drank up swiftly and once back outside on the street normality returned.

Conclusion: Bright flashing lights and musical beat pattern caused temporal lobe dissociation.

Rainy day women Nos. 12 and 35
Against what in soberer times I would have avoided, I chose one evening to sample a largish mushroom growing on a willow tree stump in our Seaton Carew back garden. Trusting my ability to match it with an illustration and description (edible and safe) in Richard Mabey's classic book *Food for Free*, and having previously been told by gypsy friend Tom Cole's wife Sharon that if the setting looks harmonious then the fungi should match that, I ate some. Little did I realise I had embarked upon a 'trip' of sorts. The next day, cycling to work along Coronation Drive, Hartlepool, I saw a jogger approaching who suddenly vanished into thin air. Later, mentioning this to my son Ian, he pinpointed the exact location and said others he knew had been the subject of similar weird experiences there; on one occasion two youths tripping on the drug LSD were passed by a jogger at this spot soaked to the skin and with rain falling on and just around him, but not on them or elsewhere. That lunchtime I had a couple of pints in the Jackson Arms and as I climbed the short flight of steps to the front door of the *Hartlepool Mail* offices, someone came out with a hand covered with and dripping blood – or so it seemed to me. During that afternoon I was in the toilet urinating when the door opened and I turned to see reporter Paul Wenham, who began to shrink and took on the partial form of a zebra before unexplainably exiting.

Conclusion: these seem to describe involuntary drug-induced 'flashbacks' rather than any form of temporal lobe dissociation.

But do my experiences appertain to a 'unified theory' for all paranormal events, as attributed by some to temporal lobe dissociation and neurological trauma theory (or for that matter electromagnetic pollution or tectonic stress in the Earth's crust). Forteana mates with neurotheology.

Don't think twice, it's all right
Or has what has been described been a sequence of brief psychotic events as initially diagnosed in me by psychologist friend Neil Robson, PhD., but who is not absolutely certain,

though adamant I do not have temporal lobe epilepsy. Nor mad. I once asked Neil where on a scale of one to ten I would stand as regards one for totally sane and ten for stark staring bonkers. We were playing dominoes, and he replied: "Two or three, but all four of us sat here would score either two or three. Nothing to worry about, Paul." Well, that was a relief.

This appendix is based on what I have called my exegesis, or neurological status report, on trying to make some sense out of strange personal experiences. During its evolution I have shown it to, and sought comments from, a few trusted friends.

Mr Tambourine Man

Earth mysteries, ufology and consciousness author Paul Devereux reckoned my experiences were:

> ' ... just altered states triggered at different times by different things. You may be particularly prone – you probably would have been a shaman in another culture/epoch.'

John Michell, the radical-traditionalist, whose book *The View Over Atlantis* massively influenced the Sixties counter-cultural generation, wrote to me:

> 'You are, as I've recognized all along, a man of deep perception, with insights and experiences that cannot be well expressed – a shaman, if you like. But there's nothing unusual in being "gifted." It's how you use it that counts. I liked reading your accounts of your mental adventures and thoughts on them. You have made use of them rather than becoming their victim – which is the hallmark of a real shaman. I hope you'll continue writing and make your knowledge and enthusiasms of use to other people. There is no one else like you.'

Much of my experiences are echoed in two works of fiction by Philip K. Dick, *Radio Free Albemuth* and *VALIS*. Dick deserves the last word as he sums up my current state of play trying to make sense of my place in the world:

> 'Every day he developed a new one [theory], more cunning, more exciting, more fucked.'

My back pages

When this appendix appeared in my book *Crossing the Line: Trespassing on railway weirdness*, publisher Bob Trubshaw voiced some misgivings, but I prevailed – at least the first incident did at least occur on a train. On reflection, it does appear incongruous in context, and far better fitted to appear here. To be honest, I now find its original placing embarrassing. None of the reviews – all positive – mentioned it. Maybe they didn't get that far? Nevertheless, it imparted personal information I wished to see in the public domain. It also explained why I had embarked on a new thrust to revive my moribund literary career. It also has some significance as a catalyst for my research into temporal lobe epilepsy (I prefer dissociation rather than the emotive word epilepsy, which is inaccurate), particularly inspired by a special inquiry in *Fortean Times* into this contentious neuroscience subject by Joe McNally. It led to us doing some collaborative work on a book on the subject, but he got a better offer of a fortean TV series in his native Ireland and seemingly lost interest. Frankly, it was probably for the best as I was beginning to have misgivings about my self-diagnosis.

One other curious point. In an author's note to what amounts to a second edition of 1966's book *Margaret Clitherow* (retitled *Saint Margaret Clitherow*, published 1986), the writer reveals Katharine Longley is her real name and she had written the original version under the pen-name 'Mary Claridge.' It was the first version I saw distinctly in my vision.

Lastly, it was humbling of John Michell and Paul Devereux to separately mark me out as a shaman. I feel unworthy. I make no claims for this myself, but am comfortable if my peers judge that I should deserve such distinguished status.

PART FOUR
ALTERNATIVE HISTORY

CATCOTE "DIG" INSPIRES SOME THOUGHTS ON THE RO- MAN OCCUPATION

(*Mail*, Hartlepool, 6 April 1964)

The Catcote 'dig' on the [Hartlepool] Owton Manor estate must have aroused considerable interest – even if some people think it was only to condemn the spending of £900 to dig a dozen or more rectangular holes which appear as graves awaiting coffins. Some, however, like myself, may have been fired with sufficient interest actually to read something about the subject. The majority of books dealing with the Romans and their occupation of Britain ridicule the democratic Ancient Britons, who are portrayed to the world as 'woad-painted savages.' Such books then induce us to admire the qualities of totalitarianism and power of the Romans. The cruelty, ruthlessness, greed and unfairness of the Romans was discreetly omitted and emphasis placed on the glory of their conquering strength, and the fact that they pacified the whole Mediterranean basin, France, England, and a large portion of Central Europe. It was the result of unrest among their warlike neighbours that the Romans first began their subjugation. Greed and lust for power caused them to spread their boundaries. Their unquestionable organising ability gave the misguided impression that they were merely on a civilising mission, but they plundered and milked their provinces dry. The Roman poet Virgil wrote:

'Let others study Art and Science; Rome has somewhat better to do,
namely War and Dominion.'

Had Hitler invaded and subjugated this land the effect would have been comparable to the Roman occupation. Not only was Britain a relatively settled country at the advent of the Roman invasion, but was thriving agriculturally, and had trade in exports of spinning, weaving, glass-making, pottery, carpentry, bronze and iron, with the Mediterranean lands. Towns existed and a great road system, so often attributed solely to the Romans, radiated strategically from London, providing quick movement of the Britons' chariots. In fact, the Caradoc – last Bronze Age king of Britain, mustered 4,000 chariots under his banner and as Britain was then thickly forested they could travel only by the well-planned roads. The Romans merely paved this system of roads, in order to make them easier for their infantry to march on. Paving would have been a hindrance to the unshod horses pulling the Britons' chariots.

To conquer Britain the Romans sent their best general and the Britons put up the strongest resistance to the Romans since the time of Hannibal. The conquest of France had taken four years, but it took over 18 years for the Romans to advance from the Thames to a line drawn between Gloucester and Ely, and nearly 40 years to occupy Yorkshire. Many generals returned to Rome after short terms in Britain, amongst whom were Agricola and Suetonius Paulinus, the latter's greatest achievement being the massacre, on Nero's orders, of the elderly and un-armed Druids. This near-extermination of the Druids caused the Britons to flock to the wid-owed Queen Boadicea for revenge. She addressed her army in these stirring words:

> "I rule over Britons, little versed in craft or diplomacy, but born and trained to die for their country. I implore aid for freedom, for victory over enemies infamous for the wantonness of the wrongs they inflict, for their perversion of justice, for their contempt of religion, and for their insatiable greed; a people that revel in unmanly pleasure, whose affections are more to be dreaded and abhorred than their enmity. Never let a foreigner bear rule over me or these, my countrymen; never let slavery reign in this island."

For three-and-a-half centuries Britain was an unfortunate province of the Roman empire, always unsettled in its 'peace.' Alan V. Insole, in his book *Immortal Britain*, commenting on the Romans writes: 'To any people they intended to enslave they declared that they only came to impose peace.' The Britons were peace-loving before the Romans arrived, but the experience of having their homes looted and menfolk slaughtered, caused them to fight the Romans valiantly. Those Britons not slaughtered lived in fear of being shipped to Rome to die as gladiators. The gladiatorial games, where men were torn to pieces and eaten alive by wild beasts became major massacres as time went by. The barbarity of the Romans appeared also in their system of law where the right of appeal only applied to a privileged few. Those condemned to death were first publicly flogged, followed by a tortuous death such as strangulation, live-burial, or worst of all, crucifixion.

The Romans achieved a splendid architectural style, which owed much to the Greeks, and although their buildings were magnificent it must not be forgotten that, like the pyramids of Egypt, it was slave labour which built them. Stonehenge, in Britain, was built without slave labour, and the trouble taken to transport the huge stones from Pembrokeshire matched any feat undertaken by the Romans. The Druids supervised the construction of Stonehenge and were the spiritual guides of the Britons. Their moral values were much the same as those of the Christians. They taught that there was one God in existence who was one unity; whole and indivisible, representing all things in existence, goodness, truth and beauty. The Romans, however, claimed that to advance in civilisation the Britons must fall down and worship the busts of repellent Roman Caesars.

The Druids stood against slavery and human sacrifice. The gladiators represented human sacrifice in Rome, and even today our hanging of criminals remains as a remnant of this practice. One archaic religion surviving at that time, however, did permit a human sacrifice every seventh year, but this was carried out with a <u>voluntary</u> victim and the sacrifice of an animal instead followed quickly. Christianity added to the persecuted peoples enslaved by the Romans. Slaves were at the mercy of every whim of their master or mistress of the household in which they served.

It was the Caradoc who became the only important prisoner whom the Romans feared to have publicly flogged and killed in the brutal traditional manner. In a speech before the Roman Senate, as reported by Tacitus, the Caradoc said:

> "I was lord of men, horses, wealth: what wonder if at your dictation I refused to resign them. Does it follow, that because the Romans aspire to universal dominion, every nation is to accept the vassalage they would impose? I am now your prisoner, betrayed not conquered. Had I, like others, yielded without resistance, where would have been the name of the Caradoc? Where your glory? Oblivion would have buried both in the same tomb. Bid me live and I shall survive in history as the sole example of Roman clemency."

Such were the brave, sarcastic remarks of a captive king attacking the totalitarian principles of Rome; words far removed from the illiteracy of a 'woad-painted savage,' as we would be induced to expect by so many perverse writers glorifying the Romans. Let us finally remember the words of a contemporary king of the Picts in Scotland, who declared:

> "To robbery, slaughter, plunder, the Romans give the lying name of Empire; they make a solitude and call it peace."

This piece was my first published work of any consequence. Its genesis was inspiration from reading a 'heretical' book by Alan V. Insole, *Immortal Britain*, a very different slant upon ancient history to that which I had become accustomed. Secondly, my ambition lay in the direction of journalism and I hoped to impress the editor of our local newspaper. I don't recall any particular praise from that editor, Frank Dines, only him telling my father that the only thing wrong with my piece was that I had committed the sin of splitting an infinitive. Another lesson learned: editors can be petty and unappreciative. What I did not anticipate, but with foresight should have expected was, the reaction at West Hartlepool Grammar School, where I was in the senior arts sixth form. The head of Latin, an Army man, Major Gavin Donaldson, admirer of Roman brutality and - as Philip K. Dick was later to warn - a believer that 'The Empire never ended,' summoned me to appear before his sixth-form Latin students and mocked my article publically. I told him what I thought of his bullyboy methods and kangaroo court style of leadership and eventually walked out. The next morning the headmaster, Edwin Houlton, ambushed me after assembly, asked me if I "believed the Moon was made of green cheese" and chastised me "for being rude to Major Donaldson." In my defence, I told him I thought his head of department had overstepped

the mark and assured him I held no such belief about our satellite's physical composition. The matter did not rest there as Major Donaldson utilised another tactic in his campaign to subjugate me. He recruited one of his pet senior pupils, the odious collaborator James R. Atkinson, to have published a rejoinder in the local newspaper. I certainly learned that there's another side to every story and the temporarily civvy street warrior had made a strategic advance, but overall I felt like the Caradoc, bowed but not down, proud and un-shackled, betrayed by a Quisling, not triumphant, but the moral victor.

Although my article was not wholly accurate and I had taken Insole's 'facts' at face value, his unorthodox perspective for 1952 when the book was published was one which was to gain ground with my generation. I had already learned the valuable lesson that there was more to history than the victor's viewpoint. Also that Rome's imperial ambitions were not to be admired but deplored. More importantly, Albion's resistance was what mattered; Britons were freedom fighters, not terrorists; Druidry was superior to the worship of multi-ple gods, including dead emperors; and that Roman roads were only a literal resurfacing of something far more archaic.

I had started my journalistic career with a vengeance and a baptism of fire of sorts. It could only get better. Almost half-a-century later, and personally convinced time is not linear but cyclic, I believe Alan V. Insole has just been exonerated by *UnRoman Britain* (The History Press, 2010) authors Miles Russell and Stuart Laycock, who have swept away the notion of a civilising era in Albion of poncy togas (think David Beckham's sarongs) and villas with under-floor heating (Coleen Rooney's pampered pooches satirical urban myth); though they do allow that the Romans helped the native populace cash in on exporting their in-vention of the woollen hoodie (back in fashion with Wayne Rooney) while importing whores (ditto W. Rooney). Exploitation was rife, becoming more naked as taxes rose, as did resentment. No wonder another parallel was drawn by the book, that the West's in-volvement in Afghanistan, particularly NATO military occupation of Helmand province, was a perfect analogy for 'our boys' and their thankless and futile presence, just as the Romans were not welcome in Britannia and failed to fully subdue the indigenous population.

ASTRAL WEEKS, HOLLOW WORDS, FIELD OF DREAMS

(*The Ley Hunter*, No. 117, 1992)

If I ventured in the slipstream / between the viaducts of your dreams / where immo-
bile steel rims crack / and the ditch in the backroads stop / could you find me? /
Would you kiss my eyes? / Lay me down in silence easy / To be born again.
— Van Morrison (*Astral Weeks*, 1968)

During the early Seventies a modest figure on the UFO scene was Dan Butcher. Wheelchair-bound Dan, of Ash Green, Hampshire, wrote a number of articles for *The Ley Hunter* under my editorship and I wish to draw attention to them as they relate to the paradigm shift being initiated by the current editor of *TLH*, Paul Devereux. I've never believed in spoon-feeding my readers, so this column will only drop hints; but the points I'm making may be worthy of further thought and research.

Dan, who may well now be dead, was particularly interested in astral travel. I suspect, from reading between the lines of his articles and his disabilities, he was a practising out-of-the-body experienced initiate. One article (*TLH*, No. 15) discussed astral travel at three speeds and linked its straightness, UFO sightings and behaviour and also the possibility of UFO/ human following leys. He suggested a shaman would use this gift to survey and choose where a tribal migration should follow. As for the vision of Macsen Wledig, as recounted in *The Mabinogion*, he believed this was similar, with Macsen spending a year searching for the route he saw originally in a **[lucid?]** dream. Eventually he traced it to the fair maiden he had earlier seen in a castle on an unknown island. This turned out to be Anglesey. Dan then went on to discuss 'the ancient practice of incubation, or going to some sacred spot such as a mound, a stone or cairn to sleep the night in the hope of obtaining a dream of guidance. Such incubation dreams as are on record read very much like out-of-the-body experiences...'

His following article, 'The Wandering Turf: or the Psychography of Leys' (*TLH*, No. 17), discussed the importance of gates and gaps in hedges. He believed an apparently ordinary field could be inter-penetrated by an unknown *milieu*, and a ley could be a favoured locality for a psychic experience. Dan subsequently followed up by writing of Helen and straight roads (*TLH*, No. 20) and earlier of an alignment in the Western Desert of Africa (*TLH*, No. 12) going from nowhere to nowhere but linking places that may possibly have been used to obtain significant dreams.

Here we must leave Dan Butcher's intuitions, though he deserves to be better recognised as one of the truly seminal figures in earth mysteries rather than overlooked as a peripheral and undervalued character in ufology. The material by Dan I consulted did not connect his observations to tracks associated with the new death roads paradigm in ley hunting, nor am I going to make such a connection here. I had, I admit, tended to translate 'dod' as 'dead,' and will endeavour to give Paul Devereux's new projection for alignments a fair assessment as he publishes all his material.

To close, I want to throw some personal observations in the air and see how they come down: be there a pattern or otherwise. In Hartlepool, when I was a lad, we would go in the summer months to a depression in a hillock called Dead Man's Hollow. It had scrawny decaying dead trees and an eerie feel with Summer Hill to the north where there was a depression in the ground (which my late father said was a crater where a German bomb had been jettisoned). Dead Man's Hollow is labelled 'old gravel pit' by the Ordnance Survey. One evening while out with my 'Just William' chums, the one who was a 'Cowboys and Indians' fanatic called Derek Hugill decided single-handedly to round up the cows in the field, much to the farmer's chagrin.

One afternoon I found circular areas of scorched earth near Dead Man's Hollow, and having consumed a copious quantity of alcohol that evening at his party, confided in my friend from a rival newspaper that it had probably been caused by a flying saucer. I was flabbergasted that he took me seriously and the next day, a Sunday, when he was on duty and perhaps still inebriated himself, he investigated my drunken surmise and spoke to the bemused farmer, who explained he had been burning piles of stubble.

Dead Man's Hollow also figures in the lives of two girlfriends. Stainsby girl [reference Chris Rea song] Marilyn Pillar and I had our one and only fight there during a three-year courtship, knocking the proverbial shit out of one another and landing in a hedgerow ditch. There a couple of years later, my wife-to-be Pauline saw herself as an astral body cross over a stile into the next field to the west. In the opposite direction lies the site of the Romano-British settlement of Catcote, which I have posited as the Arthurian battle site of Cat Coit Celidon [see p.146], and to the north, as a sixth-former a fellow pupil regaled our common-room with the news that earlier that morning a cycling transvestite gunman had fired at him!

I've many happy memories about Dead Man's Hollow and the field where it stands. I hadn't realised until penning this column just how it played so many roles during my rites of passage. A place of craziness, of hurting the one you love (actually to be honest, it was all the fault of my petty jealousy, leading to pushing and shoving and in a tussle of me coming off worse – ok, she rather beat me up - as we tumbled scrapping into a large blackberry bush clump, where I now recall that years earlier, on a walk with my father I had seen my first red admiral butterfly) and an out-of-body experience for a wife-to-be. Such a concentration of memories and weirdness. A field of dreams.

This article from the period when Paul Devereux edited *The Ley Hunter*, subtitled *The Journal of Geomancy and Earth Mysteries*, was written in response to the paradigm shift whereby the previous notion of leys being either or both trackways or energy lines was being challenged by speculation of them as corpse roads, fairy paths or routes of astral/shamanic flight, being one of my Long Man of Wilmington columns, which numbered 43 between 1976 and 1999. As for Dan Butcher a sweep of the internet revealed that it seems his one and only book was entitled *Water and its symbolism in UFO encounters* (1971), but more tellingly he described a skywatching vigil as '... in the nature of a séance, a circle composed of some mediumistic people ... in which anything can happen.' (*Pegasus*, 1971)

ROBERT THE BRUCE – HART-MAN

(*Mail* (Hartlepool), 3 September 1988; *Folklore Frontiers*, No. 25, 1995)

R obert the Bruce was born in Hart. Fair enough there is no evidence to prove this, but equally no other place in England or Scotland can prove for definite to be his birthplace. So let's hear it for Hart, County Durham.

He was one of Scotland's greatest heroes, but few people realise that in addition to owning estates in Annandale and Carrick in Scotland, he was also Lord of Heortnesse – this tract of land including Hart and Hartlepool. Scottish nobility such as the Bruces were an obvious example of people well at home in England. The Scots hero was the eighth member of the family to be called Robert, five of whom are buried at Guisborough Priory, North Yorkshire, founded by the second of the line, including the hero's grandfather. The lordship of Annandale was conferred on the second of the Norman family of de Brus by King David, who when he died left two sons, one of whom, Robert, received the Scottish and Heortnesse estates.

Another noble with fiefs in both Scotland and Northumberland was John 'Red' Comyn, who fought for Henry III at Northampton and Lewes. Robert Bruce cut Comyn's throat in a fit of temper and became a hunted outlaw. As such he appealed to the patriotic section of the Scots; in our parlance he and William Wallace became freedom fighters, or if you were on the opposite side, terrorists. Bruce boldly canvassed his claim to the Scottish throne – and had his lands in Heortnesse confiscated by King Edward I. In two minor engagements, Bruce was defeated but eluded capture. It was at this juncture that the spider of legend enters history – or folklore. There are two versions of a tale where Robert the Bruce was hiding in a cave. In one he watched a spider laboriously making its web and having many mishaps with its intricate construction. Through a variant of 'if at first you don't succeed, try, try again' he was inspired to keep his ambitions alive and press on to eventual victory. In the other version the spider spins such a large web as to completely cover the entrance to the cave and lead his pursuers to assume there was no one within it and go away. Interestingly I was told a similar tale as to the latter version in Aberdeenshire with Bruce replaced by Rob Roy, and anyway could a humble spider spin such a huge web across a cave entrance?

Bruce went on to ravage England's northern counties, exacting a terrible revenge. In 1314, the two-day Battle of Bannockburn left the English army in tatters. It vindicated Bruce's claim to the Scottish throne and his revolutionary bid for leadership of the Scots. Peace was made between the countries in 1327. To this day visitors to Hart will have pointed out to them the de Brus wall, where supposedly Robert the Bruce was born, and one of his ancestors supposedly lies in the de Brus tomb in St Hilda's Church on Hartlepool's historic Headland.

I republished this *Mail* article in *Folklore Frontiers* in response to a piece by Mick Goss, then writing a regular column in the magazine under the title 'FolkJokeOpus,' where he argued (same issue) that Robert the Bruce was a fellow Essex Man, born just outside Chelmsford. In another article on Robert the Bruce ('Kilts off for the Lassies,' *FF,* No.48, 2004), who was the central character in *The Scottish Loveknot* (2003), I recorded how at £12m this thistles and sporrans epic was the most costly pornographic film made in the UK. Not exactly *Monarch of the Glen*, Lady of the Loch actress Jodie (34D-26-27) Moore extolled its historical and creative credentials as "more mainstream ... not just putting a cock in your mouth." Still, from the excerpts on the brief-run, highly-amusing and much-admired TV smut show *Ban This Filth* (C4, 26 October 2004), it was more declarations of lust rather than the missing Declaration of Arbroath, and the programme helpfully informed those more familiar with documentaries by Starkey and Schama that Bruce died on 7 June 1329 of leprosy rather than gonorrhoea. Born 11 July 1274, son of Robert de Brus and Marjorie, countess of Carrick, he was married twice, and reigned from 1306.

HROTHGAR AT HART
(AN ANGLO-SAXON WETHERSPOON'S)
(*Folklore Frontiers*, No. 27, 1995)

L ast issue, FolkJokeOpus columnist Mick Goss put forward an Essex contender as the true Robert the Bruce and I countered with the local hero from Hart, County Durham. Serendipity, not awkwardness, comes into the frame here. In his latest contribution, Mick's claim of a great mead-hall of King Hrothgar located in Denmark is, I would argue, just as geographically incorrect as Essexman Robert the Bruce. Hrothgar was also located in Hart, County Durham. No joke – folk, opus or whatever!

Hart had an Anglo-Saxon church and Hartlepool itself grew as a satellite of the village. Check the Venerable Bede, who was certainly a careful historian and so was my late, old friend Robert Wood, headmaster and author among several books of a history of West Hartlepool. Bob Wood didn't have much time for Hartlepool's monkey-hanging legend, so when he located *Beowulf* locally we should take notice. He wrote:

> 'The famous King Hrothgar from whose hall the hero Beowulf sallied forth to kill the monster Grendel at the bottom of a dismal swamp is supposed to have had his palace at Hart. Villagers will still point out to you the field known as Palace Garth or King's Meadow, and I can remember many years ago an excavation in that field revealed the post holes of a huge hall of the type mentioned in *Beowulf*. Hartlepool Slake could well be the home of Grendel.' (*Northern Daily Mail* (Hartlepools), 17 April 1964)

An explanation: The Slake was a muddy estuary, now part of the port of Hartlepool, and at Hart the name Palace has been applied to a new road. Sounds like the hall was of the dimensions of these new Wetherspoon-style superpubs built in the likes of former warehouses. You can just imagine the scene as similar to the Intergalactic Bar in the film *Star Wars*. And that's before Mick Goss, me or Grendel arrives.

Again an alternative history argument and again Mick Goss challenged. What was not revealed in my brief piece was that Robert Wood's and my stances were based upon a theory originated by Daniel Henry Haigh (1819-1879), the noted Victorian scholar of Anglo-Saxon

history and literature, who wrote two influential works, one of which, *The Anglo-Saxon Sagas*, published in 1861, set the landscape around Hartlepool (then Heretu) as the scene for the events in *Beowulf*. (Haigh's book can be downloaded from Christina Debes's occult and religious books site, darkbooks.org/pp.php?v=713811136). This interpretation by the amateur with no academic training is out of favour today. Also in 1861, the dedicated self-taught scholar published *The Conquest of Britain by the Saxons*. He also wrote several monographs on his other interests, runic inscriptions and Anglo-Saxon numismatics. When a second *Beowulf* film, starring Ray Winstone, was released, I was interviewed on the saga and spoke of Haigh and the hall at Hart (*Hartlepool Mail*, 14/11/07). What the reporter didn't quote was my moan that we wait one thousand plus years for a film set in Hartlepool and two come along at once! And that's also quite a double: both Robert the Bruce and Beowulf originating from Hartlepool. Pity the town has not cashed in on these historical connections – but that's typical Hartlepool. A town with no appreciation of its heritage or pride in its legacy. Except the monkey...

CRIMDON AS CAMLANN

(Pendragon, Vol. XX/1, 1989)

Today Crimdon is best known for its annual August Bank Holiday beauty contest. During the last war, munitions Minister and local Member of Parliament Emmanuel Shinwell played truant from his duties to judge the Miss Crimdon spectacle, leading to the headline 'Shinwell puts legs before arms.' After the war Crimdon, then in South-East Durham, was dubbed the 'Pitmen's Riviera.' Today, continental package holidays have made it a shadow of its former glory and Costa del Crimdon is distinctly tawdry.

It overlooks a scenic deep-sided valley: these gashes into the coastal limestone being known locally as 'denes.' The name Camlann is supposed to translate as 'the crooked glen' and this is exactly what Crimdon Dene is. In fact, an old map of the district, dated 1801, has the name Kamlan where Crimdon now stands. The story of King Arthur and his Knights has for centuries been associated with nearby Castle Eden and Blackhall. It was to record this lore, that Blackhall Rocks historian Reg Wright set to compiling information, and had it privately printed. Much of what Wright records is anecdotal, and his style is woolly and repetitive, but it is good that someone has taken the trouble to record the lore before it is lost forever. The Kamlan map name is certainly revealing, but can we substantiate it further to the site of Arthur's last battle? According to the Matter of Britain, Arthur's crown had been seized by his son Mordred, progeny of unwitting incest between Arthur and his half-sister Morgause. Arthur, returned from France, and the two armies met in the mighty battle of Camlann, where Mordred was killed - but Arthur had been struck a fatal blow.

Wright claims to substantiate Crimdon as the scene of this carnage, for above the grand sweeps of the dene gorge lie massive burial sites surrounding Benridge Farm. Skeletons of men and boys huddled together as if originally having been pitched into hasty graves were found, and Wright believes the site should be examined professionally. [1] Among collected reminiscences published by Wright is this one from 'an old farmer' regarding the bodies:

> '...in my young days when I first started farming hereabouts, many's the day I've ploughed up skeleton after skeleton, sometimes single and others in batches as if they'd been thrown in. I once found what looked like an old sword but I lost it again. The reason I never told anybody was because of the "red tape." The

councils at the time would have held up my work. I couldn't afford that. I had to make some money. I was newly married. Of course I found bits and pieces of this and that and the other. These I used to leave lying about the barn or stable window sills. Don't know whatever happened to them though.' [2]

As he lay dying, Arthur instructed Sir Bedivere to retun his sword Excalibur to the Lady of the Lake. Could he have tossed it into the Black Pool at nearby Hart? Then Arthur was ferried on a barge to Avalon as his final resting place. Wright reckons that there are records maintaining the old town of Hartlepool to be Avalon and he associates the borough's stag emblem with Merlin. Another Arthurian battle was Cat Coit Celidon and a Roman-British settlement was excavated in the town's Catcote area. Catcote has a Dead Man's Hollow and Blackhall Rocks a Dead Man's Bank: local lore also states that Arthur played games with the Devil on the cliff-top at Blackhall Rocks, which has left places there called Devil's Ditch, Devil's Dyke, Devil's Leap and Devil's Path. One of the caves on the beach at Blackhall Rocks is called Arthur's Cave: according to folklore it led to an inland safety escape grotto used by Arthur and his en-tourage. Two miles west of Castle Eden there is a large cavern called the Knights' Hall, ru-moured to have been one of Arthur's meeting places, and which is the site of an Iron Age set-tlement. In Castle Eden village itself, at the T-junction leading to the present day castle (a ma-norial hall), it is said that during the hours of daylight the spirits of Arthur's knights disguised as a clutch of chickens often frequent this spot.

Just down the A19 at Hutton Henry crossroads is Arthur's Tor, a small rocky hill where in 1832 a cairn on its summit was excavated and the skeleton of a man with a breastplate was discovered. It is said to still contain buried treasure, guarded by giants of soldiers from the Dark Ages. Also the valley which once swept down from here to Sheraton was known in olden days as the Valley of the Graves. In answer to a request for information, Wright was informed by Hartlepool poet Elizabeth Davison that 'King Arthur once shaved his head before walking through Castle Eden Dene.' Also it is said that at Garmondsway, King Canute camped and shaved his head to walk barefoot to St Cuthbert's shrine in Durham Cathedral.

Coming to the present, Arthur's hillfort above Castle Eden Dene, formerly named Yohden, traditionally can be seen rising in the mist above the postwar new town of Peterlee every Mid-summer's Eve. Evocative? If you ever saw Peterlee you would know why the past would want to escape the present.

References:

1. Reginald Wright, A *History of Castle Eden Lore in Search of King Arthur*, published privately, 1985
2. Reginald Wright, *Black Hall Rocks and Blackhall in the Parish of Monk Hesleden*, published privately, 1985

Yet another revisionist viewpoint, this time inspired by Reg Wright, an amateur historian, archaeologist, writer, poet and musician. He died in 1991. I doubt if his (or my) speculations here would get more than short shrift from scrutinising scholars, but keen amateurs do have a role to play and most disciplines have been enhanced by hobbyists, however much they may be regarded with contemptuous disdain. I think the experts should give my and Reg's speculations at least a cursory examination.

RESURRECTION SHUFFLE ...
(FROM KING ARTHUR TO ROCK 'N' ROLL OLYMPUS)

(*Pendragon*, Winter, 1989)

'Every rock star who has ever died is really still alive (and vice versa)'
— Penny Stallings [1]

If mythology has a single most important component it is death – along with rebirth. Death and shaman are chicken and egg. Who escorted the first dead human soul to salvation? Who paid the first ferryman? Who showed the first ferryman the way? Certainly a cult of the dead appears as old as man's emergence. Also it seems death has hardly seemed the final act in many cultures and societies. 'In the film, the pair, Butch Cassidy and the Sundance Kid, were pictured in a last heroic action. Like Barbarossa, King Arthur or even Jimi Hendrix, they were held by some not to have died in a hail of bullets at San Vincente, Bolivia, but to have been seen back in the U.S.A. [2] Heroes, outlaws even, are popularly imagined able to beat destiny's rap. And so this persistent story that certain individuals have cheated an obvious death resurfaces all over the world. Did many Nazi leaders begin new lives in South America and Adolf Hitler escape to Iceland in a U-boat? More persistent are tales of immortality. In its strongest form we find that persons chosen for their outstanding personal qualities are retained in a form of limbo in readiness for a time when they will again be required. This motif of the national hero who once lived and will live again when his country is in peril is immutable and universal. For 1,000 years King Arthur has been Britain's sleeping hero and today he is still extolled as a shining example of national idealism. The tale of Arthur – *rex quondam rexque futurus*, The Once and Future King – appeals to the oppressed and most strongly in times of strife or perseverance.

I will leave to others the argument as to the historicity of a real King Arthur, but stress that the tale is archetypal and widespread in its variants. Other candidates in the suspended animation pantheon have been Northern England hero Harry Hotspur and hounds holed up by a landslide at Hell Hole in the Cheviots awaiting release by a call on a hunter's horn; Earl Gerald, who lies below the Rath of Lullaghast, from which he will emerge to drive out the British and unite Ireland; Roderick, last of the Goths; Don Sebastian of Spain; Welsh heroes Owen of the Red Hand and Owen Glendower; King Wenzel below Bohemia's Blanik Mountains; Frederic Barbarossa beneath a mountain in Thuringia; and Ogier the Dane, who after 200 years in a super-natural land was required when France needed a saviour and after accomplishing the neces-sary, returned to his place of enchantment.

This motif that Arthur would return was fuelled by William of Malmesbury's statement that Arthur's grave could not be located. By the 12th century the rumours of Arthur's still being alive had spread to his having been reported in so unlikely a location as the subterranean depths of Mount Etna. Geoffrey Gaimer stated in his *History of the English* that the Welsh of that time (1150) threatened the Normans that they would win back their land through Arthur and restore the name of Britain. An early record of Arthur being encountered after his death is recounted by Peter des Roches, Bishop of Winchester, in *The Lanercost Chronicle* (1216). The story goes that he was out hunting when he came upon a splendid mansion. Here the ser-vants invited him to dine with their master, a man who introduced himself as Arthur. In order to convince sceptics of the veracity of his tale, he is said to have been given the power of pro-ducing a butterfly from his closed fist at will.

It wos Kelvin McKenzie wot wrote Gotcha!

Hundreds of sites are associated with Arthur in legend and the latest theory interprets these places as signifying locations of special sanctity. Yet basically the attraction of the tale of Ar-thur is that it fits our tradition of salvation, resurrection and immortality, and it is as strong today as when the stories coalesced into the Matter of Britain. He may have been a military leader, but he can also be seen as an immortal solar hero; his 12 battles being the astrological months and his deeds related to the passage of the sun through the ecliptic.

We may believe that nations have souls and that for Britain the archetype of Arthur is in truth an aspect of this. Nations' fortunes ebb and flow and this rise and fall through culture, eco-nomics and politics is part of the psychic flow; but should serious danger threaten, then the image of Arthur will be activated and allow for a rallying of the people. The rumour of a sleeping Arthur therefore is poetic, but also at a deeper level is a sign of our having anthropo-morphised the nation's soul. [3] That rumour becomes reality, was to be witnessed during the 1982 Falklands conflict, when two of the task force ships were *Sir Tristram* and *Sir Galahad*, named after two of Arthur's Knights of the Round Table.

Yet 20th Century belief, denying the certification as dead of various screen idols and popular music figures as untrue and the victim being secretly alive yet often tragically disfigured or masquerading in mundane employment, suggests there are alternatives to the hypothesis that it is only oppression which nurtures belief of heroes in suspended animation. Valentino's death provoked 60,000 people in New York to riot and the hysteria generated unlikely stories such as that he was buried in a huge bronze coffin, had been engaged to Pola Negri, and was a se-cret fascist and, of course, still alive. The cause of death of kung fu hero Bruce Lee is even more bizarre than the rumoured notion that a hostile oriental martial arts sect was to blame. The healthy, tough Chinese-American superman took one tablet for a headache, became aller-gic to it, lapsed into a coma and never recovered. Or did he?

For Hollywood happiness, who brought more into the lives of generations of people probably than anyone else but Walt Disney? Author Robert Anton Wilson had his dead daughter Luna preserved medically in the hopes that medicine will one day be able to bring her back to life. Luna Wilson has been preserved by the Bay Area Cryonic Society voluntarily free of charge as an expression of gratitude for the publicity her father has given to their work. Not unsurprisingly a *Fanatic* interviewer mentioned an old chestnut: "There's a persistent story that Walt Disney was one of the first to opt for cryonic burial..." *Illuminatus* co-author with Wilson, Robert Shea first interlocuted by commenting that: "One version of the rumour is that he's in a permanently locked chamber in Snow White's palace in Disneyland, because people have seen hoar frost coming from under the door." Wilson added: "The Disney Organisation always denies it. But it is a fact that before he died he made a series of films, one of which is shown each year to Disney executives as a kind of pep talk. And at the end of each film he says, 'I'll be seeing you,' which could refer to the next film or it may have referred to the fact he IS cryonically suspended." [4]

But since Disney's day, less wholesome mythologising has taken over. It's become all sex 'n' drugs 'n' rock 'n' roll. And few rolled more joints and had other drugs, plus getting his rocks off with more girls, than that other king, Elvis Presley. Seriously, how could a man make records such as *Heartbreak Hotel, One Night, Blue Suede Shoes* and even later *Suspicious Minds*, yet create that series of banal films? Perhaps his twin brother Jesse did NOT die at birth – maybe it was him who did the acting and was enlisted in the army while the real Elvis carried on the serious business of recording classic records. Moreover, could the drug-abused, junk-food-bloated body found in the bathroom have been Jesse's? Maybe old Elvis is alive and well south of the border. Or, in 1968 he paid ten million dollars to be cloned by a California genetics institute and a year after Elvis's death the young replica escaped and is somewhere in Los Angeles. Many more Elvis rumours exist and maybe the Penny dropped on April 1st. [1]

Would the real Paul McCartney have wed Heather 'Dark Satanic' Mills?

The live fast and die young philosophy usually entails a third ingredient – high profitability. The question could be asked: is the singer/investment better dead than alive? One rumour claims Bob Dylan's motor-cycle accident in 1966 claimed his life. The person who now makes Dylan records and tours is a talentless lookalike recruited to salvage record company investment. Nothing 'Dylan' has done during the past decade would dissuade those who suspect a substitute. And what of the secret ciphers on records? I have a bulging file of supposed infiltrations. Mostly they are argued to be satanic and usually you have to play the record backwards to hear the message. A Simon Bates column led with Prince's backwards Second Coming prophecy on *Darling Nikki*. [5]

Then there's the persistent rumour that Paul McCartney died in a car crash and a doppelganger substituted. So it goes, among much other circumstantial evidence, John Lennon mumbles "Paul's dead (or "Paul is dead, man"), miss him, miss him" when the *White Album* is played backwards (or between numbers when played slow), and on *Magical Mystery Tour* (or end of *Strawberry Fields Forever*) John says supposedly "I buried Paul." For many the cover of the *Abbey Road* LP itself clinched the rumour. It showed all four Beatles crossing the street by way of a zebra crossing. There was the way they dressed: John the minister, Ringo the undertaker and George the gravedigger. Only Paul was barefoot and out of step with the others. The numberplate of a car read LMW 281F - or fancifully 28IF – if Paul had lived. In America this macabre speculation created a crop of ghoulish songs, while preposterously there were cynics who suggested the Beatles themselves masterminded the scam as a publicity stunt. [6] So did Paul die in a car crash on 9 November 1966 and was he replaced by a 'double'?

The unlikely favourite candidate was a Canadian student who won a McCartney lookalike contest that year. [7]

Anyway, it seems like today's rock stars, Arthur lived fast, dangerously, died dramatically and left a highly profitable corpse/corpus. Look no further than the library or bookstore! Oh, yes, the sleeping hero aspect? Yes, well, how's about Allenshead? That's where I'm told on very good authority **[by Tom Cole]** the hero lies ... waiting. Unless, of course, you know better.

References:

1.   Penny Stallings, *Rock 'n' Roll Confidential*, Vermillion, 1985
2.   Nigel Pennick, *Anarchist Review*, No. 5, 1980
3.   Paul Screeton, 'Arthur, Merlin and Old Stones,' *Pendragon*, Vol. XIV, No. 4, 1981
4.   'Illuminatus,' *Fanatic Supplement*, 1977
5.   *Daily Star*, 9 March 1985
6.   *Look-In*, 27 February 1982
7.   *New Musical Express*, 9 October 1982

FIRECRACKER!
JORDAN – WICKER WOMAN
(*Folklore Frontiers*, No. 48, 2004)

One can only conclude that when 30,000 people turned out to cheer as a 30-foot effigy of topless totty Jordan is burned, that Guy Fawkes' role in bonfire folklore is truly eclipsed. Seeking a direct descent from prehistoric and Celtic pagan fire rituals and human sacrifice falls foul of the fact that there is no trace of late autumn or early winter bonfires in mediaeval or Tudor England (which is not to say midsummer rites could not be continuous). A Commons bill proposing a perpetual anniversary thanksgiving for the foiled Gunpowder Plot met with unanimous approval and was grafted to the reformed religion. That Jordan (the Hastings effigy spelled 'JAWDON') was chosen follows the bonfire societies of the South-East tradition of burning various caricatures. Pope Paul V was a favourite in years past, being Roman Catholic leader at the time of the plot in 1605, but more recently Lewes, for instance has built 20-foot explosives-filled effigies of Nigel Lawson, Bill Clinton and Margaret Thatcher and burned them. [1]

But why Jordan? One obvious answer – well, two actually – being her dubious celebrity and living locally (and you were contemplating her double-barrelled chest, no doubt). A banner was raised above the red-hot stunna's head which read, 'I'm a resident – Get Me Out of Here!' This being a reference to her move to nearby Maresfield and her appearance as a contestant on the reality TV show *I'm A Celebrity – Get Me Out of Here!* I trust it was not as folklore guru Ronald Hutton was told by a girl - her hair, coat and gloves alight at the time – at the Ottery St Mary tar barrel ceremony that the purpose was to chase evil spirits from her community at the beginning of 1990's winter. [2] In 2004, as the flames lit the East Sussex sky and Jordan's right breast sagged down before collapsing completely, onlooker Joanne Butler, 25, from Tunbridge Wells in Kent, said:

> "It was great fun. The effigy was really lifelike, although I'm not sure the ten-foot high boobs were as big as the real thing. Anyway they soon deflated and collapsed, which made everyone smile." [3]

The charred remains of Jordan were later ignominiously scraped off the beach front and removed in bags, but the bounteous beauty can bask in the afterglow of knowing her cremation raised thousands for charity. But back with continuity, Hastings's bonfire was only revived in 1996 after a 40-year break, before which it stretched back to 1605. Doubter that I am, I had gone so far as to borrow a book from our local library to check whether the *Daily Sport* reporter had correctly attributed Jordan's conflagration to commemorating the anniversary of the Battle of Hastings, but apparently its being held around the conflict's date of October 14 was correct. *The Times* added that it features a procession of 1,066 torchbearers and a bonfire on the beach and that enemies of bonfire get burnt too: traffic wardens and BSE-ridden beefburgers having been recent victims. Enemy of bonfire or not, burning Jordan is preferable to the fiercely sectarian olden days and spectacular struggles between the constabulary and the anarchic bonfire gangs. From drunken pyromaniacs demanding money with menaces from passersby, events today are family-friendly affairs and fun.

Although for reasons already noted I dismiss the continuity theory, Ward Rutherford sees today's bonfires as Druidic/Samhain/longevity survivals and drags in banshees from prehistoric barrows in the form of beautiful temptresses in search of mortal lovers. (4) Perhaps burning Jordan was to protect us from the modern equivalent of the belief in spirits of the dead – deadbeat D-list celebrities like her.

References:

1.   John Naish, 'Watch out, all you enemies of bonfire,' *The Times Weekend*, 2002? 2003?
2.   Ronald Hutton, *The Stations of the Sun*, Oxford University Press, 1996
3.   Richard White, 'Burn baby burn!,' *Daily Sport*, 19/10/04
4.   Ward Rutherford, 'Druids Among the Fireworks,' *Quicksilver Messenger*, Issue 1, c1980

MYLONITE MOUNTAIN

(The Ley Hunter, No. 129, 1998)

T he importance of geological fault lines within earth mysteries is now generally accepted. An article about an extraordinary temple raises some very interesting questions for hermetic topographers. Former *That's Life* television show Esther Rantzen posse personage Simon Fanshawe described for the *Mail on Sunday*'s *Night & Day* magazine readers (20/7/97) how a religious cult has built an invisible to outsiders temple under an Italian mountain. Its exact location perhaps points to the pulse of a fundamental question which an esoteric New Age community has addressed and answered. Above the village of Vidracco, in northern Italy, is the Temple of Mankind, totally hidden from the world despite having four storeys, five large chambers (the biggest of which, the Hall of Mirrors is 40ft high and has what is said to be the largest stained-glass cupola in the world) formed of marble and mosaic work.

It was constructed within the mountain in total secrecy by members of the Damahur. It went unnoticed between 1978 and 1992 and even after that it only became public knowledge because its creators revealed it. The entrance is disguised with a series of double bluffs. Damanhur, which means city of light, was founded in 1977 by a healer, painter and one-time insurance salesman, Oberto Airaudi. The 47-year-old was born in Balangevo, a village in the same part of northern Italy, and persuaded a group of New Age enthusiasts from an organisation in Turin called the Horus Centre to join him in Valchiusella, a valley about 25 miles to the north, in which five villages, including Vidracco, are scattered at the foot of the Alps. A depopulated area, they began to buy up land and later buildings. Communal living, with self-realisation, belief and ritual at the core, Airaudi said they wanted to create a philosophy rather than a religion. Starting out as 40-strong, in two years there were 150 and today number more than 700. The Damanhurians have gradually gathered influence, having 13 councillors on the four district councils in the valley and now number five self-governing communities.

Fanshawe is contemptuous of the whole project and persons involved:

> 'Whatever else you think about Airaudi, he and his mates did build an industrial-scale temple underground.[Yet] there is no escaping the fact that, at least in some ways, these industrious, creative people are completely barking.'

This is all very well, but I'm drawing attention to this marvel for a specific reason. Apparently Airaudi selected Valchisella because, he says, it lies on a 'shining knot of synchronic (whatever that means) lines,' adding, 'an intersection of various rivers of energy in which the knowledge that flows around the Earth is stored.' But if the Damanhurians are bizarre, the behaviour of the regional government seems even odder, for despite the secret temple being invisible to the outside world, it enlisted Geodata, one of Italy's leading geological and engineering companies, to examine the mountain for environmental damage. The senior geologist in charge of the survey, Elena Rabbi, described the site of the temple as 'really extraordinary.' There is, she explained, 'a zone of milonite (sic) between two plates of granite in the hill. They have built their temple right in the milonite fault. They chose the only place where they could possibly have built it.' So, what does she really know?

Fanshawe then ponders whether she believes the Damanhurians' theories, only to learn: 'It's just extraordinary that we arrived at the same place, starting from two completely different points.' On the surface, all of this is opaque. Surely we are being asked to question the exactness of location and the morphological significance. In other words, had they deliberately created some kind of mind-altering crypt? The clue is obviously the geology. Fanshawe writes 'milonite' but it's actually mylonite.

So what is mylonite? According to the only reference book mentioning it I could find after scouring Hartlepool's libraries, *The Macdonald Encyclopaedia of Rocks and Minerals*, mylonites are a subdivision of metamorphic rocks whose crystallisation came from displacement or cataclaptic metamorphism. This occurs when two masses of rock move in relation to each other as a result of geological pressure, leading to the formation of more or less minutely fractured areas and in the case of mylonite to re-melting as a result of the heat generated by friction. It is a rock of no commercial importance, but tantalisingly of spiritual value. The major examples are the Insubrica Line in the central Alps and intriguingly perhaps California's San Andreas Fault. Further attempts at analysis are beyond the scope of my fossilised 'A' level geography grade, but maybe a reader well versed in geography will be able to follow up these seeming clues to the significance of this siting. I, for one, would be grateful for any light which can be shone on this invisible temple.

Earth mysterians are not normally shy of sharing knowledge or engaging in debate, particularly if a topic is contentious, but here the magazine readership remained stubbornly silent.

PART FIVE
SPECULATIVE ARCHAEOLOGY

A NEGLECTED MASTERPIECE:

ANCIENT TRACKS ROUND CAMBRIDGE

(*Ancient Skills & Wisdom Review*, No. 10, 1980)

'For some strange reason this book has attracted no attention.'

The quote above was written by Allen Watkins, the only son of antiquarian author Alfred Watkins, in his biography of the rediscoverer of the system of prehistoric alignments (or 'alinements' as Alfred Watkins and his son argued to be the more correct term), since referred to as leys and later, ley-lines. Initial findings of precisely aligned trackways dating from a period long before the Roman invasion were presented to an unsuspecting public – and alarmed the archaeological fraternity – in his book *Early British Trackways*, when he was already elderly. Alfred Watkins was born in 1855 and his initial ley discoveries were presented in 1921. He was also a prominent Herefordshire businessman, magistrate, school governor, former president of the Royal Photographic Society, an expert on flour milling and creator of Vagos bread, brewing expert and beekeeper, yet such a man of credibility and down-to-earth interests found himself in direct opposition to an archaeological hierarchy which then – as now – vilified or ignored his findings and has regarded those who support his views as being of a 'lunatic fringe.'

Cheerfully and proudly I align myself as one of those most vociferous in supporting Alfred Watkins's thesis. But by making such a statement I do not entirely endorse every single assumption made by him. What, however, I would argue is that the intellect and lively appreciation of topography displayed in his work is in accord with commonsensical deductions. The litmus test is simple. Read his books and use them by testing his leys with ruler and pencil.

Rather than discuss the philosophy or validity of ley hunting (present views are far more occult-orientated today than they were in Watkins' own) or argue the relevance and difficulties of statistical probability analyses of alignments (a currently hotly-debated topic), I choose to put his book *Ancient Tracks Round Cambridge* into a historical perspective of its writer's work; for anyone wishing to learn the rudiments of actual practical ley hunting can easily purchase Watkins's *The Old Straight Track* (Abacus paperback) or for a wider discussion of contemporary ley thinking, my own *Quicksilver Heritage* (also Abacus; Thorsons hardback). The initial quotation continues:

> 'Yet it (this book) has many claims to be considered the best he ever wrote: it was also his last. His mind was wider and more mature than when he was writing *Early British Trackways* in the first flush of enthusiasm, and he was reaching out into the future. Discovering, discovering.'

The new discovery here was 'cardinal points alinements' and as Allen Watkins points out, his father anticipated by many years the grid pattern later emphasised by Major F.C. Tyler in his now-rare book. Sadly, Allen Watkins passed away last year. I was honoured that he was speaker at a meeting which I chaired in 1971 in Hereford to celebrate the 50th anniversary of leys and Allen was always an enthusiastic supporter of ley hunting. He was educated at Cambridge University and when working in the city professionally as a chartered accountant was visited by his father for a few days. In his book *Alfred Watkins of Hereford*, published in a limited edition of 325, he wrote:

> 'Characteristically, he was quite indifferent to the University life and buildings, but mightily excited by an obscure mound in the urban district which called itself Cambridge Castle, and spent the whole of his time ferreting round it. That was Alfred Watkins all over! He had discovered on the local map that Cambridge was an intriguing Ley-centre, so he had no time for rival attractions. In about two incredible months of feverish map-searching he had actually completed another book! *Archaic Tracks Round Cambridge* was published in 1932. It is an astonishing book especially to anyone who knew its origin: he might have lived in the district all his life. The amount of local information crammed into its 60 pages is staggering. My father had an appetite for local information; he just ate it up.'

I've climbed Cambridge Castle (or Castle Mound, as I knew it) and visited several of the city centre churches in Cambridge. Unfortunately for me there was not time to get out and about into the countryside and the same applied to Alfred Watkins. After his 1931 visit, Alfred wrote to his son asking if he would report on one of the many leys touching the mound, Cambridge Castle. Eager to test the validity of the ley, he took the day off, travelled by train to Royston and set off on foot for Stethall. As he strode through the beautiful Sky Counties scenery he noted a solitary figure ahead, walking towards him. They exchanged pleasantries about the weather, and when Allen mentioned that he had walked from Royston, the farm labourer commented: "Ah! Then you must 'a' come by the old Roman road, sir. Now when I first came to these parts some of the older folk did used to say as they'd seen another old Roman road. It went straight from Strethall Church towards Cambridge." This was Alfred Watkins's ley.

Allen Watkins, by simply indicating his route, as anyone would in conversation, had received valuable information. He commented in an article on the occasion in *The Ley Hunter*: 'He must have read my mind in the way that a native countryman often does.' Allen then asked the man if he had ever seen the second road." No sir, I never did, but I'll tell you a funny thing about that old road. You can't see it at all on the ground, but when the corn grows you can see exactly where the old road went by the poorer crop. I've often seen it."

But it is not everyone who will be treated to such agreeable beginner's luck, for as Allen wrote:

> 'I go out in search of confirmatory evidence, and at the first place I stop, in the middle of a field miles from anywhere, a man marches up and, unasked, gives me exactly the kind of evidence I am looking for – first-hand field observation. You may call this coincidence. But is it? In the ley hunter's notebook these "coincidences" begin to accumulate. My father had a score of such experiences. Nothing gives so much confidence as unsolicited evidence from an unexpected quarter. In this instance the casual memories of an elderly man unearthed a valuable clue.'

Naturally, Alfred Watkins stressed the need for fieldwork in his books, and in the chapter in *Ancient Tracks Round Cambridge* where he briefly records the above discovery by his son, he notes that corroboration on the ground normally follows map evidence.

At the end of this volume he stated: 'Adventure lies lurking in these lines where I point the way for younger feet than mine.....who will strike the trail?'

Yes, who will strike the trail? In fact, over the years thousands have answered Watkins' clarion call and he remains an inspiration for those who are attuned to the mysteries still enchanting our rural landscapes and even aligned city churches. Watkins himself is today a neglected archaeological maverick, but John Michell's proselytising brought him to Sixties/ Seventies counterculture's attention. With hindsight, he probably received too much uncritical praise from this young generation of disciples, yet he was more insightful than his detractors give him credit for. I had not previously read this, his last book, until sent a photocopy and asked to write a foreword – which forms the above – by publishers Newton & Denny. The new edition never appeared, but geomantic scholar Michael Behrend has made it available via the internet, and with my permission added my introduction. (http://www.cantab.net/users/michael.behrend/repubs/watkins_atrc/pages/screeton.html)

CRACKPOTS GET THE <u>LEY</u> OF THE LAND

(Fortean Times, No. 94, 1997)

Football, soap opera and conspiracy theory can be linked. At least in the minds of those who still believe in leys (OK, we'll call them ley-lines to suit the times). The current generation of serious geomants who have brought earth mysteries out of the ghetto are rightly indignant that however much solid research is published – just as they were once seen as the lunatic fringe of archaeology – they still have a corona of crackpots. Dowsing and the whole concept of ley-line energy has been virtually eliminated from the canon of alignment research. The current paradigm is the concept of archaic 'spirit lines' related to both the dead and shamanism. The theory has been propounded most notably by Paul Devereux, who relinquished editorship of the influential *The Ley Hunter* magazine earlier this year and who has spread the gospel through countless articles and books, which has taken the viewpoint to thousands of readers.

Resistance to change is quite natural, so long as strongly-held beliefs appear sufficiently solid. So let's look at three examples of presented ley lore where there would seem to be no such rationality:

Excuse my first example's provenance, *The Sunday Sport* (remember that half America's received wisdom comes from checkout tabloids), for I expect it will be totally alien to discerning *Fortean Times* readers. Of course, it could be a hoax or soccer fans' belief tale cynically manipulated to boost circulation, but not being a sports fan, I do not monitor all the sports diary column material, from which it might have originated. At the centre of this tale is the alleged mystery of why Manchester United get an extra two minutes when they play at home. The theory being that the alignment of structures in the new North Stand exerts an effect on referees' watches.

An engineering science expert, David Wardle, and his team carried out experiments using state of the art technology. He concluded: "The shape and materials used in the new stand create electromagnetic fields which can affect instruments. Our experiments show a timepiece could theoretically be slowed by up to 1min 40secs. This could increase to 2mins or longer when the stadium is at its full 51,000 capacity and EM fields are even stronger." A 'paranormal expert' asked for his opinion was Rudi Hench, who claimed the £28m rebuilding programme reflected the influence of ley-lines. *The Sunday Sport* then authoritatively explained: 'These are invisible sources of power that criss-cross the country, and when two or more converge, interference is strongest.' Hench believed that the Old Trafford ground is located at the junction of three such ley-lines. He then cited a game when United were playing Sheffield Wednesday and their captain powered home a header to win the game in the third minute of injury time. He added: "My findings will hopefully take some of the heat off referees who have come in for a lot of stick from opposition managers for their generous allowances of injury time."

It's not far, as the crow flies, from Old Trafford to the Granada TV studios in Salford, or a quantum leap to the rumour there that a jinx regarding *Coronation Street* was blamed upon ley-lines. The late Pat Phoenix first drew attention to this strange surmise and it was taken up by William Roache, a well-publicised Druid, and the psychic detective Robert Cracknell. The thesis being that the show's rehearsal room lies where two lines of subtle power crossed and this had caused calamities in the personal lives of the cast. Pat Phoenix surprised her audience during a question and answer session at a convent school in Altrincham, Cheshire, by saying problems arose when the cast began to use some converted stables as temporary rehearsal accommodation and changing-rooms. Her words were: "I am convinced there must have been ley-lines there or something like that." If the character of the flame-haired temptress Elsie Tanner said so, it could now easily be buried in the consciousness of millions of *Street* devotees.

Now for something even more sinister with its bizarre believers. In the Seventies, ley hunters were accused by anti-fascists of indulging in a politically incorrect study. Now a bulletin from the London Psychogeographical Society has appeared on the internet, claiming that a ley-line goes through the front room of the home of Derek Beackon, formerly a British National Party councillor for a ward on the Isle of Dogs in London's Docklands. The document claims the line has long been in the Establishment's hands and that the Greenwich section was used for astrological purposes. It then evokes feng shui to argue that the Isle of Dogs, not Greenwich, is the omphalos of the British Empire. The true omphalos is the Mudchute, an area of park which replicates an ancient hillfort, with a staircase to a cobbled circle. Here the magus John Dee conjured up the British Empire in the presence of playwright Christopher Marlowe. It gets even more sinister when we learn that every time the ley-line is used, a human sacrifice must take place, explaining Marlowe's death in a brawl and the 'accidents' that befell workers during the building of Canary Wharf.

In addition to the L.P.S. twaddle were this year's bizarre stories of a mass grave of satanic child abusers' victims at Oxfordshire's Rollright Stones; Avebury monument being built by homesick Martians; and Stonehenge being created to encircle a giant haystack. As a journalist, I have access to all the daily papers and this year I have yet to see a serious article on hermetic topography. All there has been is irrationality and sensationalism. To redress the balance, in part, maybe someone could commission an article on soap opera stars' favourite spirit paths or Page Three girls' sexiest stone circles.

Sources:

J. Simon, 'Why Do Manchester United Get So Much X-tra Time?,' *The Sunday Sport*, 7 April 1996

T. Hendry & I. Smith, 'Evil That Haunts *Street* Stars,' *Sunday Mirror*, 20 Nov. 1983

Paul Screeton, 'Ley-Line Theory To Explain TV Show Jinx,' *Hartlepool Mail*, 23 Nov. 1983; *The Shaman*, No. 4, 1984

Tom Hodgkinson, 'Surfing and Diving' column, *Telegraph Weekend*, 28 October 1995

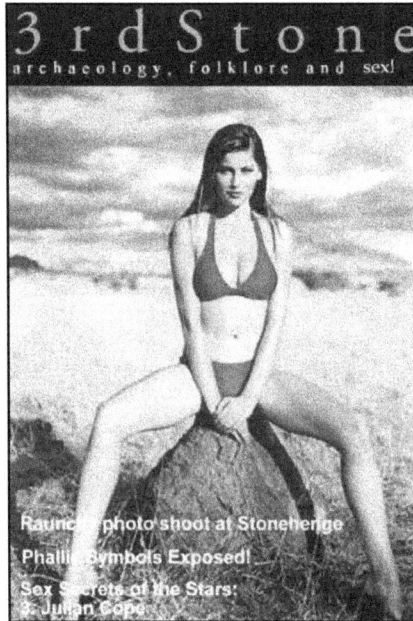

This picture from a photoshoot is almost exactly what I envisaged (except the model is not topless) in this previous article and fell into my lap(top) by serendipity! Tim Prevett came across the image – no recollection of how, why, where – and passed it to Andy Burnham. This was at the time when *Fortean Times* had been bought by a basically lads' mags publisher and Andy mocked up a spoof cover of what *3rd Stone* magazine might morph into in such a situation. It has been on *The Megalithic Portal* website since 2001 (still going strong and highly recommended). Neither Tim, Andy nor I have been able to ascertain the creators of the image. The context is intriguing. The stone looks deliberately sited but that may be coincidental to the purpose for the shoot, where the girl is obviously size zero skinny despite a reasonable enough bust and in a classic pose, but the 21st Century lass looks a little uncomfortable astride the triangular megalith in her non-Neolithic bikini (hang on, of course, think Raquel Welch...).

Having decided to use the girl-on-stone spoof and about to post the illustrations to CFZ Press, my wife and I were flicking through our albums when I found this synchronous photograph. Sorry, but I'm not in a bikini! Is this an indicator markstone or indicator of where megalithomania would eventually lead me? Me somewhere on Dartmoor in 1960. (Gordon Screeton)

FOSTERS: A CAUTIONARY TALE

(*The Ley Hunter*, No. 91, 1981)

An August field trip to Yorkshire's Upper Wharfedale recalled for me a bizarre news story from eight years ago which proved embarrassing for ley hunters and archaeologists alike. Happily since then there has been a great increase in public awareness as to what leys are and involve. Equally it is no longer regarded as eccentric to be both archaeologist, ley hunter and ufologist.

Back in 1973, the strange behaviour of a couple during what proved to be a seven-day wonder must have left many newspaper readers deeply confused and extremely wary of an interest in earth mysteries. This is the cautionary tale of the Fosters and the media. So, get a bright intro and hold the reader. That's what journalists are trained to do, and a *Yorkshire Post* reporter did just that: 'A cult which believes in flying saucers and contact with beings from outer space could figure in the disappearance of a young archaeologist and his wife, the police at York said yesterday.' Cranks, mystery and the authority figure all in the first paragraph. No sex, though? The second paragraph hints, however, in that direction: 'Workmen heard the wife screaming for help in a field near York early on Wednesday morning and found her partially dressed and in a distressed condition.' *The Northern Echo* reported she wore 'only a pair of slacks and a jumper' while the *Yorkshire Post* and *Daily Express* called them 'trousers and a cardigan.' She was Wendy Foster (variously 22 or 23) and the husband was George (23 or 26). All papers agreed that he had been working on a 'dig' in York but could not agree whether she was secretary or ex-secretary of York Archaeological Trust. Lorry driver George Shields, who took Wendy and then George to a works canteen, reported Mr Foster had told him he'd had a scare and seen "flying saucers coming out of the sky."

The couple, of Grove Street, Penley, then drove off. George's family had told police he had been acting strangely for some weeks and they issued descriptions and photographs of the couple. Voices had apparently been telling George what to do and instructed him, he said, to hit his wife, although he had told her the previous Sunday: "It will be all finished in four days." Chief Insp. Noel Digweed's comment must have enraged the academic archaeological fraternity, amused or irked ley hunters and ufologists, and bemused the public: "It is understood that Mr Foster is connected with an extreme type of archaeological study which links with the study of flying saucers being from outer space and something from the 'straight line syndrome'." A British Unidentified Flying Object Research Association official was contacted to explain what all this was about and Trevor Whittaker was quoted on othoteny and leys (UFO sightings points forming straight lines when plotted on a map). The report then quoted Dr Henry Disney, warden of a field centre at Malham Tarn, who said the Fosters had not been seen there for the past couple of days or "any flying saucers or cultists." He told the *Yorkshire Post* of the ancient remains there and its reporter felt confident to describe the area as 'thought to be connected with the cult's beliefs.' Having a second crack at the story, the *Daily Express* said Mr Foster had told friends he was from another planet and could control other people's destinies.

I don't know whether the story had a happy ending. The Fosters had actually been camping in Inverness, unaware of the search and speculation, and after being interviewed by police, wisely went into hiding. Well, the moral of the story is more than that those voices were only in George's head. Other aspects of relevance to *TLH* readers spring to mind and in my restricted space I'll share a few: would such a recurrence in 1981 cause such media and police concern and misinterpretation?; might UFOs form in part a 'choice' mechanism which leads many into E.M. studies?; is this all just another episode in what in *Common Ground* your editor calls the 'myth machine'? I understand there is now talk that because the great wave of juvenile marching bands' children collapsed at the same time as the 1980 *TLH* Mootgoers were at Arbor Low, a rumoured cause and effect has been posited. Strangely enough, in that case a UFO was said to have landed in the field adjacent to the carnival one! UFO ubiquity in urban belief tales is all around us.

As I write this, leys have been a factor in the current popular *Sapphire and Steel* TV programme and a question in a recent radio general knowledge quiz was: "What is a ley?" The competitor answered satisfactorily, so maybe we'll hear no more of straight line cultism. As for Malham, the day I was there was very misty, a cow was bellowing as if it was having an onerous calving or maybe tripping on magic mushrooms, and companion John Watson thought the site area most unpleasant. The Fosters are welcome to it.

Sources: *The Northern Echo*, 14 and 15/12/73; *Yorkshire Post*, 14 and 17/12/73; *Daily Express*, 14 and 15/12/73.

INSECTS AND MEGALITHS

(*Ancient Mysteries*, No. 10, 1981)

Mankind's feelings towards insects seem to be largely ambivalent. There are few more irritating aspects of life than the pestering fly in the sunshine, but one must admire the spider's persistence and energy. Also if studied to any extent, it will be noted that insects of the higher orders present an awareness of situations which indicate vague mental processes and ability to exercise learning, judgement, control and co-operation. They exhibit unstinting labour, shared information, care for offspring, foresight and even communal fidelity and individual self-sacrifice for the common good.

However, this is not an examination of analogous behaviour between ourselves and insects, but a few observations I have made of bugs and sacred sites. Earth mysteries researchers before me have looked to the genus *hexapoda* previously and Alfred Watkins, no less, was a keen beekeeper and made lantern slides of their activities in the hive. John Michell cited how when released away from their hives, Watkins noted how they circle and then make a 'bee-line' for home. Watkins also took an interest in patterns of ant hills. [1] As for flies, when first visiting Castlerigg stone circle in Cumbria on 24 August 1979, I was surprised to find these showing a distinct preference for the largest of all the stones. Later that year, on 28 October, medium-sized spiders did not seem hostile to the hundreds of ladybirds hibernating in the fluting of the central monolith of the trio known as the Devil's Arrows. Were these fertilised females ensconced in the crevices lying dormant until spring? No doubt this was to be home for the whole winter and recalls the nursery rhyme:

> 'Ladybird, ladybird, fly away home,
> Thy house is on fire, thy children will roam'

And so on in ubiquitous forms. The entomologist Geoffrey Taylor stated it is, 'prehistoric, in fact. And learned folklorists and students of comparative religion have traced our humble ladybird back to the august company not only of Icarus, but also the Egyptian Gods.' [2] I am not qualified to connect this sun myth with the ladybirds at the Devil's Arrows and any possible solar alignment, but note that it is sometimes called Barnaby bug and that in past centuries a St Barnabus Fair was held in a field between the monument and Boroughbridge, North Yorkshire.

The celebrated dowser Guy Underwood, who took an interest in the behaviour of wildlife associated with his spectrum of earth energies he detected, mentioned gnats and ants, but not spiders or ladybirds. However, I believe I have in some small way validated one of his claims. The first living creature he noted making use of what he termed geodetic lines was the gnat (related to what we in Hartlepool call midges or midgies). He recorded that all their dances occurred over blind springs or nodes, and if dispersed temporarily by a gust of wind they would reassemble for their circular dance over the original spot. Sometimes swarms could appear smoke-like and that the fire alarm would be sounded when insects danced above the spire (over a blind spring) of Salisbury Cathedral. [3] My dwelling is humbler, but I dug below the single point in my back garden where I observed midges' gyrations and struck water within about nine inches, which burst up just like a spring and quickly filled the hole which had to be filled in before the garden flooded. Be warned. I recently dowsed the garden and found this to be the only place where I received a reaction.

Another writer to take a great interest in insects is American scientist philosopher Philip S. Callahan. There is no space here to detail his fascinating discoveries into awesome mysteries of insect behaviour, but only mention here a possibly apposite incident. Lying on his back in the summer heat one day on Dartmoor, Callahan noted thousands of small insects hovering over the rocky tor where he lay contemplating. He followed this up, finding entomologists were aware of the phenomenon but neither its full extent nor cause. He developed a theory that they were attracted by infra-red radiation generated in huge quantities and creating 'a sort of invisible fleeting-floating energy-world' with glows like 'invisible St Elmo's fire.' [4] At this point I would hesitantly argue that certain megaliths may emit energy of a special sort attractive and conducive to insects. Obviously research such as *The Ley Hunter*'s Dragon Project would be necessary to correlate. Curiously, Callahan feels many so-called UFO sightings at night 'are mass swarms of lighted insects [glow-worms?] migrating and caught in just such a voltage field between the sky and earth.' An example my family and I witnessed at Berwick-upon-Tweed a few years ago may well have been such. And to follow the spiral further, Terry Cox, who lives on Dartmoor, has tried photographing UFOs with infra-red film with some success. [5]

Inconclusive as this article must be, I hope it might spark someone to look further into this. Insects are one matter, and I also ponder the relationship between sites and mammals often encountered there. Why two stones called the Mare and the Foal? Why do the Goatstones resemble in actuality crouched frogs? But that's another tale. As usual, more questions than answers.

Notes:

1. John Michell, *The View Over Atlantis*, Sago Press, 1969
2. Geoffrey Taylor, *Insect Life In Britain*, Collins, 1945
3. Guy Underwood, *The Pattern of the Past*, Museum Press, 1969
4. Philip S. Callahan, *Tuning in to Nature*, Routledge & Kegan Paul, 1977
5. Terry Cox, 'Infra-red Techniques in Paranormal Research, *Northern Ufology*, No. 75, 1980

Prolific amateur publisher Nigel Pennick printed this speculation of mine on earth energy and insect behaviour in his essential journal of geomancy, lost knowledge and ancient enigmas. Since the late Seventies/early Eighties, the choice of small magazines on esoteric matters has shrunk alarmingly and we are all the poorer for this sad state of affairs. As for the contents of my musings here, I can only add that friend Tom Cole stressed to me the rich heritage of cosmology enshrined in nursery rhymes; this being a means of teaching children from a very young age the laws of planetary dynamics. Such analysis of children's verses is out of favour today and commentator Albert Jack, discussing *Ladybird, Ladybird* offers optional theories for its meaning: that the 'house on fire' refers to farmers forewarning the helpful insects of setting stubble ablaze or conversely is a reference to the Virgin Mary – 'Our Lady' – offering dissuasion to Roman Catholic recusants who refused to attend Protestant services. Incidentally, Jack requested his publicist when sending a review copy of *Pop Goes the Weasel: The Secret Meanings of Nursery Rhymes* (Penguin), she include a copy of his fortean mysteries companion volume, *Loch Ness Monsters and Raining Frogs* as he reckoned I would appreciate it (actually it was a disappointment, but I thank him for the thought and have just acquired his take on urban myths, *That's Bollocks!*).

FRANK LOCKWOOD:
THE MASTER CUTLER OF LEY HUNTERS
(*Northern Earth Mysteries*, No. 12, 1981)

When ten years ago Frank Lockwood invited me to spend the day with him in Sheffield it was an opportunity to meet the man who was writing regularly for *The Ley Hunter*. I had restarted the magazine in 1969 and he, under the pen-name Circumlibra, was proving a popular contributor. I knew he was manager of a steel industry factory in the city and I was expecting to be met at Sheffield Midland station barrier, by a cigar-smoking, suit-wearing, affluent executive with chauffeur-driven Rolls-Royce to whisk us away to lunch in an exclusive restaurant.

But Frank was a humbler man. Wearing a weather-beaten mackintosh which would not have disgraced a practised flasher, I found a diminutive figure who was a shy but personable sort, and his chosen mode of transport proved to be a bicycle. He was even a member of an organisation called Rough Tough Cyclists! In fact, the last time I saw him was at the Northern Earth Mysteries Group weekend moot in April last year at Barmoor, a large three-storey house on the edge of the North York Moors, near Hutton-le-Hole, and Frank cycled there and back at a grand old age. As a fellow cyclist he had warmed to me as I, too, deplored that metaphor for 20th Century life, the motor-car.

When I first met him he was already well on in years and widowed, but still obviously very active. A couple we passed in the street spoke to him and he told me they were fellow patrons of the old-time dancing sessions he attended. As for his chosen Circumlibra pseudonym, he explained that his birth sign was the balancing scales of Libra, and that his researches rotated as if cyclically and each was interconnected.

He tells in an unpublished article (planned for *Ancient Skills & Wisdom Review,* No. 13, as a tribute) how he was turned on to leys and New Age thought. He was at New Grange mound in Ireland. There he first felt the power megalithic man utilised. Showing his capacity to construct interesting articles, his piece tells how he wondered why the custodian told him they must hurry before the power went. The electricity was about to be switched off and the guardian had candles in the event of this occurring whilst inside. But the other power, as he pointed out, cannot be turned off by man. Whilst groping by candlelight, Frank discovered why the tumulus was placed there deliberately. He went on to explain that he chose to call these sites 'etheric energy centres' and found they fell into geometrical landscape patterns and were a 'vital factor in the positioning of the "old straight track" and the basis of the celestial calculating of ancient peoples.'

He stated the actual centres were small and told me a hand would cover one unless a special structure had been placed upon it. 'In short they are points where the earth breathes in and out,' he noted. His researches suggested that there were daily divisions when the pulse of power altered and that our Saxon forebears, at least, still knew and recognised these and made sundials and engraved them to correspond to these natural sequences. These 'tides' lasted approximately three hours and peaked in the middle.

Piloting and banking assistance for one fat lady

Frank described where he had located power centres. In addition to prehistoric sites, road junctions and modern buildings are mentioned such as York Minster (my wife and I last year persuaded a guide to show us the crypt and the ley power was so overwhelming I thought I would faint), village churches, a municipal meeting room, Sheffield Cathedral (he showed me where at certain times the pulses can be felt around it), a boarding house and, 'I speak with horror for I know its implications, an old farm which is now a slaughterhouse.'

Power centres are part of the belief system of the Aetherius Society, and Frank was one of the organisation's early members. When I first met him he stated that their 12 prayers had impressed him and he recalled a 'shape power' excursion to some holy peak he had joined. He humorously recollected how an extremely fat woman required much assistance from both front and behind for her to reach the summit. The Aetherius Society is, of course, a UFO sect and Frank took great interest in the manifestation of flying saucers. Here's his belief: 'May I confirm that they do and have always [visited us] and that they use the centres and lines of power which connect them in many ways. The beings from space are our humble servants and yet at the same time are our masters, certainly our superiors.'

I must say that I felt this view was very naive, but it is also worth emphasising that he was writing in the Sixties, and it predates Erich von Daniken and also the UFO/ley surmising of John Michell in *The Flying Saucer Vision*. In the same article, Frank makes another tantalising point. Saying the New Grange incident in itself was of no great importance, it did begin 'a long and fascinating search which has revealed far more than I dare put into print.'

When we talked a great deal that day in Sheffield, he made much sense, but one comment did leave me nonplussed. Perhaps we all take our preconceived notions to Stonehenge and expect them to be reflected back. Frank's Stonehenge tale was that a certain well-known ley hunter – who shall remain nameless - then had plans to wrest control of the monument and use it to take over the country. This paled into insignificance his tales about his workplace's Nigerian cleaning lady's psychic powers, his friend's awakening at Arbor Low and learning from discarnate entities there how these Atlanteans had built the henge monument, friend Philip Rodgers's raudive voice phenomena recordings, and so on.

Little green man was mound dweller

His paranoid Stonehenge rumour I now dismiss as fanciful, but still feel his encounters with elementals as described in print and during discussion warrant serious attention. I believe that these can occur under differing circumstances. One which he described in an article now sounds more like a hypnagogic experience, whereas the other may have been of a more 'natural' order. The latter case, he told me, was of being approached in a Sheffield park by a small green and semi-physical entity which conversed with him. Frank said the entity was at pains to claim that it was human and at the end of the discussion walked away and - perhaps significantly – vanished on a truncated tumulus.

It was anecdotes such as these, which in conversation and in his written output, made him a valued and popular contributor to *The Ley Hunter*. Personal experience and its exposition is what enthuses others to follow the path of the pioneer earth mysteries investigators. Frank was a quiet and unassuming man who inspired me and I hope others during the formative period when ley hunting was getting a new wind as the Seventies began. Much of what he wrote then is now fashionable – ancient astronauts, Atlantis, ecology concern, demythologising, conspiracy, simulacra – but was then regarded as decidedly cranky. His revelations were also relatively daring for their time.

So, a (very small) factory boss, but no Savile Row suit, Havana cigar or chauffeur-driven Limo. Swanky restaurant? No, he took me to a Co-op cafe, where he tut-tutted when I ordered a meat meal and he wrongly predicted I would learn the error of my ways and become a vegetarian. One consoling factor about this obituary – and others I've penned – has been that largely ley hunting fraternity folk going to that great moot in the sky have had a good innings. Alfred Watkins was 80 and his son Allen another octogenarian, and Straight Track Club members Douglas Wintle and Charles Mayo were 97 and 94 respectively when they were called to a higher plane. Frank Lockwood gave inspiration when earth mysteries studies needed it most. His death is a sad blow.

Sadly, I have penned several obituaries in the form of feature articles: the deceased friends being Brinsley Le Poer Trench (Earl of Clancarty), Donald L. Cyr, Anthony Roberts, Allen Watkins and Guy Ragland Philips, all authors.

RECOLLECTIONS, & JOTTINGS FROM NOTTING HILL

(*Folklore Frontiers*, No. 61, 2009; *R.I.L.K.O. Newsletter*, No. 75, 2009)

COUNTRYSIDE LOVER. John Michell enjoyed nothing more than simply walking in the countryside, and I invited him up to our humble abode in November 1970. After my father gave us a lift to Hart Village, John and I trekked towards the coast. The peace was only broken when a farmer on a tractor bore down on us like Erwin Rommel leading the Afrika Corps panzer division and ordered us off his land. I patiently pointed out that my Ordnance Survey map clearly showed we were on a legal footpath, to which he claimed to have paid a small fortune to London lawyers, who had apparently verified its inauthenticity. Having conceded we were by then two-thirds of our way across "his" land, he made us repeat after him that we were technically trespassing and allowed us to go on our way. The point of this shaggy dog story is that John then confessed a similar experience at Sockburn (of dragon legend fame) when researching his first book, *The Flying Saucer Vision*, and, through the demands of a similar unsympathetic farmer, having to make an unwanted perambulation which led to him reaching Darlington so late that all hotels were closed and finding shelter in a Salvation Army hostel.

REEFER MADNESS. The next day, John was travelling back to London (Peterborough, actually, where he had got bored of driving and abandoned his car for the train), but before that we travelled by bus to Durham for me to introduce him to Tom Cole, a gypsy shaman who had landed on my doorstep previously after reading John's seminal and famous book *The View Over Atlantis*, and wanting to share with me his discovery of a terrestrial zodiac around Stanley. John and Tom got on famously (later to meet down a drove road at Glastonbury), not least because they shared an interest in the more arcane attributes of cannabis. John, until shortly before his death from lung cancer, always had a modest spliff lit, and left burn marks in a blanket at our house (which we still retain as a form of holy relic). The combination of dope and drink led me to later come to my senses wondering why I was wandering in York and phoning home to say that like ET that I would be late/laid back.

The above episodes were somehow missed from my homage, *John Michell: From Atlantis

to Avalon, while shifting material between chapters, as his life and interests could never be adequately compartmentalised. They are extracted from reflections on John's life, 'Recollections of John Michell,' which I wrote for my magazine *Folklore Frontiers* and which was reprinted among several tributes in *The Research Into Lost Knowledge Organisation Newsletter*. Also, just as John sifted through a great deal of historic Hitlerian material – jokingly described by one commentator as the Fuhrer's 'after-dinner rants' – I combed John's voluminous writings and interviews for similar morsels of wisdom from the philosopher's table. Because I had passed my 50,000-word limit for *John Michell: From Atlantis to Avalon*, the following pearls failed to make the final cut, but I feel are sufficiently interesting and worthy of publication here as an 'out-takes' postscript.

NUCLEAR POWER. While in Seaton Carew, I pointed out to John the magnificent skyline colossus of a great concrete slab which is Hartlepool Power Station and its accompanying petro-chemical complex to the west, and the gaunt towers and pipes of Lackenby steelworks across the Tees to the south. He seemed to shudder with disgust at this stark industrial landscape despoiling, for him, a fine view of the Cleveland Hills. For John:

> "Looking at it dispassionately, the whole idea of atomic power and dependence on atomic power is dangerous, evil, inhuman and incompatible with any humane way of looking at the world. It's by a reaction to such excesses that a complete reformation of the way we view things will come about".

This item has been put in context by me, but the following extractions of wisdom (or crankiness) need little such referencing, and only where apposite.

KINGSHIP/QUEENSHIP. 'A queen who does anything her government tells her is a danger to the country, because the government can then do anything in her name, and there is no appeal.' John then suggested superior candidates for the royal role. 'Yehudi Menuhin would be my choice, or Lord Longford ... or honest Ken Livingstone.' (John having a private joke? Another of his heroes was William Cobbett (1763 – 1855), who detested moralism (Lord Longford a pious advocate) and socialism (remember when Livingstone was demonised as 'Red Ken'?) Or Lady Thatcher 'who has always coveted the queenly role' or 'noble-minded' Prince Charles.

A representative of Prince Charles attended John's memorial service, but John had nil respect for the Queen, having described her as a 'sour little woman.' I had suspected John wrote the anonymous Swiftian allegory and countercultural classic *The Abdication of Queen Elizabeth II*. He denied this, but admitted to me: It inspired me to work out an anagram of Elizabeth Windsor – The Snob Lie Wizard.' This diatribe was publicised in *The Fanatic*, Number 5, and there was another anti-royal piece in that issue, *The Love Life of Elizabeth the Second*, promoting both Danish film-maker Jens Thorsen and Gnostic gospels, and which John also denied penning. Before moving on, when John emerged for breakfast while staying at our home, he said he had a good night's sleep and, "I dreamt of the Queen when she was a young chick and she fancied me."

FEMINISM. "Women keep up the customs. Usually in all societies women decide who is going to be married, buried, how one's going to eat, how one's going to do everything in society ... I know women like to deny the traditional role of women, but it seems that history demonstrates that as a fact of nature."

RACISM. "Having gone through the immigration period, I have the impression that it has gone remarkably smoothly." As for West Indians: "Unfortunately they hardly ever seem to go to the country or seaside, so they know far too little about their new island."

LIVING ABROAD. "Why then should anyone who enjoys the freedom of Britain, including the right to leave it, not exercise that right? Why linger in this sick, sour, surly society when there is no compulsion to do so? One good reason could be the life of an émigré is in most cases notoriously futile."

CENSORSHIP. In response to changes sought by an American publisher: "I think that one of my private beliefs is that any good writer coming up against any system of prohibitions can always get round those prohibitions. That is one of the hallmarks of a good writer: anything that's not allowed you can say exactly the same thing in a way which is not offensive."

TELEVISION. "It was because of them [comedians] that I allowed the hire people to take back my set some years ago ... It is a dangerous, ravening beast, the arch enemy among us." He also loathed TV for its "dollops of Darwinian propaganda doled out with nature programmes." I wonder if, before consigning his TV set back to the rental company, John ever watched *Grumpy Old Men*? If he had appeared on the programme he could have become what he loathed, a TV celeb. He certainly would not have agreed with the modern view that the television set represents the modern fireplace equivalent.

GLOBAL COOLING. Another example of John not taking global warming seriously is a comment in response to predictions in the Cambridge University magazines *Cam*. Here specialists warned of population growth, extinction of the species and a climate change crisis. John wryly noted: "The Dutch are advised to heighten their dykes and the Bangladeshis to learn how to swim."

GAIA. "I don't think there is any evil in the natural processes of the earth. Things are as they were meant to be. This is our place of birth. It can become a potential paradise."

This was the last section of Chapter Six of my celebration of the life of a good friend, *John Michell : from Atlantis to Avalon*. My publisher at Heart of Albion, Bob Trubshaw, limited me to 50,000 words and upon reaching 53,000, I decided reluctantly to expunge this as the most superficial and least crucial part of the work. It does, however, give a flavour of John's philosophy and contextualises his mixture of crankery, curmudgeon and common-sense.

WILLIAM SITWELL'S CARNAC WEEK-END

(*The Atlantean*, No. 150, 1973)

An unashamed believer in the existence of a former continent of Atlantis and colonisation there from, Brigadier General William Sitwell remains a shadowy figure of forty years ago, hardly known today, but a man far ahead of his time. Few of his archaeological theories would today be endorsed by either orthodox or even alternative prehistorians. Yet this neglected researcher has much to offer which relates to his grasp of psychic realities and understanding of the purpose of many ancient monuments. That he also made claims, which can today be refuted as entirely devoid of any rational logic - or the slightest proof - is true. He held tenaciously to a diffusionist theory – all the vogue at the time – and though recent developments in dating sites have invalidated a large proportion of his (and many others') arguments regarding the supposed migrations of megalith builders, it is he, above all, who had some inkling of the extent to which the Neolithic civilisation was basically global.

To pass from what I feel to be a certain naïveté in diffusionist indoctrination, and the untenable slavish insistence upon attributing many megaliths of c4000BC to monuments to fallen warriors or victory in post-Roman times, I wish to dwell upon his experience one weekend at Carnac, in France. The following accounts are provided in his rare and obscure book, *Stones of Northumberland and Other Lands*, which was published in Newcastle upon Tyne in 1930 by Andrew Reid and Co. Ltd. Though he somewhat unoriginally followed the conclusions of Dr Fergusson's *Rude Stone Monuments*, Sitwell - being a military man - must be given a degree of leniency for subscribing in part to the notion that some megaliths marked the sites of armies' conflicts. Yet he was also willing to admit to a world of visions and, though failing to attempt to explain the non-materialistic phenomenon of why some prehistoric stones are 'magnetic,' positively stressed this undeniable fact. This power, which at times manifests with certain stones – dependent apparently upon a flux between earth currents and cosmic power from celestial bodies, and also recognisable by sensitive individuals – is of special concern to those investigating our sacred heritage, especially the ley hunters who map the alignments of prehistoric monuments and deduce the inspirational, etheric power flowing between the ancient holy sites.

Sitwell was invited to Armorica by his friend Bernard Springett, who also believed the stones of Carnac and Stonehenge related to sun worship originating from Atlantis. He warned that 30 April was the most important day in Brittany, and Sitwell made his historic weekend visit to coincide with that date. The most significant passage in the book states:

> 'And now to explain why these stones are magnetic. The majority of them have been erected with the smaller end planted in the ground; one receives the astounding sensation that they vibrate, and with very little effort could be pushed over. This extraordinary illusion may be limited to only those persons who are susceptible to the hidden forms of nature – such as water-diviners, crystal-gazers, and the like – amongst whom I am happy to be able to number myself. Yet many who are unaware that they possess any psychic qualities have recognised and noticed this curious vibration when touching the stones of Carnac, not only at this alignment but at several other places.'

Sitwell, while seated upon a stone, witnessed a solemn procession of priests, clothed in white carrying goods among the Carnac stones watched by "small dark men, rudely clothed yet unmistakeably sailors" who could not join in the rite. Then, on the night of 30 April, Sitwell and two others set out for Le Menec at 11pm and through rain reached the 'altar' shortly before midnight.

> '... Springett then thrice perambulated the stone and offered a beautiful prayer to El Shaddai, our Creator, for protection from all dangers of the night, and that we might be vouchsafed to see whatsoever He willed. Then, when seated on the altar stone beside us, well clear of the ground, he remarked: "And now we shall see what we shall see, and anyhow the frogs will tell us all about it." Hardly had he spoken than every frog ceased croaking abruptly as though waiting for his command. There were light vapour clouds overhead ... and then we became aware that we were not alone. Coming from behind us and to our left through the gloom the Powers of Darkness were abroad. Awful primordial creatures prowled round us on every side, elemental monsters undoubtedly, and of all shapes unknown to mortal man. Some were not unlike the rhinoceros, and there were huge walking lizards, dinosaurs perhaps. The most active were black four-footed things as agile as antelopes, but with horrible heads, and these seemed to leap from menhir to menhir like goats. Yet we had no sensation of fear; they came, they inspected us and they turned away, for we were on holy ground. Then they seemed to draw off, but without haste. On their disappearance we looked upward and a vast white city came into view. Lofty walls and a wonderful panorama of stately buildings rising behind them. It might have been the New Jerusalem **[John Michell, eat your heart out!]**, and we may have been looking upon an Eternal Temple made without hands. It was quite unearthly, and nothing was vouchsafed of

what might be contained therein. Yet there it stood, greatly to be desired, and we were allowed to hope that some day we may gain admission to glories and wonders beyond all dreams. Gradually all faded away, and after a long silence Springett again stepped down and, circling round the altar the reverse way to before, gave humble thanks for deliverance from evil, and a petition that in due time we might receive the peace which passeth all understanding. Immediately all the frogs lifted up their voices as if to associate themselves with his prayer.'

That was not the end, however, for on the sacred island, Ile Longue, Sitwell's party each had strange visions within a tumulus. The psychic experiences and solar orientations described in the book are extremely fascinating, but the reader must sort the wheat from the chaff in the light of advances in scientific knowledge and 'live' archaeology. Here described are serpent motifs created upon and by stones themselves, a possible vision of the New Jerusalem, and detailed descriptions of sites. Hopefully more archaeological books such as this, combining verifiable scientific scholarship with irrefutable visionary perception, will be produced in the years to come and be acceptable to both alternative and orthodox archaeologists.

Despite the dubious ability of the discarnate entity called Helio-Arcanophus – who led The Atlanteans, a society with a philosophy offering a sensitive and compassionate approach to life – to have an uncanny knack of cultural tracking developments in the real world, channelled to his gullible followers, I rather enjoyed aspects of their magazine and contributed regularly. However, I now totally disassociate myself from the New Age content I introduced to my article here – whose merit is the weird happenings described by Sitwell – and my flaky thinking and woolly terminology used. I seem to have been brainwashed by wishy-washy mumbo-jumbo and – although I hardly ever re-read my writings – suspect my first book, *Quicksilver Heritage*, was influential in the New Age movement from feedback I have received. That being a force for good, no apologies or regrets from me. But I do advise caution with <u>any</u> aspect of New Ageism. Positivism should not be mistaken for gullibility and illusion. See how my tone had changed ten years later with the next article...

JOHN FOSTER FORBES:
ECCENTRIC ANTIQUARIAN

(*Quicksilver Messenger*, No. 7, 1982)

Vibrating old ladies finding spa towns conducive to messengers from the higher aethers, rival psychics mediating with cosmic commercial travellers offering new improved whiter than white wisdom, Ancient Ones loitering at every prehistoric site with intentions to be guides back to a golden romantic harmonious age, pendulum perambulators with prattling philosophies ... are these just jellyfish visions? Harsh, perhaps. I could argue a cogent case for charlatanism on commonsensical grounds: which would fill our open prisons to bursting point or mix the greedy and the gullible in a sociological treatise pinpointing the Salvationist message and reasons for supporting and seducing by this subtle mental blackmail. Cynicism aside, there are healthy reasons for separating the wheat from the chaff in this field of speculation. For reasons explained elsewhere, I feel there can be relevance to studying the past by paranormal means. [1]

No blanket endorsement of mediumistic practice is suggested, but at least I can say that it can on occasion provide practical results. Verification of such is an altogether more difficult matter – but not always impossible. Such an introduction has, I feel, been necessary to set the stage for a sensitive, Iris Campbell, a woman claiming literally to have facts of ancient peoples at her fingertips. Her 'mental' readings and those of Miss Olive Pixley were amplified in the brief books of John Foster Forbes, who died in Brighton.

He utilised psychometrists – seers who claimed to tap 'vibrations' at sites and 'see' the past intuitively – to garner material which he spun into the rich tapestry of his antediluvian reconstructions. A collected edition of their joint work was published in 1973, but for Sussex readers probably a particularly intriguing reference comes from an early issue of *The Ley Hunter*, published during my editorship. The article began:

> 'Once, many years ago, while sitting with a friend on the downs near Brighton, I had a vision of these lines spreading out before me. I felt then that I was seeing something which denoted great spiritual significance, but never pursued the matter further until I read of these leys in John

> Michell's book *The View Over Atlantis*. This recalled to mind the vision of many years ago and after meditation on the matter I decided to write down what came to me as I so often do when a subject interests me. Incidentally the friend with me at the time was John Foster Forbes, with whom I have often worked in connection with prehistoric sites.' [2]

The vision parallels how Michell glorified Watkins's revelation in his work of quixotic genius and it is worth reminding readers again that the Merlin of hippiedom's embellishment is as far from reality as T.H. White's version of Camelot, though as evocatively grand and mystical. No doubt that trickster allegorist Carlos Castaneda did not have access in the UCLA library to Watkins's *Early British Trackways*, but made a study note there from *The View Over Atlantis* and worked it neatly into *Journey to Ixtlan*.

Miss Campbell's article continued in an occult form, whose reprinting would be of little advantage. Well aware of its awkward woolliness, I sought an additional - more comprehensible - account and received in a letter:

> 'After 20 years I can only say that they stretched out before me as rays of light from a central point. I felt that they were very holy. I also felt that at the point there were officiating priests. I felt that the lines were not only on the earth's surface level interpenetrating; also that they manifested above in the air, but that there was no division between these three planes if one can so describe them. All were one straight line each case.'

Yet it is John Foster Forbes, author of *Ages Not So Dark*, *Giants of Britain*, *Britain the Land of Lost Magic*, *Living Stones of Britain* and *The Unchronicled Past*, who deserves lengthy consideration. Much of the following is drawn freely from an earlier account I wrote. [3] The man was a rather quirky writer; he was basically scorned in his time and has since been almost entirely neglected. His output was meagre and has remained obscure. Most of his notions appear crank fringe material and to enter his world is almost to imperil one's sanity. Nevertheless, I feel that the quicksand speculation can be crossed by a series of imaginatively perceptive stepping stones largely supporting his strong views upon the character of sacred sites. Yet as with most unorthodox thinkers he is embarrassingly imprecise when it comes to creating any attempt at an even loosely scientific medium for attracting critical support. With a wealth of weird ideas in his work, unsubstantiated one way or another, it is hardly yet time to evaluate his contribution to speculative archaeology.

To some he was a religious fanatic as he was a devout supporter of the Rev Todd Ferrier and his beliefs concerning the correct placing on the globe of the various races makes him sound fascistic today. Archaeologists would have winced at his 'cyclopean walls' imagined to have connected the Devonian tors and 'water worn remains of shaped statues of prehistoric animals.' Also he was a poet and preacher, a prehistorian and a painter, a schoolmaster and a broadcaster. Eccentrics do often attract a brand of admiration and he gives the impression of being an antiquarian screwball by all comparisons. Yet in the late 1930s, when his slender output found the light of day, he was a Fellow of the Royal Anthropological Institute and Fellow of the Society of Antiquaries of Scotland. Additionally, as a great believer in a previous

Golden Age and the Fall of Man caused by abuse of knowledge, he not surprisingly believed in this context that a cataclysmic disaster overtook a one-time vast continent of Atlantis. Later Atlanteans sought to abuse their powers contrary to the divine law of the universe and brought about destruction. The early Atlantean civilisation, he believed, was only a largely successful attempt to regain lost status of harmonious perfection in any event. To him the Golden Age was a distinct reality:

> 'Atlantis in Britain was an amazing attempt at a resurgence of this age at a time white men found themselves driven from a doomed land and took refuge on what was to them virgin soil and on which they superimposed and interfused such marvellous spiritual conditions as have, in many places, persisted until these days.'

How far we might agree with his statements is for personal predilection. An unnamed psychometrist led him to conclude a fluted pillar near Trebeurden, Brittany, was all that remained of a giant bird temple whose enormous figure had six wings. Covering a vast expanse of ground, this eagle-like bird had its head orientated towards the north, 'the seat of all power.' With two groups of rocks forming the angles of the base of the triangle whose apex was its head, the fluting of the lone remaining pillar being part of the winged formation of plumage. The Devil's Arrows at Boroughbridge, Yorkshire, were accorded a similar explanation. Bird temples! Flights of fancy?

John Foster Forbes was the youngest of the six children of Colonel Forbes, whose family seat was the Castle of Rothiemay. In his book on his Aberdeenshire home and its surroundings, he described various stone circles. In fact, the castle – now demolished – was built upon the site of a prehistoric earthwork. J.F. or Jock, as he was generally known, not only wrote about megaliths, but every one of his inspirational paintings had an ancient stone or more depicted. At around 30 years of age he married a wealthy and considerably older woman, Caroline Gwynilda.

The marriage, though reasonably happy at first, broke down and they went their separate ways. The breach was undoubtedly partially caused by his eccentricities. He outlived her and died in 1958. One evening that summer he gave a lecture entitled 'The Spiritual Nature of Sussex' to the Sussex Vegetarian Society in Brighton. Patrick Benham, a teacher and Glastonbury activist, knew him during his last couple of years and wrote about J.F. for *The Ley Hunter*. [4] This was followed up by the county's well-known writer and witch, Doreen Valiente. [5] Also, the psychometric team of Campbell and Forbes were a liked feature of early editions of *The Ley Hunter* (reprints in issues 42 and 72) and Miss Campbell also wrote a short summary of their work. [6] Such writings – typified perhaps by Mollie Carey, proved immensely popular – but now seem eclipsed in modern mysteries magazines.

Though much of Forbes's output makes today's speculative antiquaries' notions conservative by comparison, he must be applauded for both drawing attention to the mystical nature of prehistoric sites and encouraging through sixth-sense seer companions a new approach to the works of the megalith builders.

References:

1.   Paul Screeton, 'A Psychic Approach to Ancient Technology,' *Terrestrial Zodiacs Newsletter*, No. 8, 1980.
2.   Iris Campbell, 'The Straight Lines or Leys,' *The Ley Hunter*, No. 10, 1970.
3.   Paul Screeton, 'John Foster Forbes and the Tragedy of Atlantis,' *The Atlantean*, No. 165, 1976.
4.   Patrick Benham, 'The Ancient Site of Brighton,' *The Ley Hunter*, No. 41, 1973.
5.   Doreen Valiente, 'More About Old Brighton,' *The Ley Hunter*, No. 43, 1973.
6.   Iris Campbell, 'Some Memories of John Foster Forbes,' *The Ley Hunter*, No. 12, 1970.

This piece was specially written for *Quicksilver Messenger* with a Sussex bias as it was based in Brighton. I also wrote about J.F. in *The Atlantean*, the magazine which published the previous piece. It is interesting that the Rev Todd Ferrier's views rather chime with the Twelve-Tribe Nations and races concept connected with a form of *genius loci* manifestations propounded by John Michell and Christine Rhone.

MARGARET CLITHEROW AND A SHAMBLES

(*The Ley Hunter*, No. 74, 1977)

Ley power, earth spirit, telluric current, geodetic force, naiad field, electromagnetism... As with the billion names of God, the interpenetrating subtle emanations allied to the concept of leys have been identified time and time again throughout history and each time received a new name. Isolating sites with the power, noting its fluctuations and analysing its nature is no simple matter. However, my own experience is that this subtle energy withdraws under examination and its vitality can relate to some aspect of the individual. Consequently, I was most pleased to encounter the elusive charge twice during my holidays.

Strolling down The Shambles in York – restored (to extremes, some regard) in postwar years with crooked mediaeval gables leaning across the narrow street – there are among the quaint, tourist trade oriented shops a former butcher's shop now transformed into a shrine. The tradesman and city counsellor's wife, Margaret Clitherow, was accused of harbouring Jesuit priests and allowing her home to be used for the celebration of Mass. Her penalty in jail was to have a stone placed beneath her back, a door placed over her and then sufficient stones placed upon it to literally crush her and her unborn child to death. This was in 1586; in 1970 she was canonised by the Roman Catholic Church.

My wife, three-year-old daughter Kathryn and I entered the gloomy shrine in the lower room of her old timbered home. There seemed to be a distinct tingling in the air; akin to the pins and needles effect I have experienced in the presence of earth energy. The atmosphere was distinctly 'alive,' as can be experienced at, for instance, the crypt in North Yorkshire's Lastingham Church. Both my wife and I were intensely aware of the presence of the power, but did not stay too long as we realised Kathryn was carrying an ice-cream which was desecratingly dripping its contents despite the extreme cold which accompanied the emanations. I have not had the opportunity to check the ley potential – if any – of the site, but in a tourist guide noted the shrine lies on a line linking the ancient Clifford's Tower and an old city church.

The following week we had visitors, Philip Heselton and Jimmy Goddard, both of whom were

191

intimately connected with the first series of *The Ley Hunter* during the 1960s. Among the North-East England sites we visited was the Lady Chapel, near Osmotherley, and above Mount Grace Priory – whose dissolution date was 1539 – on a platform overlooking the Vale of York. The Lady Chapel was founded in 1515 and before its newness could wear off, along came the Reformation and it became deserted, derelict and crumbled to a desolate ruin. Yet despite this, pilgrims crossed the moors to kneel before its desecrated altar. Supposedly insignificant, without tradition, the embarrassing nature of the site so disturbed the magistrates of nearby Northallerton that they threatened imprisonment and levied punitive fines. During this century it has been returned to Roman Catholic ownership and has been repaired to appear substantially as it was in 1515.

It was a warm afternoon when we entered the small chapel and earth power was apparent to each of us. I felt a distinct spiral of it rising from beneath the ground. A leaflet in the chapel suggested that the site had a sanctity far predating the building of the chapel. Returning home, I recollected a *Dalesman* magazine article on the chapel, and after a lengthy search through my shambles of Sagittarianly higgledepiggledy files, located the 1964 article. There to my amazement was the revelation that one theory to explain the great religious significance of the Lady Chapel was that here lay buried Margaret Clitherow. Did something happen between 1539 and 1586 to attach special sanctity to the spot? What is the secret? Whatever the explanation is, the synchronicities struck me.

This was one of my Long Man of Wilmington columns for The *Ley Hunter* after I relinquished the editorship. Whenever I'm in York I make a point of visiting Saint Margaret Clitherow's shrine (though modern scholarship doubts the present site was formerly her earthly dwelling place but elsewhere in The Shambles). I take this opportunity to bring the story up to date with a short extract from a recent article of mine:

'Upon learning that her withered hand is preserved in York and can be observed by appointment, I just had to see it. It was at the Bar Convent. Unfortunately there is no bar (a cafe, yes) as the name suggests, so I crossed the road to imbibe in The Punchbowl until my 1.30pm rendezvous with a nonagenarian nun and we climbed the steep spiral staircase for me to view the relic. The mummified hand was a disappointment, but had I expected anything other? The photographs I took were blurred, but I blame that upon the light, location, camera and ineptitude or combination rather than that phenomenon which makes shots of UFOs, anomalous big cats, lake monsters and ghosts so elusive. Anyway, I do have a book with a clear depiction of the hand. As for the complete body, when dug up six weeks after her death it was still uncorrupted, 'without any ill smell...' and removed by night. The Bar Convent hand is traditionally hers and there was once a relic of her hair at Westminster Cathedral. (Katharine Longley, *Saint Margaret Clitherow*, Anthony Clarke, 1986). But there still remains the mystery of where the rest of her martyr's body lies. Of the reputed locations, I have reasons to strongly favour the Lady Chapel, above Osmotherley, North York-shire, but that's another story entirely.' (From 'Relics (of past and present ages),' *Folklore Frontiers*, No. 63, 2010).

Of course, this piece was selected to amplify the observations presented in Interlude One earlier in this work.

PART SIX
UFOs, ROCK 'N' ROLL
& more LEYS

SKY WESTBURY AND CROOKED

(*Amskaya*, No. 57, 2004, and *Touchstone*, No. 64, 2004)

These somewhat random thoughts were inspired by my latest UFO sighting last autumn. Unlike a similar West Country sighting around ten years previously, this blink-and-you-miss-it aerial manifestation has had a deeper influence on my psyche and raised more questions. As I'll endeavour to explain later, there appeared to be an – albeit tenuous – religious dimension. Anyway, there's a touching scene which opens the film *Sky West and Crooked*, where teenage actress Hayley Mills buries small animals such as moles, and asks her local vicar if they have souls. In our politically-correct society Ms Mills' character would be described as having 'learning difficulties,' whereas back then she was given the local rural term 'sky west and crooked.'

Without straying too far from the subject, the Beagle II project raised questions of 'are we alone?' and as there is no mention of Mars in the Bible, would faith be in crisis if interplanetary life was to be discovered. John Polkingthorne, a theoretical physicist and Anglican priest, says: '"It is quite an old problem in theology, actually. After Galileo's discoveries, people started to speculate about whether there were Martians or Venusians, and whether they were saved. The theological argument was did Christ die for the Martians?" (*The Times*, 3/1/04)

Frankly, I have no idea what the origin of UFOs is; regarding the extraterrestrial theory least likely and a psychosocial one most promising. One writer on the subject who has studied the phenomenon for a great many years had wise words for his readership. John Michell wrote: 'One of the things I have learnt is that UFOs are habit forming. After you have seen one you are likely to see others.' And: 'Quite often, UFO sightings are followed by good luck and happiness.' (*Daily Mirror*, 9/10/03) I mention this because I'm a 'repeater' UFO spotter; the most recent occasion being on 24 September 2003 as my train arrived at Westbury, Wiltshire. A gleaming circular 'daylight disc' crossed the sky and vanished into clouds. Why me?

I have pondered if by some strange process it had anything to do with my inward journey from Devon to London Paddington; from Reading I was joined by two Alpha Course (evangelical charismatic) Christians, one of whom insisted on giving me a blessing despite my having insisted that they were preaching to the converted and I explained my take on Gnostic Christianity, which believes in Jesus and salvation. They told me they were off to the famous Holy Trinity, Brompton, and I rather excitedly asked if they knew Samantha Fox, celebrity cele- brant there and they seemed not to have heard of the Page 3 topless model and singer, so I dumbly added "big tits," even making a descriptive 'figure eight' movement with my hands. Alas, no. Since then I've discovered former Spice Girl Geri Halliwell, and Sinitta are also con- verts there. (I might add that my daughter Kathryn was Alpha Course baptised in Yorkshire's River Ure last year and my wife Pauline has now joined). As for the UFO, it was only in view for a few seconds, though for some reason I subsequently got it into my head that this flat disc had filigree edging. It would seem to have been heading from the direction of Westbury White Horse and, of course, this is an area which encompasses that Sixties centre of skywatching and strange happenings, Warminster. So, naturally, I consulted the works of that shamanic journal- ist Arthur Shuttlewood for clues. His *The Warminster Mystery* (Neville Spearman, 1967; Tan- dem, 1973) did not help nor *UFO Magic in Motion* (Sphere, 1979). However, in *The Flying Saucerers* (Sphere, 1976), Shuttlewood claims 'that most sightings and all reported landings of UFOs in Britain stemmed from the guidemarks of seven White Horses situated west to east, from the one at Westbury to that at Uffington.' My silver disc appeared to be heading from Westbury White Horse towards Bath (coincidentally once the home of John Michell).

My previous sighting was also a late afternoon one. Having alighted at Tiverton Parkway, after half a mile I stopped to ask a gardening householder the bus times into Tiverton itself. As she flicked through a timetable, I glimpsed a similar silver disc, which was much higher in the sky than the Westbury one, and politely listened to the woman's directions and unfortunately did not see the UFO emerge from the clouds into which it had passed behind. As for Michell's comment regarding UFO sightings and good fortune, as I waited in the dark on the Paignton- bound platform at Newton Abbot, I was astonished to witness heritage 'Deltic' diesel-electric locomotive 9016 *Gordon Highlander* pass through, having delivered another preserved loco- motive to the South Devon Railway, running ghostly quiet and becoming my second spotting highlight of the day.

Do UFOs come from the past, present, future, another dimension, our unconscious or even as a Martian heritage class of spacecraft? Maybe we aren't alone.

Mmm! I'd previously seen a 'daylight disc' in Wensleydale aged around 11 and not long afterwards two cigar-shaped craft over my home in West Hartlepool, also witnessed by my bemused father, who served in the Royal Air Force during World War II. I suspect the for- mer experience was part of an initiation process (perhaps being isolated in a bedroom for six weeks when I was aged fourteen with scarlet fever was another contributory factor), or - as I tend these days to refer to it - as being 'Zap'd!' As mentioned previously (Interlude – One), it was another Paddington to the West Country train journey where I was even more dramatically Zap'd. Coincidentally, the two magazines where I shared these thoughts are both published by Jimmy Goddard, the man whose lecture in London 'turned on' John Michell to UFOs and leys, and whose skywatch notes were utilised by the wily Shuttlewood.

COSMIC ROCK:
ROCK DISCS AND FLYING DISCS
(*The Mail*, Hartlepool, 25 January 1985; *The Shaman*, No. 10, 1985)

An album by a band of unknowns called Klaatu – whose debut album had the inspired title *Klaatu* – sold in huge quantities. This was not on the strength of any musical merit but because an American disc-jockey started a rumour that it was a secret set by The Beatles. These guys, whoever they were, wrote the song *Calling Occupants of Interplanetary Craft*. The Carpenters had a hit with a cover version and all this led John Squire to study the hieroglyphics on their next album *Hope* and conclude from 26 pages of his data, that the band was not pseudonymous Beatles, but were extraterrestrials. Another investigator, Steve Burgess, reckoned he had tracked Klaatu down to a group formerly called The Stampeders. But if Klaatu was an anagram, it could be Aakult, and that is like occult, and ... anyway they were not being that original as they took their name from the humanoid alien protagonist in the 1951 sci-fi film *The Day the Earth Stood Still*, with Michael Rennie playing Klaatu. Nor were the band The Beatles in disguise, but Canadians who formed the progressive rock group in 1973.

The reason for the pop world's fascination with matters occult or regarded as fringe or pseudoscience is open to conjecture. Opposing viewpoints are that it would represent a retreat into a state of ephemerality equal to that of the transience of pop itself or on the other hand a seeking for realities higher spiritually than the mundanities and inanities of rock 'n' roll. Of all professions, it would seem the rock business has the greatest proportion of persons interested in flying saucer phenomena. A sociologist would probably offer an erudite explanation for this fact. I won't – all I shall do is present a selection of examples. Neither do I think it necessary to offer an explanation. Are unidentified flying objects from other planets, a psychosociological crisis in people's minds or misidentification of familiar objects? Your guess is as good as mine. Just let's see what our whacky pop stars make of the conundrum!

Arguably the most emotive song associated with flying saucers is *After the Goldrush*. It is my favourite composition by Neil Young and is best known in this country through the acapella version by Gateshead trio Prelude, who have twice taken it up the charts. It is a strange song which shifts its timescale from mediaeval knights in armour to lying in a burned-out basement and then to a futuristic vision of silver spaceships. Young's fellow C.S.N.&Y. compatriot David Crosby had already dealt with the subject in *Wooden Ships*, and Young extended this idea to taking selected people from Earth to form a perfect civilisation on another planet. The final image is an elitist and apocalyptic vision of carrying the seeds of the hippie generation to 'a new home in the sun.' In an interview with *New Musical Express*, Young stated: "If anyone wants to take me [in]to space I'm ready to go. I'd like to take my family too. We have to go somewhere else eventually." Adding: "I think there'll be rock 'n' roll on other planets. Maybe there is now."

Plenty of records have been about flying saucers, from Cat Stevens's *Moonshadow* through Dennis Linde's *Under The Eye* to Johnny Rivers's *U.F.O.* Wishbone Ash's LP *Argus* had a sleeve designed by Hipgnosis of a shining holy grail, George Adamski sighting-style UFO on the back.

Mick Jagger had an electronic flying saucer warning instrument in his house, but it always went off while he was out. Fellow one-time Rolling Stone Mick Taylor went sky watching at Warminster, the one-time Clapham Junction of UFO flight paths. On another level there are those with suspicions that there are aliens among us from the stars, and stars who think they might be aliens themselves. Multi-talented Lene Lovitch, for instance, has voiced her anxieties thus:

> "I've never felt at ease in this world. When I was a little kid I was from an-
> other planet. When I was seven or eight I was obsessed with space stories. I
> thought I was an experiment, a visitor sent from another planet to try living
> on Earth. This experiment wasn't working too well. I'd hang out of the win-
> dow every night, searching the sky, looking for the aliens to come down and
> take me back home..."

A similar bizarre tag has been put on Blondie's Debbie Harry by her lover and bandmate Chris Stein. She said:

> "Chris thinks I'm definitely an alien because I fit the description of a race of
> females who were put on this planet from space."

Stein, knowing Debbie was adopted when she was three months old and has not discovered who her real parents are, chose this theory, whereas Debbie herself has an only slightly less exotic explanation: "Personally, I always thought I was Marilyn Monroe's kid."

And on the same theme, guitar hero Jimi Hendrix told film director Chuck Wein, creator of his *Rainbow Bridge*, of "being from an asteroid belt off the coast of Mars." Chuck said the film was about removing "the mass paranoia against the arrival of the Space Brothers." Incidentally, only hours before dying in Monika Danneman's flat, Jimi wrote a poem with the words: 'Angels of heaven, flying saucers to some, made Easter Sunday the name of the Rising Sun.'

However, the band most deeply steeped in ufolore are The Stranglers. It was Jet Black who first developed the interest which saw its fullest expression on the album *Themeninblack*. The

Men in Black in question being mysterious persons who threaten UFO witnesses with dire consequences. Whether they are from government agencies or supernatural realms provides a happy hunting ground of speculation for conspiracy theorists. Strangely, after the group first became interested in the MIB during 1979 a tormenting sequence of misfortunes befell the group. Jean Jacques Burnel has written an article on the subject, 'A Strange Chain of Events,' in the band's admirable 'enthuzine' *Strangled*. Having created a state of paranoia and , perhaps, a wish to investigate further the subject of the sinister, silencing Men in Black, the reader is warned not to purchase a book with the title *Men in Black*. Why? The subtitle should suffice – *75 Years of New Zealand Rugby*.

[There were also a couple of extended captions to go with pop figures]

DAVID BOWIE ... played the role of an extraterrestrial in the excellent science-fiction film *The Man Who Fell to Earth*. In real life he was also involved in the subject. He told a magazine writer: "I used to work for two guys who put out a UFO magazine in England about six years ago (1969), and I made sightings six, seven times a night for about a year when I was in the observatory. We had regular cruises that came over. We knew the 6-15 was coming in and would meet up with another one. And they would be stationary for about half-an-hour and then after verifying what they had done that day, they'd shoot off."
POLY STYRENE ... found spiritual matters dominating her mind. "I got into it when I saw a UFO in Doncaster after a gig on our last tour. I just had to go searching for more knowledge. Inevitably it's going to lead to religion in the end." It also broke up her band, X-Ray Spex. And whatever happened to Ms Styrene (Marion Elliot)? Oh bondage, up yours!

Not surprisingly, other ufologists have latched on to the cultural influence of the flying saucer phenomenon and musicians; notably Jenny Randles and Andy Roberts have both written articles on the connection.

THE BALLAD OF GRAM PARSONS AND GEORGE VAN TASSEL

(*Folklore Frontiers*, No. 54, 2006; *Amskaya*, No. 68, 2006)

From rock 'n' roll to Giant Rock. A country music fan and a flying saucer fanatic. Perhaps, not such an unlikely combination. I have no evidence that genius musician Gram Parsons ever met enigmatic aviator George Van Tassel, but they were both at the same site in the Californian desert and would surely have had much in common. This article celebrates an episode in both flying saucer contactee lore and the life of a country-rock music legend. This is the story of a putative movie involving junkie-alcoholic Gram Parsons and UFO-contactee George Van Tassel.

GEORGE VAN TASSEL (12 March 1910 – 9 February 1978) was one of many people who became known in UFO literature as contactees: persons who claimed to have met extraterrestrials, and in many cases travelled with them in their spacecraft, visited other planets and been communicated pearls of cosmic wisdom. Totally out of favour today with ufologists at large and ignored by cosmologists, I suspect that they are overdue a revival as the scientific community squabbles over any and every new theory regarding the origins and development of the universe.

Born in Jefferson, Ohio, in 1910, after leaving high school, George became an airline mechanic with test flight experience for 16 years with Douglas Aircraft, Howard Hughes and Lockheed. He had the idea of running a small airport and café with his second wife Dorris at Giant Rock, in the California desert, which opened in 1947. Eventually the venue became the focus for many UFO conventions. The first of these took place in 1954. A veritable who's who of the contactee universe passed through as speakers, including Orfeo Angelucci, Daniel

Fry, Truman Bethurum and George Hunt Williamson, giving informal lectures during the day and channelling sessions after dark. George Adamski addressed the 1955 gathering, before his subsequent notoriety and playing a Rasputin role at the Dutch royal court. Spiritual messages from blond Nordic-looking humanoids were seen as wryly amusing, annoying, deflecting, anti-semitic or downright dangerous to serious UFO research. They brought dire warnings of concern among a galactic federation regarding the arms race and fearful prophecies of ecological catastrophes, whose aftershock is only now being given expression in the barmy doomsaying of the manmade global warming loony lobby. Van Tassel wrote two books on his adventures and imparted wisdom, *I Rode a Flying Saucer* and *This World And Out Again*. Giant Rock was the scene of a retro event earlier this year and was officially commemorated as an historical site in 2005.

GRAM PARSONS (5 November 1946 – 19 September 1973) never had a hit record, but his country-rock fusion started a revolution. Posthumously, his star has burned bright. Born in Waycross, Georgia, a rich kid who lived hard, his life literally burned out in the southern California desert when a friend tipped his corpse out of the casket and set it alight. What Parsons shared with Van Tassel was an interest in UFOs. In a masterly biography, Ben Fong-Torres tells how Parsons was attracted to the Joshua Tree national monument in the Mojave desert, outside Hollywood. He went there with Byrds and Flying Burrito Brothers band member Chris Hillman and later Keith Richards of the Rolling Stones, where 'they'd stay up all night, zonked out of their minds, looking for, and sometimes spotting flying saucers.' Parsons also went there to make a movie with Michelle Phillips, willowy blonde songstress with the Mamas and Papas.

GIANT ROCK was the location for the film, a huge boulder with a cave or room carved at ground level. Visitors claimed it felt very powerful and here Van Tassel carried out thought communication sessions with space people; an early example of what New Agers would term channelling. The film in question was being made by Tony Foutz, who had created special effects for Stanley Kubrick's *2001*, and he planned to make his UFO movie, *Saturation 70*, in the Joshua Tree area. Foutz and Parsons had shared a suite and the filmmaker made Gram one of the main characters. Fong-Torres wrote:

> 'Few participants could recall a plotline, if, in fact, there was one. Ann Marshall, a friend of Michelle's, thought Tony's film was based on his knowledge of George Van Tassel, author of *I Rode a Flying Saucer* and proprietor of the College of Universal Wisdom, better known as the Giant Rock airport … Van Tassel had built a domed structure he called the "Integratron," which he described as a "generator of bioelectrical energies" that had regenerative powers and made its operator capable of time travel. It looked like a Hollywood prop from *Flash Gordon*, and it worked about as well. As Tom Wilkes, the A&M Records art director who was with the crew to shoot still photos, pointed out: "It was supposed to rejuvenate people, but it didn't work for George; he died of old age".'

He died aged 68 in 1978; but Van Tassel estimated the Integratron to be only 82% complete. It was certainly in the right place for scanning the heavens. Skywatch participants of yesteryear will emote with Ann Marshall, who recalled:

> "The sky is very clear, very high in the desert, and there is no light pollution. You can see more of the sky than you can from the cities. These people with Airstream trailers and other recreational vehicles met every year at Joshua Tree because they felt they had definitely seen unidentified flying objects. They were very normal people, not hippies at all. Family people who would just take their vacations going into the wilderness."

Another first-time actress, photographer Andee Cohen, believed Foutz's notion was, to quote Fong-Torres:

> '...to use one of George's annual UFO Sighters Conventions in Joshua Tree as a real-life back-drop for a story about "four cosmic kittens who were banished in outer space and came here to clean up the planet." All Michelle Phillips knew was that she was asked to make a little movie. She piled into a Winnebago with Gram and several others and took off to Joshua Tree. The cast and crew stayed at a simple roadside motel that Gram had come to know: the *Joshua Tree Inn*.'

Once in the Mojave, Foutz spotted Linda Lawrence's (Gram's latest girlfriend) son Julian (father Brian Jones of the Rolling Stones) on set, first seeing him as an alien, but changed his mind and cast him as the movie's star. This casual, contradictory approach annoyed the producer (as did a scene shot in Los Angeles involving a dead Vietnamese man at a meat counter); it also scared the backers and sadly the film was all for nothing. Tantalisingly, had it been completed, my thoughts are that today it could be a cult classic. It would have featured the legendary Gram Parsons in his only feature movie role and a UFO connection like no other. Any footage still extant? Any songs written for the soundtrack? Contactee revival anyone?

COSMIC CONNECTIONS link Gram and George and the similarities might help flesh out why Parsons was attracted to the film project. Despite taking drugs on a heroic scale, Gram spent a period at Harvard as a theology student and later returned to religion, being influence by Gnostic Christianity. 'Meanwhile, Van Tassel was awoken on 24 August 1953 while sleeping outside by a humanoid. Solganda, wearing a natty one-piece blue suit, invited the Earthling aboard a nearby spacecraft, whose machinery was to remind George of the 'wheels within wheels' in the Book of Ezekiel. Biblical influences both. Another of Van Tassel's contacts was called Ashtar; this same Ashtar would become one of the most widely-channelled extraterrestrial intelligences in contactee circles. He also claimed to receive telepathic messages from the alien commanders of various starships.

Whereas Gram's quasi-Christian take on life can be seen in such compositions as *She* and describing his records as 'cosmic American music,' Van Tassel, it seems recorded linear flows of energy in space, believed the solar system runs as a motor, may have predicted the Van Allen Belt, but believed our Sun is square! Van Tassel also wished to rejuvenate the human body, and to this purpose was building the Integratron, a large observatory-like building about three miles from Giant Rock, 38ft high, 55ft diameter and described by one commentator as the only all-wood, acoustically-perfect sound chamber in the US.' It was supposedly a 'Venusian Gift to Mankind,' the plans for which were implanted in his brain as a high-voltage, electrostatic generator designed to recharge human cell structure, also warp time and remove gravity. Parsons, on the contrary, seemed hell bent on destroying his body. On the day he died at Joshua Tree Inn he had mixed morphine while chain-drinking Jack Daniels. There have been various accounts of the macabre and unsuccessful attempts to revive him, most of them unsavoury, such as a girlfriend stuffing ice cubes up his anus while engaging in fellatio in a vain bid whereby she had heard this was a tried and viable procedure, but all versions for revival proved fruitless.

Subsequently, as the body was about to be shipped back to Georgia for burial, it was tricked away from the airport. Having made a pact with the victim, Philip Clark Kaufman, Gram's best friend and road manager, set the corpse alight in the desert on a massive slab of stone called Cap Rock. Campers nearby thought it was a log on fire. Giant of rock, R.I.P.

Sources:

Ben Fong-Torres, *Hickory Wind: The Life and Times of Gram Parsons*, Omnibus Press, 1991
Gregory Bishop, 'Calling Occupants.' *Fortean Times*, No. 118, 1999
Jimmy Goddard, *Earth People, Space People*, STAR Fellowship
Penny Stallings, *Rock 'n' Roll Confidential*, Vermillion, 1984
Susannah Rosenblatt, 'E.T., there's no place like dome,' *Los Angeles Times*, 27 September 2006
Chelsea J. Carter, 'Signs of Life – UFOs, interdimensional travel and one Giant Rock,' *River Falls Journal*, 1 May 2006
Amskaya, issues 19, 28, 42, 43, 44, 47, 50 and 55, STAR Fellowship

Although incomplete upon Van Tassel's death in 1978, the Integratron was bought in 2000 by three sisters who transformed it into a wacky bed and breakfast establishment sleeping thirty (Bettina Kowalewski, *Bed in a tree*, DK Eyewitness Travel, 2009). It had already been honoured with a plaque in a joint dedication for cultural importance by the Morongo Basin Historical Society and the Billy Holcombe Chapter 1069 of the Ancient and Honorable Order of E. Clampus Vitus, a fraternal society whose members wear red T-shirts and black hats, though it is unclear whether they are a historical drinking society or a drinking historical society (Sra Munro, 'Earthlings extol Landers rejuvenation machine,' *Hi-Desert Star*, 3 May 2005). At a boozy weekend party the co-owners were honoured to have Van Tassel and the monument to his vision honoured. The plaque reads:

> *'The Integratron is the creation of George Van Tassel and is based on the design of Moses' Tabernacle, the writings of Nikola Tesla, and telepathic directions from extraterrestrials.'*

ROCK 'N' LEYS:
THE OLD STRAIGHT TRACKS

((The) *Mail* (Hartlepool), 28 December 1983; *The Shaman*, No. 5, 1984; *N.E.*, No. 4, 1984)

> *Thinker came down from his place in the mountains,*
> *All he had was upon his back,*
> *He journey'd far and his legs were light,*
> *For he knew to follow the old straight track.*

The most celebrated book on leys – the heretical theory of aligned ancient sacred sites – is *The Old Straight Track*. It was written by Alfred Watkins and published in 1925, four years after he first noted that prehistoric sites and pre-Reformation churches such as stone circles, standing stones, hillforts, beacon hills, fords, ecclesiastical properties, crossroads and some sections of road fell into long, dead-straight alignments. Four or more such sites in a line he termed a ley – a word frequently encountered upon such lines and of Anglo-Saxon origin. Watkins, a Herefordshire businessman, believed leys to be early trackways, hence the old straight track. During the heady days of psychedelic hippie-dom they took on the aura of a mystical concept. Largely responsible for fostering this view has been John Michell, a writer whose book *The View Over Atlantis* became a counterculture classic when published in 1969.

To the trackway idea became added the notion of some magical force transmitted in linear form across the landscape and it has been embraced by many musical personalities, and acted as an inspiration in their songwriting and stage presentation. The original concept even became the title of the album *The Old Straight Track* by Jack the Lad. This Geordie folk-rock band formed from the original disintegration of Lindisfarne and the LP was released on the Charisma label in 1974. The title track is an evocative celebration of Watkins's revolutionary insight. When the band played their farewell concert at the Longscar Hall, Seaton Carew, I knew the co-organisers, so my wife and I went back with them and the band to a hotel for after-hours drinks. There I discussed leys with Simon Cowe and he recalled living in a farmhouse in Northumberland with a ley running through the building. He was inspired to write the song there. Leys have also been called dragon lines, as a telluric serpent power is believed by many to pass along the alignments, either at certain planetary, seasonal or processional periods or generated and directed by magicians of either white or black persuasion. The Jack the Lad album even has a song called *The Wurm* about the Loathly Worm of Spindleston Heugh, and the band do this bizarre and compelling Northumbrian folktale justice.

Despite the name, Jack the Lad take the subject seriously; not so *New Musical Express*. The music paper's piss-takes have been frequent and generally trivial, ranging from mocking duo Ramases and Selket over their single *Crazy One* (apparently a C.B.S. records employee mis-understood the designated title *Quasar One*) with 'Felixstowe is not on a ley-line with Cairo' to commenting in parentheses after noting Steve Howe had chosen Yes Tor as location for album cover photography '(On a ley line is it? – Ed).'But Steve Hillage has been the focus of most comment for his earth mysteries interest. Chris Salewicz went walking with Hillage in Wiltshire, ambling down 'the path/ley line' to the 17th century cottage he shares with Miquette Giraudy in Great Bedwyn. An R.A.F. fighter zooms above. "Chasing UFOs, I expect," mutters Hillage, apparently matter-of-factly. Around this time, Angus MacKinnon, reviewing Hillage's *Motivation Radio* in *NME* without sarcasm, suggests the reader 'go visit a standing stone and see what you feel,' while attacking the 'sensationalist chicanery' of those buffoons Berlitz and von Daniken. In 1978 a *NME* sub-editor had fun at leys' expense in a standfirst: 'Bob Edmands (the man who thought ley-lines were queues outside brothels) meets Steve Hillage (the man who's into communication with cauliflowers)' which suggested by way of the actual article's taking seriously Hillage's theory to do with leys and the earth being out of axis, that the sub-editor was the closest to being a vegetable.

NME likes to describe such people as Hillage as 'boring old farts' and no doubt Stevie Winwood also qualifies. Through the Spencer Davies Group he was driven to join Traffic, whose *Shoot Out at the Fantasy Factory* album had a track entitled *Roll Right Stones* about the Oxfordshire stone circle of that name. An Angus MacKinnon article of 1977 remarked upon Winwood's knowledgability of leys and astroarchaeology. Another stone circle figures in a tale about Echo and the Bunnymen. Echo supposedly being more than a margarine or newspaper published in Sunderland, but is apparently a Norse rabbit god. Member Will Sargeant and manager Bill Drummond were in a party which took a moonlight drive to Callanish, on the Isle of Lewis. In typical *NME* fashion we learn that Drummond 'lay prostrate at the circle's centre, absorbing quantities of magical vibration and damp peat. Scoff if you will ...' And so from Scotland to Ireland, and the greatest Boyne Valley mound inspired Clannad to write *Newgrange*, while farther afield in Peru, Jaz of Killing Joke studied astronomy and traced the fantastic figures of birds and animals left on the Nazca desert by a lost civilisation. Back in rural Britain, three members of the recently-disbanded Doll by Doll – Jackie Leven, Jo Shaw and Dave McIntosh – came together in 1977 after living two years previously in two farmhouses in Dorset situated on the same ley. Leven writes weird lyrics and retains a mystical attachment to his half-Romany birthright and the Doll by Doll single *Hard Travelled Roads* is well worth checking out.

Returning to *NME*, a 1974 tribute upon the death of Graham Bond related how the album *Holy Magick* followed his band's trekking the leys of western Britain. Incidentally, during my tenureship of the editor's chair with *The Ley Hunter*, I published an extraordinary article of coincidences/synchronicities centred upon Bond and asylums. I also reported how Martin Stone, then in Mighty Baby and later Chili Willi, had got such a buzz at a prehistoric site in Cornwall that he said he found it akin to a drug experience. Guitar maestro Robert Fripp discussed leys with Anne Nightingale at length on a radio programme a few years ago. He once wrote to me that the picture of me grinning on the back cover of my *Quicksilver Heritage* hardback ley book, 'does not give the stamp of moral authority to our subject. Were you drunk?'

[The last sentence did not appear in (The*) Mail* **(Hartlepool) version where I edited it out, but does appear in *NE* magazine. (The)** *Mail* **version had other minor variations and was somewhat shorter. I can't understand why in *The Shaman* I did not continue the Fripp story. My response to Bob's light-hearted admonition was to reply with a comment along the lines of: 'On the subject of famous people and retaining dignity, I've just been reading the in-depth two-parter on you and King Crimson in *NME*. There's the account of your next-door neighbour leaning over the fence and calling out "Bob, did you know you've got Dutch elm disease," while you were busily engaged in *alfresco* copulation. I don't see that tale lending moral authority to your musicianship.' Touché.]**

Back with the radio, I came home one teatime and turned on Radio 1 to hear Marc Bolan extolling the virtues of ley hunting and he also mentions John Michell. Which neatly brings me to mentioning that when a few years ago I was staying with John in Bath, by chance I noticed a discarded and untouched contract on top of a wastepaper basket. It related to a possible recording deal involving Adrian Munsey (remember his offbeat *The Lost Sheep* single?). Michell laughed off any possibility of involvement with the music business and added that he had just rejected an approach from someone who had wanted to put some of his writings to music. He had never heard of the person and wondered if I had. Did the name Mike Oldfield ring a bell?

Of course, not everyone shares the opinion that ancient sites are aligned deliberately. A new book attacking ley theory, *Ley-Lines in Question*, notes the concept of alignments as established fact for the Sixties generation, and its presence in their culture, art and - particularly - music. Tom Williamson and Liz Bellamy note that the cover of the first album by the Albion Dance Band, *The Prospect Before Us*, is a drawing of Alfred Watkins experiencing his controversial 'Imagine a fairy chain' epiphany. 'The fact that this is unexplained assumes a familiarity with ley theories amongst at least some of the buyers of the record,' they write. Other ley references occur in folk and rock bands; repertoires and they cite Fairport Convention's *Journeyman's Grace* and Jethro Tull's *Cup of Wonder*. Females have had little musical ley involvement, but Kate Bush figures. Her *The Dreaming* is a great shamanic record and her hit *Wuthering Heights* is another personal favourite. In his book tracing the 50-year history of E.M.I.'s Abbey Road studios, Brian Southall writes: 'Kate Bush, who knows about these things says there are ley lines underneath – strong magnetic forces. She feels their vibes when she is working there.' Abbey Road is, of course, best known as the recording home of The Beatles, so it befits this brief survey to align as mark points, John, Paul, George, Ringo, that rumour-ridden zebra crossing with the Fab Four in line, the *NME* and its scribe Paul Rambali with the latter's conclusion to a book review, '...wherein Strawberry Fields and Abbey Road are not merely familiar and typical examples of a recurrent landscape but are powerful cathedrals on the ley lines of popular culture.'

Yet I suspect that as Bob Dylan stated: 'None of them along the line know what any of it is worth.'

Earth mysteries had a great influence on popular music and three famous rock stars subscribed to *The Ley Hunter* during my editorship: Robert Fripp (guitarist, King Crimson, now married to Toyah Willcox and living in Worcestershire); Martin Stone (guitarist, Mighty Baby, Chilli Willi and the Red Hot Peppers, etc., international notoriety as a bookscout and living in Paris; and Tim Hart, multi-instrumentalist founder of Steeleye Span, died 2009. Also interviewing Quiver guitarist Tim Renwick, when he mentioned he was from Cambridge I told him I thought it a beautiful city and that I had climbed Castle Mound. "That's where I first felt a girl's breast," he shamelessly informed me. Wow! Those debauched rock 'n' rollers.

INTERLUDE TWO
PSYCHOGEOGRAPHICAL CONUNDRUMS
PETER McMAHON: LEY TRAMP
(*Folklore Frontiers*, No. 21, 1993)

I became fascinated with the subject of Peter McMahon in 1989. He was Hereford's best-known tramp and in the footsteps of that city's most famous son, Alfred Watkins, he too was obsessed with travel in straight lines. Over the years it became my aim to track him down. I had been alerted to McMahon's existence by a reference in *The Telegraph Weekend Magazine*, in which travel and historical writer Charles Nicholl reported that Herefordians seemed more concerned about Peter's welfare than that of the city's Mappa Mundi estoire. According to Nicholl, 'they say' Peter was a well-born man who suffered a tragedy in his youth. Early in 1989 he disappeared. Alan Williams, a fish and chips shop owner, offered a £50 reward for information as to Peter's whereabouts, 'Wanted' posters were printed and letters to newspapers published. Eventually, a police patrol found him in Anglesey. All he would divulge was that he liked walking in straight lines. Following this clue, I surmised (*The Ley Hunter*, No. 115, 1991) that he could have been following Sarn Helen, the supposed ancient dead straight highway created by the king Macsen Wledig following a lucid dream or astral projection. However, Nicholl seems to have confused Anglesey with Abergele, so that was a false lead. Also the maverick ley hunter Gordon Harris, with whom I'd crossed swords, challenged me to get more information from this straight-walking gentleman of the road.

The opportunity to visit Hereford finally presented itself and on the overcast afternoon of 27 April [1991] I alighted at Hereford railway station. I had been mentally preparing myself for a possible encounter with Mr McMahon. Hopes high, I seated myself in the nearest taxi and asked the driver to take me to Alan Williams' chip shop on Commercial Road. The taxi driver laughed and told me to get out – my destination was a mere 100 yards away; the shop around the corner from the pub he pointed towards across the car park. I rounded the corner within less than a minute to see just beyond the hostelry a shabbily-dressed man drinking from a mug.

"Are you Peter McManon?" I asked rather abruptly.

He acknowledged he was. There followed the most unenlightening and tedious interview it has

211

been my dubious privilege to conduct, despite all my preparation. I asked many questions but got no real answers and when he did speak I could not understand what he was saying. I asked him about his past, but more importantly about the legendary trek and supposed obsession with straight-line travel. The single fact I elicited was that the linear linkage was "rubbish." I returned to this aspect several times and each time the term "rubbish" was emphasised. He also denied any knowledge of Herefordian Alfred Watkins and his Twenties discovery of the old straight track, or ley-lines as they are now more familiarly known. Having got basically nowhere, or at least to my satisfaction, I asked if he would submit to being photographed. To my surprise there was no reluctance, but then disaster struck. The camera refused to function. (There was nothing paranormal about this: I had dropped it earlier in Newport-upon-Usk and had put the battery back, wrong way around). I frantically tried to make the camera work but Peter became impatient, muttered and huffily headed off.

Sat in a field where he would have died

Demoralised, but at least having attempted to get my story, I walked a short distance and bought some chips, asking if proprietor Alan Williams was on the premises. An affable man, he invited me into the back of the shop for a chat and to my relief rebutted Peter's disclaimer on his straight-line fetish. The 1989 marathon tramp had taken Peter not to Anglesey but to

Alan Williams kindly organised someone to take this photograph of him and Peter McMahon outside Mr Chips in 1993.

Abergele, on the North Wales caravan coast. When Mr Williams eventually found him, Peter had been sitting alone in a field for two days. Police from Llangollen had apparently earlier picked him up and given him a meal and shelter. They said they had never come across any-one before who would not give their name and he would only reveal that he liked walking in straight lines. On his extraordinary odyssey "he covered tremendous mileage," according to Mr Williams. He had gone missing while Mr Williams was on holiday and he spent three con-secutive Sundays seeking him. Each time he followed reports but Peter got farther away. He placed an advertisement in a North Wales newspaper and received many reports from the pub-lic. In fact, the police had also had a report that his appearance had frightened sheep and he was taken into [protective] custody.

Alan Williams travelled to pick him up, but Peter was reluctant to discuss the walkabout. "He had got as far as he could go. He'd reached the coast and just sat in a field in Abergele for two days. If I hadn't picked him up he would have just sat there and died," concluded Mr Wil-liams.

This begs the question of why so reclusive and uncommunicative a person should attract atten-tion. The kindly Mr Williams is not alone in charitable affection for Peter. He feeds him, so does a cake shop and when I met him outside the jeweller's, they had given him a mug of tea. When I mentioned that I had invited Peter for a drink in the pub next door, Mr Williams said that Peter does not drink alcohol. He does, however, smoke and signs on at the dole. He lives in a bus shelter in Elston Street nowadays. Mr Williams got him into a night shelter for two years after the Welsh adventure, but Peter left and would not have anything to do with official forms or charities such as Age Concern. A woman takes him to the local baths for a wash. He has been in Hereford for almost 20 years and there are many theories about his presence and predicament. These range from his wife and family having been killed in a car accident, to his having been a solicitor, a solicitor's clerk, teacher and his wife leaving him. Scruffy he might be, but it would be insulting and wrong to compare him with your average wino down-and-out.

The world according to Hereford's Mappa Mundi

Why Peter should choose Hereford as home is problematic. It is a relatively small and unre-markable market town on the Welsh Marches. There is the expanding Bulmer cider company, several museums and the See of Hereford is one of the oldest in England, being substantially Norman with a 13th century lady chapel. The crypt houses the unique Mappa Mundi together with an interpretive exhibition. It is quite expensive to view, but exhibitions officer Dominic Harbour explained this was because of the astronomical insurance premium. The Mappa Mundi was created by Richard de Haldingham, a Lincolnshire man, in about 1290 and shows a flat, circular world with a sea all around it and Jerusalem at its centre. There are puns in the drawing; Noah's Ark is docked neatly at Mount Ararat. In truth the Mappa Mundi is really not a map at all, but – in the maker's own word – an estoire. Charles Nicholl writes:

> 'It is a story, an effort to make sense of it all. You can call Jerusalem the centre of the world, or London, or you can walk in a straight line until you come to the edge. We are all busy piecing together our mental mappa

mundi, and Herefordshire is as fine a place to do it as any.'

I viewed the Mappa Mundi and then Mr Harbour took me the short distance to Harley Court, where Alfred Watkins had lived. I had made a pilgrimage to the house in 1971 and was then disappointed there was no plaque to mark the former residency of the founder of ley hunting. Today there is a fitting memorial to his tenancy. Watkins was a brewer, photographic equipment inventor, councillor and magistrate. Late in his life, through a flash of inspiration, he concluded that prehistoric sites, pre-Reformation churches, crossroads, fords and other countryside features fell into straight lines. He surmised that early man used these lines as trade routes. Calling them leys, he argued his case persuasively, though met with rancour and opprobrium from the academic archaeological establishment. That Peter should be drawn to the city of the ley man seemed to put a strain on coincidence. Also remember how Charles Nicholl wrote of walking a straight line to the edge, in fact, just what Peter did upon leaving Hereford, the centre of his world and personal mappa mundi.

Before leaving Hereford, I called at 42 Commercial Road and talked to jeweller Robert Broadfoot and his wife Philippa. I learned from them that Peter's 1989 walk to Abergele was not the first time he had gone missing. "The first time he just went straight on," said Mr Broadfoot. "He was found 40 to 50 miles away in Wales. The second time he said he was looking for something familiar." And Mrs Broadfoot added: "He has set procedures. In places he will not walk on the other side of the road and he will make ninety-degree turns." To give an unequivocal answer to the linear riddle, Mr Broadfoot assured me: "He definitely walks in straight lines."

References:

Charles Nicholl, The View From Here column, The *Telegraph Weekend Magazine*, 29/7/89
Paul Screeton, 'Keeping Straight,' *The Ley Hunter*, No. 115, 1991

Footnotes:

I sent copies of this article to the Broadfoots, Williams and Harbour. The latter two rang to confirm its factual correctness and Robert Broadfoot wrote to the same effect. Oddly enough, the day I posted the draft article, I read *The Sun* (2/8/93) and found this synchronous item:

> 'Fish and chip shop owner Alan Williams is giving his rivals a battering following the lead of your price-busting 20p *Sun*. Alan, 38, has slashed the cost of a portion of chips from 55p to 20p at Mr Chips in Hereford. He said: "The *Sun*'s price reduction is a brilliant idea. It's the only way to beat the recession and it's inspired me to be a price-buster."

Dominic Harbour dropped a note later to say one Friday evening / Saturday morning he was 'fed with chips' by Mr Williams for 7p! When the chips are down, Mr Chips rises to the occasion.

Apparently Peter McMahon died in May 2006, but the mystery of his presence in Hereford was only revealed in 2010 by a local journalist. He had been a familiar figure for more than 20 years, 'standing like a sentinel,' as reporter Liz Watkins put it, near Commercial Square and occupying a bus shelter at the top of Aylstone Hill. Ms Watkins mentioned in her article Peter's disappearances and straight routes preference. She wrote:

> 'He rarely spoke, never drank, caused no trouble, asked for nothing and the people of Hereford took him to their extended heart. People in Hereford allowed Mr McMahon to live life in his own strange way, caring for him in their own way.'

Her piece recalled chip shop owner Alan Williams and his father Ken taking Christmas dinner to Peter's shelter, only to find others had been there earlier, leaving wrapped gifts on the seat. She revealed that Peter would only listen to May Goode, of the Salvation Army in Hereford, who made arrangements for him to have regular baths or showers, plus haircuts, and ensured he had suitable clothing to protect him from the elements. The loner finally succumbed to society's bosom one very wet day when he was found collapsed on a roadside verge and taken to hospital. After much persuasion he agreed to accept a place at Manor Rest Home, where following a brief illness, he died.

Liz reported the aspect of the 'many sentimental myths and stories' which had attached to the reason he chose such a solitary sojourn in Hereford. Apparently members of Peter's family from South Wales had been trying to trace him and the trail took them via the police and *Hereford Times* to Alan Williams and they were then able to meet the people who had befriended their missing relation, visited his old haunts and the cemetery where his ashes had been scattered. Critically, they were able to satisfy people's curiosity over the recluse's life. The facts, as related by his 67-year-old brother David, are that Peter was born in Cardiff, the seventh of nine children, was employed at GKN steelworks, but suffered head injuries when a runaway wagon knocked him down. He was awarded compensation and it was believed he spent it on clothes and going out every night. He received mental treatment but after ceasing to take his medication his condition worsened, he left home and his family lost all contact until they came across an article about his being found in Abergele. A sister and brother travelled to Hereford, but Peter did not seem to recognise them or communicate so they thought it best not to interfere again in his chosen way of life. (Account condensed from Liz Watkins, 'In his black coat, he stood sentry in a Hereford bus shelter. Now his story can be told,' *Hereford Times*, 8/1/10) And Liz <u>Watkins</u>, what an appropriate name for the investigator of a man who walked in straight lines and how fortean that the Welshman chose the city of Alfred Watkins birth and death for his linear perambulations base.

* An abridged version of my article appeared as 'Quest for the Hereford tramp,' *The Mail* (Hartlepool), 12/1/94; and in a different form as 'Straight Lines and Two Herefordians,' *The Ley Hunter*, No. 120, 1993/1994.

PART SEVEN
FOLKLIFE

A LOCAL LEGEND

(*Fortean Times*, No. 63, 1992)

The subtle codename 'Operation Napoleon' was well chosen. Keeping the location was secret. A red alert test of emergency services to see how they would cope with a simulated railborne nuclear consignment being damaged had to be kept under wraps. When it took place recently, the cryptic historical connection became clear. It had to be at Hartlepool.

According to the legend, the fishermen of Hartlepool hanged a monkey which had been washed ashore on a spar of ship's wreckage. This was during the Napoleonic Wars and the monkey was mistaken for a French spy. Chattering away in what was deduced to be a foreign tongue and dressed in a military-style uniform, it was decided as a precaution it should be hanged. This is the basic and simplistic version of the legend. Hartlepudlians, wherever in Britain or abroad they travel, are remembered and recognised for this deed and dubbed 'monkey-hangers.' The majority take no offence; indeed, they regard it more as a compliment. However, on occasions when a questioner might have sarcastically inquired, "Is this where they hung the monkey?," the reply would be, "Why, have yer lost yer father?"

Delving into the archives, I was able to find an account several times removed from an original witness, giving details of the shipwreck on the Longscar Rocks of a French privateer named *Chasse Maree*. The spoils from the warship included the bedraggled, shivering monkey. A 'lobster pot court' was held and the verdict was that the stranger was a foreign spy. A coble's mast was erected on the Fish Sands and the monkey duly hanged. Problems with the story arise immediately, as inquiries have failed to establish the historicity of the *Chasse Maree*, despite the account's keen observation and technical detail. In any case commonsense dictates that any monkey found floating on a piece of timber would be a small breed and familiar as a ship's pet, whose size and innocent appearance would not qualify it as a French agent. More reason for doubt is that none of the prominent regional folklore collectors of the period found the story worthy of mention, had they heard it. Unless, of course, they considered it as historical fact?

So, if documentation of the monkey-hanging legend from the Napoleonic era speaks volumes by its absence, then there is a tantalising reference made in a political pamphlet of the 1840s to 'aquatic monkies.' Accounts of the historical development of railways throughout the North-East rarely touch upon the intense rivalries which were stirred. It was the battle to export coal more cheaply which led to railway companies converging upon Hartlepool, creating the larger and more prosperous West Hartlepool (the two boroughs amalgamating eventually in the 1960s). Initials on the small bill announcing 'aquatic monkies' doubtless stand for those who favoured the West Dock scheme. But if these people can be regarded as Johnny-come-lately charlatans, then we can deduce that the 'aquatic monkies' jibe turned on association with 'Jenny Hanivers.' These mermaid-type creations – half-fish, half-monkey – were popular in the last century. The bill was dated 1844 and we know that showman Phineas Barnum was exhibiting an example in 1842. Indeed, in Hartlepool, even today a small skate is folded, smoked liked a kipper and can then take on the appearance of a small monkey, demonstrating a possibly unbroken tradition of 'aquatic monkies' in the town spanning 150 years. But what most firmly established the legend was a song composed by Ned Corvan (1829-65). Corvan's policy was to discover some local tale and exaggerate it into an epic. This he would declaim with suitable gestures and those dramatic asides so essential to music-hall gatherings when everyone was suitably merry from drink and bonhomie. Corvan's song includes:

> "Still you may hear to this day,
> Boys crying, 'Who hung the Monkey, O?'"

There was also a popular play at the time called *Jack Robinson and his Monkey*. One rival railway had a Stephen Robinson as engineer; was his opposite number a 'monkey'? Robinson's monkey was called Mushapug; Corvan called the monkey Pug, as shortened in the play. The song made its stage debut at the Dock Hotel Music Hall, Southgate, Hartlepool, on an unspecified date. The ballad sheet contends it was greeted with immense applause, but it has also been suggested Corvan was run out of town for performing it. Whether Hartlepudlians liked it or not, they had to be resigned to the fact that Corvan had put them on the map.

However, it is only fair to record that Hartlepool is not alone in having a monkey-hanging legend. Another features Boddam, Aberdeenshire, where the delightful inhabitants lit beacons deliberately to lure cargo ships to be wrecked on the rocks. When a monkey was washed ashore, it was hanged, as there were fears that as the sole survivor it would claim the remaining merchandise as was standard in maritime law. Boddam fishergirls followed the herring fleets and would have gutted fish ashore in Hartlepool. Perhaps this could be the genesis of the tale – migratory legend, it's called. There again, the tale surfaces on Clydeside at Greenock, in distant Cornwall in Mevagissey and even inland in a Derbyshire village, as John Michell discovered.

Just as legend relocation is common, so are examples of *blason populaire* – a simple expression for a distinct form of local tradition, a jeering slogan or jibe, a taunt levelled in semi-malicious fun, by the inhabitants of one community, town or region against those of another. In fact, both Hartlepool and Boddam also share a catcall – "I hear they're painting the end of the new pier red to save lighting the beacon at night." More than 100 years ago Robert Chambers observed:

'There is a nationality in districts as well as in countries: nay, the living on different sides of the same stream, or of the same hill, sometimes entertain prejudices against each other, not less virulent than those of the inhabitants of different sides of the English Channel or the Pyrenees.'

West Hartlepool born and bred, I must record that there is still rivalry between the people of the former boroughs of Hartlepool and West Hartlepool; equally, a mutual insularity shunning connection with either neighbouring Teesside or South-East Durham. More positively, Poolies can laugh at themselves and have capitalised upon the monkey legend rather than decried it. The monkey today is mascot in sporting and military contexts; regaled in modern traditional songs; used in advertising promotions and even for sugarcraft modelling; and has appeared in the name of a strong beer. A century ago, the tale gained national prominence when Hartlepool Rovers Football Club was having a glorious period during the 1890s. A stuffed monkey was hanged from the crossbar before a match and national newspapers reported this novel behaviour.

The club still associates itself strongly with the legend. When recently a Rovers team went to a match at Twickenham, they had a live monkey as a mascot. On the return journey the bus crashed and the only survivor was the monkey. A police officer tried to communicate with it to ascertain what had happened. Eventually he had some success, and when asked what was happening at the rear of the coach, the monkey made a gesture indicating people playing cards. In response to the question of what was happening in the central portion, the monkey gesticulated as if singing and waving a scarf. As for those at the front the monkey demonstrated the drinking of cans of beer. When asked about the driver, it held up its hands as if reading a newspaper. Lastly, the police officer asked what the monkey was doing itself. Its hands moved as if controlling the steering wheel…

In this 'Forum' piece for *Fortean Times* I set out the main elements of the Hartlepool monkey-hanging legend as a 'taster' for my book *Who Hung the Monkey?* The book has gone through several reprintings (including 1,000 copies deliberately discounted for sale by my then employers at the *Hartlepool Mail*). It has never been out of print and is available from Printability Publishing, c/o Atkinson the Printer, 11 Lower Church Street, Hartlepool, TS24 7DJ. This following passage is drawn from the conclusion to the book:

It is a fallacy of conventional scholarship to distinguish between these aspects with rigorous discipline and distinction. For folklore is the psychic life of a people and cannot be separated artificially from shared events. Legend may seem like lies but they always have an element of truth. Even when exaggeration and embellishment are applied, even to the extent of deliberate falsification and invention, such 'lies' of a people are not wholly gratuitous. They refer to some strata of communal reality where underlying fears, deficiencies, desires and dreams require exorcising or compensating. Their falsity makes them real; their power makes them true. In this way a self-definition of a community is created; a collective identity occurs just when and where it is needed. It can be a truth without true tangibility. So "Who hung the monkey, O!" We did.

(*Who Hung the Monkey? (A Hartlepool Legend)*, Printability Publishing, 1991)

MOCK MAYORS OF
MIDDLETON

(*Aspects of Teesside*, Wharncliffe Books, 2002)

The tradition of 'mock mayors' is one of folklore's lesser-known and least explored outposts. Possibly the only remaining example exists in the tiny community of Middleton, in Hartlepool, focussed upon the Smallcrafts Club, hidden away from the touristy commercialisation of the burgeoning marina. Mock mayors in days of yore were generally elected as being the greatest drunkard or most derelict individual in the community. Thus it was a deliberate demonstration of non-conformism or putting two fingers up at snobbish society and authority.

The Middleton mayoralty is only relatively recent in its inception, but it derives from a noble and ancient tradition. It is probably unique in the 21st Century. It is also special in that its genesis was wholly spontaneous. The notion of electing a mayor in Middleton came about without prior knowledge of the historical antecedents of such an unofficial office. Middletonians lived in smart cabins (some having been there for sixty years) by the harbour and they socialised in the Smallcrafts Club, the former *Prince of Wales* public house. Their very existence and rights were often under threat from the port authority, council and developers, so the residents banded together for mutual support and were led by what was known as the Banks Top Committee. It was the trusty triumvirate of trade union official Owen Richmond, engineer George 'Geordie' Grainger and coal merchant Bertie Cox who sparked off the idea of having their own local mayor. Owen Richmond was the first to hold office in 1970, and was particularly proud to hold the office again during 1982, as it was also Maritime England Year. In all, he has held the post of mayor four times. Of the inaugurators of the honour, Bertie Cox was installed in 1971 and George Grainger held the title in 1975, 1978 and 1979.

Lavatory chains and regimental shield

The first Middleton chain of office followed the tradition of mocking ceremony and authority by being formed of two lavatory chains being attached to a Durham Light Infantry shield. The current chain is more presentable and has a special coat of arms with a proud emblem. Between the townships of the ancient borough of Hartlepool and the upstart West Hartlepool there was a marshy area known as The Slake. Long before a road, harbours and shipbuilders' yards were created, each summer around July, a large flock of herons would roost every night on this stretch of mudflats. Apparently the Middletonians – there were several rows of houses and a handful of public houses – became so attached to this migratory occurrence that they adopted the birds as an emblem. Perhaps the herons followed the shoals of herring from Scotland to the Thames, stopping off awhile at The Slake. Whatever, the bird is honoured on the chain of office by the ancestors of the Middleton residents who took the graceful wading birds to their bosom.

Author Paul Screeton proudly displays the Mayor of Middleton's
badge of office in the Smallcrafts Club in 2001.

Many mourned the demolition of the housing in Middleton, leaving as its only reminder the Smallcrafts Club. Long-distance lorry driver Jackie Knight, mayor in 1988, commented at the time:

> "We can't preserve the community - the people were moved out - but we can preserve the spirit of Middleton. That is very much alive. I think that will give you some idea why it is so important to have a mayor and honour tradition.

Doubtless, as with all things, there is a collective noun for mayors – in this case a 'mocking of mayors' might be appropriate. As for the mayor's parlour, as mentioned this is the Smallcrafts Club in Commercial Street. While the marina developers have created a new world vision, the 'Smallies' is the embarrassing old world reality – where Small really is beautiful. The Small-crafts Association started life in a cottage owned by the father of the renowned boxer Teddy Gardner. After searching for suitable premises, the organisation settled on the then *Prince of Wales* pub, which was rented out to it by Cameron's Brewery (which even donated a barrel of beer to kick the group off in fine style). Over the decades, the members worked hard not only on repairs to their clubhouse, which they were eventually able to lease after lengthy negotia-tions with Teesside Development Corporation, but to raise cash for various charities. It is here that people with a love of all things nautical can swap yarns, have a few beers and play pool or darts.

Having been running smoothly since 1970, in 2001 the ceremony got off to a bad start with a couple of embarrassing hiccups when the traditional Easter mayor-making was missed. The women's committee, which apparently was supposed to organise the event, was blamed for the oversight. I then stepped in myself as an interested observer to urge that the ceremony should still take place even if a little late. On the rearranged Bank Holiday Monday, planned recipient Jimmy Hall failed to appear, not knowing that it was to be his big day, the choice of recipient being kept a closely-guarded secret. Owen Richmond finally did the honours by plac-ing the chain of office around Jimmy's shoulders on a later day of my choosing. Owen made a brief speech, and afterwards said that Jimmy had been chosen because he's a grand chap and probably the only person in the association alive who was actually born in Middleton. The mayoralty was saved, but in 1999 the 48 cabins were moved from their original site to another quieter location with a splendid view over Hartlepool Bay. Everyone seemed quite happy with the new berths.

A national phenomenon

My fascination for the Mayors of Middleton put me in touch with a retired polytechnic lec-turer and fellow student of folklore and mock mayors, Derek Froome. I have him to thank for summarising material he has collected from the North-East. Durham City had its Duke of Bau-bleshire, a character who was ennobled as a tribute to his eccentricity. Newcastle Boys' Gram-mar School often elected a boy mayor. At Embleton, Northumberland, there was a regular election of a tramp or other derelict as mayor after having been made drunk, but the local vicar had the tradition banned. Also in Northumberland, at Ford, there was an annual election of a drunken mayor. In Victorian times, the custom was often met with hostility from the clergy or police. The Mayor of Middleton was new to Derek and he wrote to me: 'Mock mayors are very fugitive and their discovery is more often than not a pursuit of serendipity.'

Fellow folklorist Peter Christie has researched the mock mayors of his native North Devon. He has found several spoofs of the real thing, where election days seem to have been an excuse for a holiday spent in drinking and making speeches attacking real or perceived abuses of power by local councils and the government. During the 19th Century he found references to these functionaries at Bideford, Parracombe (where by tradition the mayor was pushed around in a wheelbarrow and tipped into the mill pond at the end of the day), Torrington, Chittlehampton, Buckland Brewer (the nomination going to the most notorious wife-beater in the village), Derby and Bradiford (both suburbs of Barnstaple). The Mayor of Derby showed the office was not just a jovial one by writing letters to the press calling for work to be carried out to improve the roads and drainage in his area. He even went so far as to lead a crowd, with an attendant band, in a mass trespass along a disputed footpath to Landkey. In an echo of this 1840s political act, Smallcrafts activist Owen Richmond led a similar protest against Tees and Hartlepool Port Authority when it sought to bar walkers from a disputed right-of-way across Hartlepool Docks.

Postscript

The First World War probably put paid to these traditions and as I have suggested, Middleton's mayors are probably unique in the 21st Century. Yet it would be remiss of me if I did not acknowledge that there might be some semblance of other continuing traditions. The host of the television quiz show *Countdown*, Richard Whiteley, joked on air that he would like to be Mayor of Wetwang, in the heart of the Wolds in East Yorkshire, and villagers took him up on his offer at a ceremony in June 1988. It's a post, I believe, he still holds and he is part owner of a racehorse named Mayor of Wetwang.

As seen, generally mock mayors have been traditionally selected in the past from the less salubrious sections of society. *The Sun* newspaper, at some date in 1991, had a single paragraph announcing that 18-year-old builder Fevin Oatley is a fool – officially – clinching the village idiot title in Croscombe, Somerset. Also a 1999 international news snippet reported that the townsfolk of Porto Alegre, Brazil, were fed up with their local politicians and decided to teach them a lesson. For a joke, they nominated a pig in the town's elections, but the joke backfired when the animal was elected after polling 2,573 votes. As I write this, the public of Hartlepool has voted narrowly to choose a high-profile town mayor along the lines of New York and London, against the advice of all three major political parties on the council. Shades of the mock mayor tradition of power to the people!

This piece was one of two (the other being on the monkey legend) which I contributed to a book of 'discovering local history' edited by Maureen Anderson. I have since learned that to customise traditions to produce false concepts of the past and the patriotic is known as folklorismus. Doubtless mock mayors give an impression of giving a hamlet some inflated importance and the recipient elevated through dubious status. Any involvement by folklorists themselves disturbs the purists, but I was proud to have played a role in saving the Middleton tradition. In the social sciences, such action upon a social group by a student observing it is known as reactivity. When an urban anthropologist such as myself is conscious of his reasons for engaging to stamp his wishes and maybe some (folkloric) authority

on the proceedings of those he is researching and influencing, it is known as reflexivity. I simply call it going native. Sadly, after my intervention in 2001, it marked the end of a brief era, as I understand that was the last occasion upon which Middleton held a mayor-making. But as one door shuts another opens. The whole of Hartlepool got its first publically-elected mayor and it beggared belief that the electorate chose football club mascot H'Angus, aka Stuart Drummond, over his opponents. Seemingly against the odds, Mayor Drummond has proved a worthy recipient, learnt the ropes, has won a third term and remains in the post to this day. In 2010 he was voted tenth best in the world at the civic job. (*The Sun*, 11/12/10; *The Sunday Times*, 12/12/10). As they say, you couldn't make it up.

THE MAN WHO ATE
A DOMINO

(The Man Who Ate a Domino, Private, 2002)

An on-the-spot joke by a domino player had him knocking on an operating theatre's door. For he had to be cut open by surgeons three months after having swallowed one of the pieces in 1986. To save the funster embarrassment (though he was named by the *Mail*, Hartlepool), we will simply call him Derek (after Eric Clapton's band Derek and the Dominoes of *Layla* fame).

The chain of events began when 29-year-old Derek was playing a game in the *Horden Hotel*. Jobless Derek popped the piece in his mouth as a party trick. However, the joke became a serious affair when the domino remained stuck inside him. Speaking briefly to the *Mail*, he related: "I swallowed it in May, but after a while I began to feel terrible. It was making me so ill, so I went to the hospital." Staff at Hartlepool General Hospital gave Derek a series of X-rays when he sought medical help for his stomach pains. During the August of 1986 he was admitted to the hospital and had the domino surgically removed.

Derek's mother told the *Mail* the domino – which he was carrying about with him – was partially digested. "He was very lucky," she conceded. Approached by *Mail* reporter Peter French, the landlord of Horden's. *Horden Hotel* refused to comment, but another village pub licensee revealed it was not the first time Derek had performed his domino-eating stunt. Readers doubtless chuckled at luckless Derek's expense. Silly season story if ever there was one. But that's not the full story. Oh, no.

It came to the newspaper's attention through another aspect. Let's now go into *Have I Got News For You?* mode – the 'alleged' aspect, that is. Scurrilous surely; untrue, er hum; possibly, perhaps. Let's face it, when a man undergoes surgery it's no joking matter. So what of the rumour which actually initiated the journalistic investigation, but which was judiciously absent from the report? I mean, who would seriously accept that dedicated professional nursing staff and doctors would actually organise a sweepstake to guess what the dots were on the domino which a patient in their care had swallowed? Doubtless, wreckless Derek was disbarred from entering? **Source:** *Mail*, Hartlepool, 19 August 1986.

The Man Who Ate a Domino

The Man Who Ate a Domino. A bizarre reconstruction by cartoonist Paul Jermy of the operating theatre scene surgery.

As the sub-editor handling this item I knew the real and potentially embarrassing background story, but had the unenviable task of writing an innocuous headline to hide what might have been misconstrued as serious misconduct if the full tale were to have been fully revealed. My bland headline became the title of a self-published book which carried the subtitle *Humorous Excerpts & Stories from the Newspapers*. Not my choice, as I included some tales which were original and not published. It was planned for the book, being local, to be published by Printability Publishing, as was the monkey-hanging one, and had been typeset. So when for no apparent reason it was aborted, I acquired the proofs and organised publication myself, running to two imprints (slightly different back covers). It was illustrated by a talented *Mail* colleague, Paul Jermy, to whom I fed the contents as the project went along.

VIRGIN ON THE RIDICULOUS

(*The Man Who Ate a Domino*, Private, 2002)

Some years ago, in conversation, I mentioned to a friend that the three red sandstone lion statues outside Hartlepool's Lion Brewery, currently owned by Camerons Brewery Company, were alleged to roar if ever a virgin passed by.

My pal added that the statue of the founder of West Hartlepool and its first Member of Parliament, Ralph Ward Jackson, was supposed to rise from his seat if a virgin walked past. At the same time the statue was being moved temporarily to make way for the City Challenge improvements to Church Square.

Hartlepool Mail diarist Phil Hickey, fascinated by my revelations, penned a short item about the consequences councillors had not foreseen. He posed the question:

> 'How will the likely lads know the virtue of local lasses heading for the Church Street drinking dens on a Friday night if they don't have that test any longer? Note for students of Hartlepool history. No-one has ever seen the statue stand up.'

These comments landed Phil in deep trouble. From the editor? Press Complaints Commission? No, worse than that. His wife. She thought it was sexist. Why should it just apply to women – and not men?

But hang on!

Ralph Ward Jackson is actually already standing! It's not Ralphie but Sir William Gray who is seated. No-one bothered or knew better than to remonstrate with his column that Phil had the wrong august local entrepreneur.

Or maybe no-one read his column. Also a regular weekend act of jocularity has been to climb upon Gray and place a traffic cone on his head or Jackson hold a potted plant or some other object in his hand. Perhaps in these circumstances a condom might be appropriate.

Source: *Hartlepool Mail*, 18 March 1994.

Virgin on the Ridiculous

Virgin on the Ridiculous.
Again the illustration is by Paul Jermy
and also from the book *The Man Who Ate A Domino*.

DON'T MENTION THE WAR

(The Man Who Ate a Domino, Private, 2002)

Hartlepudlians seem to have had a mixed relationship with the Germans over the years. The animosity element came back into focus when the leader of the council, Bryan Hanson, launched a double-fronted attack upon a kraut – his term, not mine. But before getting into the recent whys and wherefores, let's consider:

1. We once overlooked not the North Sea but the German Ocean.
2. On 16 December 1914 three of the Kaiser's warships pounded Hartlepool and West Hartlepool, slaughtering among others the first serviceman to be killed on British soil in World War I.
3. On 27 November 1916 a zeppelin was shot down over West Hartlepool by Lieutenant I. Pyatt, of No. 36 Squadron, based at Seaton Carew aerodrome. Raids continued until March the following year.
4. Town servicemen gave their lives in two world wars defending their country.
5. Then some Poolies plundered Hitler's yacht, the Grille, when it was docked in West Hartlepool, perhaps exacting some small retribution and restitution.
6. Peace broke out in 1974 when the amalgamated Hartlepool became twinned with Huckelhoven in the German North Rhine-Westphalia region.

Boorish behaviour on holiday and still, one suspects, imperialist ambitions, for some Germans just cause our hackles to rise. Definitely a certain Fred Zeugner got on the wrong side of Councillor Hanson, who, in a stunning verbal assault for someone in so lofty a civic position, referred to the emigree as a "kraut" and accused him of once being in the Hitler Youth. The controversial outburst came after *Hartlepool Mail* reporter Neil Shaefer put to Councillor Hanson an accusation by Herr Zeugner regarding a remark made by the former at the 1996 annual general meeting of City Challenge. Zeugner claimed Hanson refused to answer a question he put and made a reference to bombing buildings. Zeugner told the reporter:

> "I decided to walk out of the meeting, but before I left, I told Councillor Hanson that although I had a German accent, I knew what was going on in Hartlepool because I have lived here for more than 20 years. Councillor Hanson told me 20 years in Hartlepool was nothing compared to his 35 years as a local councillor. I said if I had been in the town that long, I

might also have a building named after me, but Councillor Hanson told me I would have been more likely to bomb it."

The combative councillor then shot the messenger, figuratively, telling young Neil that he stood by his original comments, before firing another salvo:

"I don't expect a kraut to come to Hartlepool and complain about the state of the town. That man is an arrogant pig and I don't know about the Gestapo, but he was probably in the Hitler Youth. I am not anti-German, and I have a lot of German friends. But although this man has lived in Hartlepool for 20 years, he gave the impression that he was anti-British and anti-everything."

At 55, Zeugner was hardly likely to have been aware of the war. He was currently living with his wife Muriel on Hartlepool's Owton Manor estate.

This was all grist for the Tory mill and a *Mail* telephone 'You Decide' phoneline registered 1,143 callers voting for Hanson's resignation and 204 for him to stay. More crucially perhaps, within political and journalistic circles, there has been speculation that a knighthood for Hanson was imminent. Sounds as feasible after this debacle as him being awarded an Iron Cross!
Sources: *Hartlepool*   *Mail*, 14, 15 and
21 May 1996.

Paul Jermy takes a satirical poke at Field Marshall Bryan Hanson, seeing the explosive

council leader as a WWII tank commander routing Erwin Rommel's Afrika Corps.

This is a rare 'original' for this compilation, for it was dropped from the book as Bryan Hanson O.B.E. was such a big-wig on Hartlepool Borough Council, with whom Atkinson the Printer (basically owner of Printability Publishing) did half its total business with the local council. Luckily I had retained a copy of the controversial section and although I did not restore it to the 2002 privately published editions, it is here in all its historic glory. As for Hanson, after a distinguished career in engineering and local government, like Mandelson and the mushy peas and Marianne, Mick and the Mars bar, 'Our Bryan' is nowadays only remembered for calling a German a cabbage ("kraut") and swinehunt ("arrogant pig").

THE 'GAY' GHOST SCAM

By Paul Screeton and Peter McCusker

(*Folklore Frontiers*, No. 25, 1995)

Would you Adam and Eve it? A ghost in Eden Street? This haunting from Horden, County Durham, in 1967 plays a small part in a cautionary tale. Unable to access Peter Underwood's *A to Z Gazetteer of Ghosts*, I have had to 'rely' for information on this beginning of the saga from the ludicrously-titled *World's Great Ghost and Poltergeist Stories* by Sarah Hapgood (Foulsham, 1994). Apparently a miner and his wife were disturbed by inexplicable events at their house and, although reluctant to discuss what happened, called in the local vicar, the Rev T. Matthews, to perform an exorcism. His prayers failed to halt the events and the couple moved out, still reluctant to describe what had occurred, except to say that 'ghostly presences' had made themselves felt.

The scene now turns to our place of employment, *The Mail*, Hartlepool. In case the editor would disapprove of the story which reporter Peter McCusker had written, deputy editor Harry Blackwood allocated the bizarre exclusive the privileged Page 3 lead story slot on 9 December 1994, a Saturday when the editor was having a day off.

Spook keeps stealing my boyfriends – by Peter McCusker

A gay ex-miner says a jealous ghost is chasing away his boyfriends – and has left him for his former lover. Ronnie Pratt, 55, who lives in the Oxford Road area of Hartlepool, says the ghost has been with him since they became friends when he was eight. But the ghost has now left him and is living with Ronnie's former boyfriend. And Ronnie said: "When I get a new man he will come back and chase him away like he did with the last one. He is a good ghost, he is my best friend but all of my life he has chased away my best mates." The former miner says he was born in a haunted house in Eden Street, Horden, and when he was eight the ghost abused him – the house is listed in the A-Z of British ghosts, he says. Ronnie, who worked down Horden pit for 28 years, has lived in seven houses since and he says the ghost has followed him to every one. The father of two from a 28-year marriage, explained how the ghost spooked his former boyfriend so much that he left him. "He was in the house and the lights in the living-room went out and all my hair went on end and he went all shivery. I told him it was the ghost that had done it. "The ghost hasn't got a name, but I know it's a good ghost and I won't have him exorcised, although a priest is coming to the house soon. I know when he is around because I go icy cold. On other occasions the video switches itself off when he is around, and there are other things which have happened which I just cannot speak about." He added: "I am not frightened about coming out and saying I am gay. I lived a lie for 28 years but at the end of the day you are what you are."

Never trust a stranger who comes to you with a story too good to be true – Paul Screeton

So far so good. No comeback from editor Chris Cox. In fact, we all in the editorial department expected great media interest, with the story appearing on television and spread salaciously with smutty headlines in the tabloids. The silence was not only deafening – it was suspicious. I told Peter of my scepticism, and he admitted that what he wrote was, as it turned out, not the whole truth.

RONNIE PRATT ... claimed his life was disrupted by a gay ghost.

<u>This</u> is actually the true story – reveals Peter McCusker

"It had all the ingredients of a brilliant tabloid tale, but it turned out to be a complete non-sense. In fact, a total pack of lies. It all came about because the bloke at the centre of the tale wanted to get back at a man he claimed was a 'rent boy' who had ripped him off financially." Apparently Ronnie Pratt had called at the office twice to tell a tale about the 'rent boy' who stole his money, allegedly. "It was never followed up," said Peter, "so Ronnie came back a third time and mentioned the gay ghost. Now that was a story!" Mr Pratt telephoned after the story's publication to say he was pleased with its presentation. "But the following day the truth came out. Ronnie came into the office to say it was all a pack of lies, concocted to get publicity. His logic was erratic. It had something to do with flushing out this rent boy through publicity." As a postscript, apparently Mr Pratt's family were unhappy with the news story, but an approach to the Press Complaints Commission was thrown out because Pratt himself had approached *The Mail*. Also, Pratt was not born in the haunted [No. 4] Eden Street house – but next door.

Naturally there are other ramifications to this scam. Certainly knowing the scissors and paste nature of much paranormal publishing, although as far as is known it has only been publicised in the *Hartlepool Mail* so far, doubtless the story will do the rounds eventually, each time sup-posedly true, doubtless with embellishments. Yet it was wholly untrue. Journalists are always wary when anyone approaches them: is there an ulterior motive, unseen agenda, manipulation, revenge motive, or whatever? Not that there is any implication here, of course, but a cynical motto goes along the lines of 'never let the facts get in the way of a good story' and never could there be a truer word said than this tale. It was a good story, but not a ghost of factuality. The deputy shot himself in the foot, but the sheriff, sorry editor, would have sensibly spiked the story.

Ronnie Pratt continued to be the subject of controversy. He even made the 'splash' in the *Hartlepool Mail* on 18 September 1999 when he claimed he was beaten up and had his car damaged by 15 'gay bashers' after drinking in a Hartlepool town centre bar. He reported the alleged attack to Hartlepool Police, who appealed for witnesses. He was again in the news the following year when two brothers were sentenced to jail after he had £290 stolen from a bank card and his car wrecked after drinking sessions. (*Hartlepool Mail*, 9 May 2000) And finally, by coincidence, I have discovered by chance that 'England's stately homo' Quentin Crisp's real name was Dennis Pratt. Small (fortean) world

BOOBS & BOOZE!
(Tits out for the folklorists)
(Folklore Frontiers, No. 30, 1997)

Since the days of serving wenches with big busts, taverns have used titillation to encourage trade. Certainly the regulars at Mick Nolan's *Victoria* pub in Batley, West Yorkshire, were falling over themselves to get another round in when a new 22-year-old, six-foot Aussie barmaid called Jade whipped off her shirt to pull pints. But her taxi had dropped her off at the wrong *Victoria* pub, and after a few minutes Mick took pity and told the stunner: "Sorry love, you're in the wrong pub." Mick commented:

> "She bounced through the door and came straight to the bar and said, 'Where do I get changed?' I twigged straight away that she should have been down the road, but I thought it would be a smile for the lads so I said 'upstairs.' She came down topless and got behind the bar. The lads thought it was marvellous. She was really beautiful. I let her serve for a few minutes before I told her that she was at the wrong place. At first she wouldn't believe me, but then she called me a mongrel."

Mick said he might hire topless barmaids in future, while the landlord of the other Vic, Chris Ingram, responded:

> "The regulars were a bit down when Jade didn't turn up. I was pleased when she did. It wasn't her fault. I was angry that the other pub kept her." (*Daily Star,* 1/7/95)

Also in West Yorkshire, but at the *Prince of Wales* in Castleford, two £30-an-hour topless barmaids went on strike when the boiler broke down. Stella Mitchell said: "We were getting so many jokes about cherries and how outstanding we were." Mai Ling added: "When you are just wearing shorts, you can catch a chill in some very unusual places." The strike meant takings plunged, having rocketed in topless times from £30 to £1,500 a night. (*Daily Star,* 27/12/96)

Rather the opposite occurred in Norway, where it was claimed topless barmaids distracted customers from buying beer and caused 'sexual stress' so were to be banned (*Daily Star, The Sun*, 5/7/93) Meanwhile, in Adelaide, Australia, topless barmaids were banned by an Industrial Commission edict, so they wore clown suits to outline the absurdity. (*Aberdeen Press & Journal*, 8/10/92) Now one for the photocopylorists where the familiar line-up was used to advertise the regular go-go dancers at the Queen Anne, Vauxhall, London, by showing 21 different types of girls' knockers **[not reproduced here]**. Most regulars go for 'oranges' said landlady Denise D'Courtenay. Our front cover, however, shows April Glazebrook and you can judge for yourself which are her fruity wares from the 21 shapes. (*The Sport*, 27/9/96)

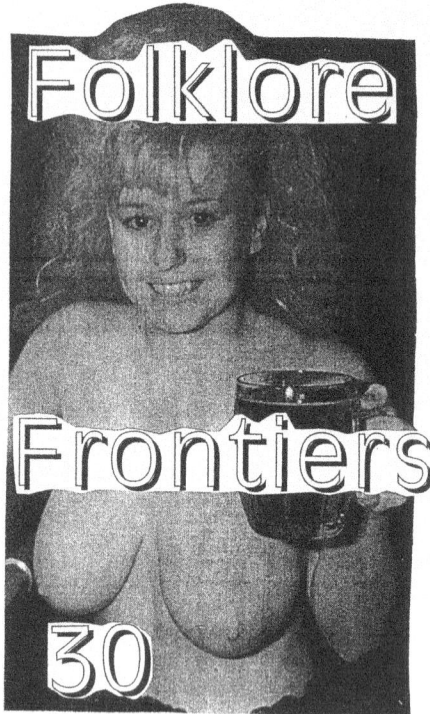

You don't get many of those in a pound! With 'water melons' breasts, April Glazebrook serves up a pint. She graced the cover of *Folklore Frontiers* No. 30. Chest the job!

The telltale 'who refused to be named' gives the game away that the newspaper was desperate for an angle not there when it wrote up a story about a pub where women met weekly after a swimming session and some breast fed their babies. The get-togethers were at the Aunt Sally, Sheffield. (*The Sport*, 1/8/97) But true prudery applies to a woman who grew hairs on her chest as a result of drinking 'more body more taste' Tennent's lager, which caused a flurry of protests in Eire. Displaying a healthy hair growth on her well-developed chest, it was claimed the model and advertisement were sexist and offensive. The 'It will put hairs on your chest' campaign was abandoned. (*Morning Advertiser*, 27/8/93) However, there were no complaints, it seems, when busty Page 3 girl Sarah Hollett peeled off for a red-hot Johnnie Walker whisky commercial when her boobs doubled for sand dunes. (Daily Sport, 12/6/96) But controversy came when Elvira, of TV's sexy *Mistress of the Night*, was dumped from a Coors beer advert because her boobs were too big. Her replacement? *Baywatch* babe Pamela Anderson – hardly flat-chested herself. A Coors executive told Elvira: "We're selling beer, not breasts." Exactly! (*Daily Sport*, 12/6/96) And while on the subject of big tits and advertising, 'face' of Wonderbra, the 34C chest of Eva Herzigova, 24-year-old Czech supermodel, was created she says, on her grandfather's advice that to get big breasts she'd have to drink beer. I've seen better, but... (*News of the World*, 1/5/97) Staying with 34, 34DD-23-35 blonde Page 3 Vicky Lee, after appearing in a Guinness TV commercial said: "Not only do I drink lots of Guinness – I rub it into my breasts. Since I started they have actually grown a lot firmer." (*Sunday Sport*, 17/3/97)

Calm down! Back to the boozers and barmaids who want their 'bee stings' enlarged. Two stories appeared about pint-pullers wanting boob jobs. Joanna Sant, of the *Graziers*, Wakefield, West Yorkshire, (what's it about the former West Riding? Small wonder I chose a wife from there...) had a 'titty kitty' provided from contributions from pubgoers.. (*Daily Sport*, 26.9.95) and Jenny Clark, of the *Queen's Head,* North Kelsey Moor, Lincs., paid £2,500 to expand her 32AA chest into a DD and got her tits out for the lads in the pub. (*The Sport*, 24/3/97)

Large or small? Just as there are opposing opinions on everything, here's a case in point. Girls had to have at least a 36-inch bust to get into the popular *Big and Lovely* nightclub in Sydney, Australia, and bouncers would turn away those who fell short. (*The Sun*, 27/5/96). However, club boss Paul Murray of nightclub *Quids Inn*, Scarborough, North Yorkshire, blamed losses on big boobs. He said:

> "The trouble with big chests is they take up too much space on our 40ft by 20ft dance floor. By allowing small to medium-breasted girls in, I've worked out I can get ten per cent more people on the dance floor."

Topless 37FF model Linsey Dawn McKenzie mocked: "Most men go to nightclubs to look at big-breasted women" (*The Sport*, 3/7/97) and stupid, stingy chauvinist Murray rescinded his mega-boobs ban after 36D-24-34 Adele Stephens, of Wakefield, West Yorkshire, removed her bra in his club and smacked him across the kisser with it. (*The Sport*, 7/7/97)

Anyway, let's look at something more important than sex. Booze. But we'll stick with female anatomy, of course. Moles brewery boss Alan Morgan, of Melksham, Wilts., spotted a pub landlady as a stripper he'd watched in 1987 and named a strong cider after her. "She was wearing no knickers then," he said, "so the name for the new cider came to me in a flash – Black Rat." So get ratarsed, I say. (*Daily Sport*, 25/2/95) Staying with the naming game, Steve Madley was promoting a 'cask-conditioned Czech pilsner' from, er, Burntisland, Fife. Near Rosyth naval facility, it had the name Dockyard Rivets, but actually all is not as it seems, for the name was local slang for a woman's nipples. (*The Sport*, 31/1/97; *What's Brewing*, February, 1997) Also, an Australian beer was named Elle Ale after the top Oz model, Elle Macpherson, for being 'well-endowed with abundant flavour and possesses a marvellous body.' (*The Sun, Daily Star*, 4/8/93)

Surely all folklorists of worth will have noted a recent explosion in two sectors. One is the upsurge of moral panics; the other is the proliferation of new traditions, with the derided and sadly neglected by the folklorist mainstream and forteans alike tabloid *The Sport* [aka *Daily Sport*] at the forefront. As demonstrated by its frequency in references here, this really is required reading, despite the salacious adverts. Do I suspect Whitehousian prudery, perhaps?

Chastisement over, boobs and booze crazes next:

1) Shotgunning. The rules are: get super-strength lager – shake 'til ready to explode – hammer a nail in – gulp as fast as you can – have sex on motorway bridge in public. (*Daily Sport*, 25/5/94)
2) Nippleprinting. Blackpool pubs and clubs supply colours from black to day-glo and girls paint a nipple and press it to a card to send back home. (*Daily Sport*, 7/5/96)
3) Gar-ts. A crack team of topless beauties was touring pubs and clubs with a wacky new version of 501 darts called gar-ts. They chucked frozen garfish – imagine miniature swordfish – at the dartboard. (*Sunday Sport*, 3/12/05)
4. Strip-'r'-oke. A naughty Nineties version of karaoke, brain (if that's the word) child of Manchester comic Scully, where people strip to their favourite song. (*Daily Star*, 17/6/94)

Also novel was a wacky decorating job where a pub toilet was papered with *Sport* stunnas. I trust the regulars at the *Queen's Head*, Wing, Beds., only had a leak or a dump and nothing Onanistic! (*The Sport*, ?/9/97)   And lastly, Hollywood heartthrob Johnny Depp puts his liking for alcohol and tobacco down to a lack of breastfeeding when he was a child. "Breast deprivation can lead to a fondness for alcohol," he diagnosed. (*Daily Sport*, 12/6/93)

My magazine *Folklore Frontiers* has proudly flaunted pulchritude at every opportunity. Non-PC, anti-matriarchal and proudly sexist, male readers have complained jokingly when the nipple count lowers and reader Lucy Fisher, without my encouragement, even wrote to disclose her vital statistics (unfortunately there was no accompanying photo to authenticate her claim). In fact, the only complaints have been women readers wanting hunky fella shots and a sour missive from *Pipes of Pan* magazine. At the time I was trying to interest publishers in a project for a book to be entitled *Tits Out for the Lads*, for which this was a sample, being Chapter Eight of the potential breast-seller. Their loss is your gain as it forms an 'out-take' here, too.

PART EIGHT
URBAN MYTHS & MEDIA
MONITORING

INTRODUCTION

This preamble has been necessary to introduce my first foray into urban myths and breaks my usual convention in this book of providing both fore and after contextualisations, whose purpose will become self-evident, I hope. The chosen article here is one of my 'Long Man of Wilmington' columns published in *The Ley Hunter* shortly after I handed over the reins to Paul Devereux. I selected it for inclusion as it not only shows my naïveté in 1978 regarding such tales, but because although I was making tentative steps towards a full-blown, over-arching focus upon contemporary legend to the almost complete exclusion of earth mysteries and traditional folklore, the academic study of urban belief tales was itself only in its infancy and I would respectfully suggest currently at a remedial stage compared with the dogged, committed and perceptive amateurs studying, analysing and cataloguing the material. But this is par for the course with any discipline: trust me, I've been a hobbyist activist modern antiquarian. So, here's my novice's attempt at comprehending the strange world that is the enigmatic apocryphal.

ELEPHANTS, PENGUINS AND A COSMIC CHAMELEON?

(The Ley Hunter, No. 79, 1978)

T wo recent books dealing with UFOs and psychism both stress that these related phenomena seem to deliberately create a large percentage of these occurrences to appear absurd to the sceptic. [1, 2] A great deal of basic folklore of the 'faery' variety shares this in common. It is as if we are part of a bizarre game of hide and seek the cosmic riddle, being manipulated into false cul-de-sacs, largely at the mercy of the phenomena, and each time a new breakthrough appears to have gained us ground, we face a chameleon response.

It has occurred to me during writing my book *The Living Stones* **[on folklore associated with megaliths and other prehistoric structures – Janet & Colin Bord and L.V. Grinsell, separately just beat me to the post, so it remained unpublished]** that the reductionist approach to the traditions of the megaliths may be too simple as applied, say, in *The Secret Country*, [3] yet alternately, that as we have concentrated increasingly upon what appears valid folklore there has begun a noticeable reaction to sow the seeds of doubt about folklore's value and cast it into the realm of ridicule and fantasy. I hardly think I am alone in finding myself an involuntary spectator in this process. Though seemingly unrelated to the earth mysteries, I believe we are witnessing a new breed of tale designed perhaps to confuse our reaction to folklore. The three motifs I wish to discuss may cause us to reconsider the perspective of folklore, its living and evolving nature, and ask the question as to its relevance, for these three engender characteristics which may give clues as to the mechanism of the phenomena. They are:

A)   The Destructive Elephant;
B)   The Smuggled Penguin; and
C)   The Stolen Corpse.

I first came across this as a small boy when a circus was in Hartlepool for a week and the Mini car had just been introduced. It was claimed that as the elephants were being led to the Big Top, one mistook the small, brightly-painted car for its performance platform and mounted and squashed the vehicle. The irate owner was then stopped by a policeman on his way home and asked to explain the damage. The officer found the tale implausible. In a different guise, the motif reappeared when a councillor repeated to me a story a friend of a friend told him as to a family in a safari park who trapped an elephant's trunk by winding up a car's window and the distressed beast did a fair bit of damage before its release. Again the law is involved, armed with a breathalyser, which is used (and proves positive) when the hapless driver's explanation for the damage proves far-fetched. The story was written up by a colleague. [4]

This colleague also chose to regale readers with how he was among many in the media to have followed up Flamingo Park Zoo's infamous penguin story. The zoo's Mr Kevin Taylor explained that the penguin in question which had been taken away and found suffering from heat in a duffle bag was, in fact, a Penguin biscuit. Our chief reporter being one of a long line of journalists since March checking this item of rampant folklore. [5] It may be only coincidence, but Penguin biscuits are a minor element of the Hexham Heads saga. [6]

This tale has a healthy pedigree and is well documented in a scholarly work, [7] recorded universally since 1963, and according to the book it originated in Leeds, was later (separately) being collected by a Leeds University student and was recorded in Copenhagen by Bengt Holbek (a district of Leeds is Holbeck!). I heard last year of a Hartlepool man who had relations on holiday in Ireland whose companion died, and, being in a remote area, wrapped the corpse in a carpet, put it on the car roof-rack and drove it to the nearest police station, where whilst reporting the death, the car was stolen and neither car nor corpse was ever seen again. Last week the chief sub-editor announced that a couple had an identical experience, except that the stopping point was a bar in Spain. It had happened a couple of months previously and so was regarded as un-newsworthy and anyway actual names were not known.

From such tales, I wonder whether there is a calculated conspiracy to confuse and cause us to condemn folklore in general and the megalithic tradition as part of this?

References:

1 Stephen Jenkins, *The Undiscovered Country*, Spearman, 1977
2. Jacques Vallee, UFOs: *The Psychic Solution*, Panther, 1973
3. Janet & Colin Bord, *The Secret Country*, Elek, 1973
4. 'A Day He'll Never Forget,' *Mail,* Hartlepool, 22/8/77
5. 'The Day we Were Had By A Penguin,' *Mail,* Hartlepool, 11/7/77
6. Paul Screeton, 'Heads & Tales, *The Ley Hunter*, No. 77, 1977
7. Katharine Briggs & Ruth Tongue, *Folktales of England*, Routledge & Kegan Paul, 1965

Once I felt I had sufficient grasp of contemporary legend my ambition fell to getting a book into print on the subject. On reflection, I was at that stage way out of my depth, but I was keen, willing to listen and learn and brimful with enthusiasm both for the subject matter and the project to get myself into print. During 1978, somehow I came into contact with a BBC film editor, Richard Seel. We agreed to collaborate on a book and he provided a great deal of analytical material through correspondence and meeting once in London when I

was fortuitously on a course; our abortive book on contemporary legend having the working title *Rumours*. By 1980 it became clear we were too divided, both in terms of approach and style and at Richard's instigation went our separate ways. I heard from him again briefly in 1986, when I started publishing *Folklore Frontiers* and he was in the last throes of writing a book on fatherhood for Gateway Books. I ploughed on alone, even receiving encouragement from some publishers, but the appearance of Jan Harold Brunvand's first book in 1983 damned my efforts in their eyes. I had even had the idea of presenting my material in a format similar to the popular *Phenomena*, by Bob Rickard and John Michell, to which ends I approached John as a possible collaborator. On 18 January 1982, John replied: 'Thanks for your offer to share *Rumours*. I'm tempted but don't feel activated yet — other things now on." My motto could have been these lines by Alexander Pope:

> '*The flying rumours gathr'd as they rolled,*
> *Scarce any tale was sooner heard than told;*
> *And all who told it added something new,*
> *And all who heard it made enlargements too.*'

I plodded on determinedly and by 1987 the work-in-progress had a new title, *Autohenge*, reflecting the primary role motor cars play in modern lore and the 'henge' part my dogged wish to incorporate traditional folklore associated with prehistoric sites. The cover would have been a US sculpture of cars made to look like Stonehenge. An alternative title was *Paradise by the Dashboard Light*, in honour of the Meatlaof song and showing how themes of cars and sex are central motifs to urban myths. Bob Rickard had agreed in principle to publish it as part of his Fortean Tomes venture. Sadly by 1989, financial resources could not be found to progress the book: although Bob kept faith with the project by seeking a separate publisher and editing commission, but to no avail. When it became obvious no publishing deal was forthcoming, I concentrated on publishing the material I was writing and analysing in a new magazine of my own, *Folklore Frontiers*. Here I could also indulge my interest in publishing and broadcast media material (so akin to folklore as generally perceived), often contributing to *Dear Mr Thoms* and its successor, *Letters to Ambrose Merton*: two other forum magazines which dealt with such subjects as moral indignation, tabloid alarmism, social panics, revenge, photocopylore and so on. I also share those magazine editors' interest in media monitoring, popular belief and contemporary custom, particularly mock mayors. As I write this, *FF* has been going since 1985 and reached issue 65, my age.

My faith in my ability to write successfully about contemporary legend has since been vindicated with my groundbreaking hybrid book of railways and folklore, the popular *Crossing the Line: Trespassing on railway weirdness*, and the highly-acclaimed yet unremunerative collection of essays which focussed upon named celebrities rather than nameless foafs (the general anonymous friend-of-a-friend urban myth convention), *Mars Bar & Mushy*

Peas. Along with my homage to a counterculture hero, John *Michell: From Atlantis to Avalon*, these formed a loose trio published by Bob Trubshaw's Heart of Albion Press (though strictly speaking the latter came from his Alternative Albion imprint). Speaking on the phone to Bob one afternoon on a totally unrelated matter, he asked what I was working on and I shared my tribulations, whereby my pet project of the moment was being deemed too railway slanted by folklore specialists and railway publishing houses baulked at the folklore content. Bob showed an interest and to make a comparison, just as Rick Rubin revitalised Johnny Cash's career, Bob did the same in reversing my fortunes. HoAP is still functioning but on a more limited scale and Bob has aspirations in the direction of documentary film making, for which I wish him well and am eternally grateful for his faith, guidance and friendship.

DUBIOUS TRANSMISSIONS

(Fortean Times, No. 67, 1993)

The congregation in an Oslo church were halfway through singing the hymn *Nearer My God to Thee* when they heard a voice booming, "Get ready for take-off." The church's electronic organ had, by a technical freak, picked up an air control tower 13 miles away. As with many stories we read in newspapers, this one is doubtless apocryphal. As a collector of modern folklore, I have dubbed this motif the 'dubious transmission.' Forteana deals with the anomalous, and the rare but feasible act of one piece of machinery being activated by another is not impossible. An oft-repeated tale concerns a woman whose teeth begin to play music. Electronics experts would deduce that a radio signal was being picked up by her gold and amalgam fillings, combined with saliva acid, creating a primitive crystal set. These could very well be true stories. I will shortly place this in context, but would like to draw attention to modern folklorists' methodology when confronted with such a claim.

One has only to look at a recent issue of *Dear Mr Thoms*, a modern folklore miscellany, covering alien big cats, travelling garden gnomes and the kitten in a spin-dryer. Academic folklorists seem too ready to place all manner of themes common to forteans – such as ice falls, 'Saharan' dust, entombed toads, rat kings, spontaneous human combustion – within the contemporary folklore canon. They seem reluctant to consider anomalies as true and repeating events of phenomenal reality; and they make no attempt to ascertain the veracity of unlikely events aired by the media. We can put this down to prejudice or intellectual laziness; perhaps any truth would be too uncomfortable to face.

The American guru of urban belief tales, Jan Harold Brunvand, has gone to some lengths to seek historical antecedents for today's popular legends. I would suggest that not only do all contemporary stories have examples going back centuries (prehistoric Jack and Jill went up the hill to fetch a pail of water – from a Neolithic dewpond) but that every 'new' motif which surfaces in the media, however bizarre or unlikely, will eventually be played out in reality.

To return to our 'dubious transmission' motif, the majority of tales cluster around three key elements of both life and lore. These are sex, religion and travel. All three are essential for our well-being and we might ask whether it is wise or necessary to attempt an analysis of which tales are 'true' and which 'apocryphal.'

Dipping into my files, I find religion and sex often feature together. For instance, fans of a hot-gospel show could hardly believe their eyes when a technical hitch gave them a torrid treat of topless beauties as viewers were preparing to join in the closing hymn, *Something Good is Going to Happen to You*. In another version, evangelist Oral Roberts was replaced by Lolita, Rita and Amazon and other girls for several minutes, supposedly due to a satellite malfunction. Churches keep cropping up in these stories. A couple were about to take their vows when from the organ speakers boomed a voice observing, "They're bloody well still in the bloody church." The newly-weds complained to Tameside Consumer Forum, Greater Manchester, that the taxi driver's lookout had spoiled the ceremony and officials were consequently preparing a code of practice. Then there was the interruption at St Martin's, Grimsby, Humberside, "The Lord is my ... Rubber Duck calling Balsa Bandit." The voice belonged to a Citizen's Band enthusiast broadcasting in the area and the organ amplifiers acted as a receiver.

The next two tales involve vehicles and the travel element extends to Brazilian Formula 1 Grand Prix ace Ayrton Senna. Racing along at 150mph, his newly-fitted helmet phone was meant to keep him in touch with his back-up team, but an instruction came over for fast food. "I'm already going as fast as I can," he supposedly responded upon hearing a request for the speedy delivery of six hamburgers, having intercepted a call from a Brands Hatch catering firm. Messages from taxis, police and CB have been picked up from fruit machines at four different pubs according to my files; and I have clippings of such other receivers as radios, baby alarms, double-glazing, Jimi Hendrix at the Isle of Wight pop festival and a shop's electronic cash register which would burst out with Elvis Presley's *Love Me Tender*. Then there are sexually-explicit broadcasts interrupting at vulnerable locations such as ambulance stations and air traffic control points.

Another occasionally newsworthy event is the innocent video with an incongruous insertion, usually unadulterated pornography. Particularly fortean in its irony was the evidently bona fide case of toothpaste giant Colgate Palmolive. Customers saved coupons from toothpaste tubes for a free two-hour cassette containing a ten-minute film encouraging children to clean their teeth. One of the 160,000 who received a copy realised it was a blue film and took the cassette to Lothian Region Trading Standards office. She had received one of 50 copies of *Dracula Sucks* accidentally dispatched. The evil aristocrat was seen in a sex romp with the inmates of a lunatic asylum. Colgate apologised and blamed the London firm which copies the film on to cassettes. Was this embarrassing episode an example of another familiar motif – the 'employee's revenge?' As they almost say, there's nowt so queer as folklore...

The motif of 'dubious transmissions' seems curiously dated nowadays and absent from media apocrypha – casting a question mark over each and every earlier example, as both transmitters and receivers are still very much part of our everyday lives – but not the aspect where folklore becomes reality, fiction becomes fact. As shown, although then a relative newcomer to the contemporary legend field, I had even earlier worked out for myself the prevalence of the concept which had been termed by academics as ostension. In my study of urban belief tales *Mars Bar & Mushy Peas*, I extended the range recognised by serious folklorists to identify additional sub-variants. Here I also identified a new genre which I named satirismus, whereby a story concocted as satire by the media regarding a celebrity becomes accepted and repeated as gospel by naïve plagiarists: Mariah Carey admiring the thinness of famine victims but not envying their being bothered by flies; John Major tucking his shirt into his underpants (Alistair Campbell's only scoop, unfortunately his own fictional canard); and Sarah Palin boasting of her international knowledge as she could see Russia from her Alaskan home. (For an updated take on what was discussed here, see Interlude – Three)

YOU GET A BETTER CLASS OF APOCYPHA IN BROADSHEETS

(*Letters to Ambrose Merton*, No. 17, 1999; *Folklore Frontiers*, No. 37, 2000)

The argument I will put forward is hardly contentious, but I feel it will be salutary to consider the differing quality of contemporary legends in broadsheet and tabloid newspapers. In fact, broadsheet diary columns are particularly fertile ground for a patrician style of apocrypha.

Take, if you will, this story about Derry Irvine, the Lord Chancellor. He was at the *Garrick Club* for dinner and summoned a waitress. "We'll have the lamb chops. And two bottles of claret," he requested. With his bold order he would not have to bother her again. After chatting for an hour, he was hungry and parched. "Look here," he exclaimed to the passing waitress, "I ordered lamb chops and claret – two bottles." Waitress: "Very well, sir," and returned with lamb chops and a brace of carafes – all to replace those Irvine had already consumed, doubtless too excited extolling the virtues of New Labour to notice. [1]

The Times diarist Andrew Yates continued his posh name dropping with a tale from the *Travellers Club* in Pall Mall. The grand old man of English Catholicism, Monsignor Gilbey, was ascending the stairs when he encountered the Queen Mother. "How nice to meet you," she ventured, as she descended. "I believe that we are the same age." The stooped old man dismissively retorted, "Don't be ridiculous, the only person the same age as me is the Queen Mother." Coming up, another unlikely Queen Mother yarn Yates recounts is her becoming partial to helicopter travel. "The chopper has transformed my life – even more than that of Anne Boleyn," she observed wryly. I used the word 'unlikely' expressly because the nonagenarian royal is supposed to have little or no ability for making witty remarks. The only previous quip attributed to her came when two effeminate lackeys were quarrelling and she proclaimed that, "This old queen would like some service."

From clubland to theatrical anecdotes, which Frank Johnson [2] utilised with some aplomb to flesh out his notebook column. Firstly, the late actor-manager had sacked from his company the actor playing Seton, who has scarcely more than one line, "The Queen, my lord is dead."

When Donald Wolfit, as Macbeth, asked the question as to the monarch's health in that evening's performance, the aggrieved actor replied, "The Queen, my lord, is very much better." Secondly, was one told to him about Wilfred Lawton, the actor renowned for being the worse for wear on stage. As he entered as Richard III, a voice from the audience cried: "You're drunk." He responded: "True, but wait until you've seen the Duke of Clarence." Thirdly, still working in his eighties, Bransby Williams tended to forget his lines. In some thriller, when the 'phone rang had had to pick it up. He forgot what he had to say, so he cunningly passed the receiver to another member of the cast with the words, "It's for you." Last thespian anecdote: an actor called Ralph Michael, who was playing Gloucester in *King Lear*, had a row with the actor playing Cornwall, who asks Gloucester, "Where hast thou sent the King?," to which the reply is "Dover." But that night the truculent thesp replied, "Margate."

However, I reckon TV inquisitor Jeremy Paxman managed four items of apocrypha in one column.[3] Here's your starter. Mistaken identity was the theme and boozy Sixties Foreign Secretary George Brown the culprit. The legend goes that he was once at a diplomatic reception in South America. The room was awash with admirals and generals in gold braid, diplomats, ministers and many of the most beautiful women in the country. As the band struck up a particularly jaunty tune, Brown glimpsed a vision in purple across the room. Swaying tipsily, he approached and asked, "I wonder if I could have the honour of the next dance." The frosty reply was, "No, for three reasons. First, you're drunk. Second, this is the Peruvian National Anthem. And third, I am the Cardinal-Archbishop of Lima." Paxo, pushing likelihood near the limits, then claimed he got confused with motoring guru Jeremy Clarkson. One morning he awoke to the sound of a mighty roaring outside the house. "Brought the Aston Martin," said the man in overalls who rang the bell. The presenter then regaled readers with anecdotes of people recognising and then insulting him, ending with one person's profundity, "Are you who you think you are?" Lastly, he reported a royal belief tale which I'm sure I first read in *Private Eye*. When King Constantine was being brought into the Television Centre for an interview early one morning, the driver explained to the security guard on the gate, "I've got the King of Greece in the back." The guard consulted his clipboard, found no note of the scheduled arrival, poked his head into the car and asked, "Where did you say you were king of, mate?"

At the other extreme, national and local tabloids, and Tyne Tees Television, had a field day when it leaked out that my drinking buddy George Scott had held a 'party for his penis' in the *Station Hotel*, Seaton Carew, the night before he had an operation for cancer. Happily for Scotty, all has seemingly gone pretty well, but it has taken Viagra to perk him up fully. Actually, the point of this story is that there is no point; George was not rendered impotent (bet you're glad, Diane!) and it was a gratuitous tabloid tale about a willy and a serious illness; and the broadsheets would certainly have baulked here. But it has relevance as a folklife talking point with elements suggestive all may not be as presented. I'll say no more. A more sober slant on Viagra stories is typified by this broadsheet treatment of US authorities. Mimicking the old pilots' dictum of 'eight hours from the bottle to the throttle," telling aircrew not to take Viagra within six hours of flying because it might impair their ability to distinguish blue and green in cockpit lights and on taxi-ways. Some airlines are already ahead of them with pilots banned from using the drug for 24 hours before flying, through awareness of reports that Viagra makes three per cent of those using it see through a blue haze. [4]

Meanwhile, the tabloids will treat us to stories of hoax army conscription call-ups, poop-scoop dog-dirt thefts, foul-mouthed aural simulacra, collapsing hypothermic shoplifters, couples stuck in sexual congress, pet dogs being in reality sewer rats, swapped samples showing men are pregnant, forgetful boxers entering the ring without shorts, and so on.

References:

1.   *The Times Weekend*, 9 January 1999
2.   *The Daily Telegraph*, 16, 23 and 30 January 1999
3.   *The Sunday Telegraph Magazine*, 21 October 1998
4.   *The Sunday Telegraph*, 1 November 1998

SNIPS AND NITS:
A BECKHAM'S TALE
(Letters to Ambrose Merton, No. 23, 2000)

An astonished nation awoke on 18 March 2000 to devastating front page news. Tabloid headlines of sufficient size as to report the Queen's Mum's death or a military coup in the UK horrified breakfasting Britain. 'Skinhead Beckham' screamed *The Mirror* [1] and 'Short Beck N' Sides' shouted *The Sun.* [2] Fed-up Manchester United ace David Beckham, it was claimed, had given his flamboyant hairstyle the chop. According to *The Mirror*, the reason for the dramatic Number One crewcut was that Manchester United's midfield maestro was sick of fans copying his floppy hairstyle. *The Sun* blamed the flyaway nature of the bottle-blond mane.

The 24-year-old had the most influentially-shattering clip since Biblical era Samson (team, position and age unknown; WAG Delilah) on 16 March. In modern-day Manchester, a stylist named Tyler of Vidal Sassoon cut the famous locks. He had driven 300 miles from London to spend ten minutes snipping the hair and charged £25million-priced Becks £300. A friend of Beckham reportedly told *The Mirror*: "David is extremely uncomfortable at the idea of being some sort of fashion icon who (sic) people copy. He's a professional sportsman, not a model." Which explains why he was wearing a sarong in 1998 and wore a bandana to a top London event last year.

Folklore spin-offs to this dramatic event included rival Leicester United fans poking fun by wearing 'baldilocks' headgear and a panic sweeping salons which feared it would cost businesses millions in lost revenue (a copy of Becks' old style cost £55, whereas the new one was a mere £6). [3] A football culture course is to be held at the University of Staffordshire, where course lecturer Professor Ellis Cashmore said: "Beckham has become the icon of icons. We may even begin to gauge our times by his haircut ... Nobody embodies the spirit of our times as well as David Beckham." [4] Wife Victoria, aka Posh Spice, has also just had a new hairstyle. Not dissimilar to the new image of Sporty Spice, aka Melanie Chisholm, it has been cropped spiky and bleached.

Every news story has its own lifespan and diarist Ian Hyland rebooted Becks' new look by claiming the shorn soccer star had wanted to look as tough an alpha human male as possible for when he met a pair of tigers. According to his less than impressed team-mates, Becks took his family on a secret visit to a wildlife park near Victoria's parents' home in Hertfordshire on 19 March. Brave Becks, if you believe the story, persuaded the keepers to allow him inside the Tiger House to feed the beasts close up. [5]

But there is another version to all this which *Letters to Ambrose Merton* can exclusively reveal. According to legend in Hartlepool, when the Beckhams' son Brooklyn had his first birthday party, the proud parents were horrified to find one of the guests – age and gender unspecified – had head lice. In reaction to this taboo topic, Victoria had a bleached cut so as to kill any nits and both father and toddler had crewcuts to rid them of possible infestation. And how could I know this? My wife Pauline's hairdresser told her so. [6] At the time, Hartlepool was in the grip of a nits panic of epic proportions. It began in early March and included tales of a woman humiliated after being asked to attach samples of lice to a sticky tape, while another parent hit out at a headteacher who was alleged to have used the same brush to 'tidy-up' a group of pupils' hair. A public meeting and clinics followed. The nits headache almost made national news when a television crew from Channel 4's *Big Breakfast* show, with Richard Bacon, were to speak initially to passers-by about the town's nightmarish outbreak and ask people to test out possible solutions. However, they switched the topic at the last moment to discuss the sale of British car company Rover to German BMW and instead stopped car owners for their views. [7]

Meanwhile, calls for 'Nitty Nora' to return were turned down as head lice clinics did a roaring trade. My wife and daughter were on a packed bus to Middlesbrough at this time and could find no alternative seats to get away from a couple in front with hair swarming with creepy-crawlies. But what was regarded as an epidemic may also have betrayed elements of social panic. At a public meeting, health officials stressed the monkey-hanging fame town was not the Nits Capital of the Universe, but that the problem was nationwide.

Anyway, my lady hairdresser had not heard any head lice and Beckham rumours unfortunately, but I'm sure this contemporary legend connection surfacing in Hartlepool will not be the only place where it has been heard. Oh, and if you're interested, I had a Number Two on the sides, a Number Three on top and its cost was £3.50, plus 50p tip. A snip at the price!

References:

1. *The Mirror*, 18 March 2000
2. *The Sun*, 18 March 2000
3. *Sunday Mirror*, 19 March 2000
4. *Daily Sport*, 30 March 2000
5. *Sunday Mirror*, 26 March 2000
6. Pauline Screeton in conversation with Janet of *Spirals*, Elwick Road, Hartlepool, 23 March 2000
7. *Hartlepool Mail*, 17 March 2000

ALCOTOTS AND TELETUBBIES:
TWO NEW MORAL PANICS
(Letters to Ambrose Merton, No. 12, 1997)

C ertain adults are in a lather over two very different phenomena creating a moral panic. On the one hand, popular alcopop drinks are either a cynical manipulation or a response to a perceived market, whichever view you prefer, but no doubt seriously and successfully market-tested in advance of mass advertising. As for the equally popular Teletubbies, they have been accused of childishness (though aimed primarily not at teens or adults, but nursery-age kiddies) and drug culture stigma. Not much difference there then. Now one of the *Teletubbies* programme actors has been sacked and the media, with its blurring of news and entertainment, almost suggested Tinky Winky itself had been given a P45. As for alcopops, purely for research purposes, you understand, my wife and I have just consumed the contents of a bottle of strawberry-flavoured Two Dogs. Very nice, too.

Before we go any further, you do know why it is so named? If not, its origination – a rude joke – goes like so. This Native American – bugger political correctness – this Red Indian lad, he asked his father how he got his name. "Well, son," said the brave sternly, "When your sister was born we looked out of the tepee and a bird was flying overhead, so we called her Little White Dove. When your brother was born, we looked out of the tepee and saw this grizzly passing by so we called him Running Bear. Anyway, why do you want to know, Two Dogs Fucking?"

So where did this agent to screw up our kids come from? Like with all the worst programmes on TV, blame Oz. One lonely lemon farmer in South Australia, sitting on a glut of lemons one harvest time, ultimately became responsible for an internationally-successful drink category. The hapless farmer's next-door neighbour was an extrovert businessman, Duncan McGillivary, who was running pubs at the time and reckoned he and his mate could make a killing from the excess lemons by creating an alcoholic drink. Naming it Two Dogs after the punchline of that joke was another stroke of marketing genius, but proved to provide a moralistic backlash – and even more publicity. Another interesting twist in the saga came when of all the guardians of right-wing fundamentalism *The Daily Telegraph* coined the term 'alcopop,' so disproving the adage that an earnest broadsheet journalist cannot think tabloidese. (See *The Licensee and Morning Advertiser*, 22 April 1996). Even the cynical drinks industry seems to have been caught on the hop (no pun intended) with alcopops' popularity. The cognoscenti liked what they were drinking, but already an apocryphal tale was circulating. Heaven forbid some consumers, it was suggested, were under the legal drinking age. Seduced, so the argument ran, in that this new tranche of demon drink was packaged as lemonade or cola or something else equally harmless aimed at their as yet inchoate palates. While self-appointed moral guardians pressed hard upon the panic button, commonsense rules that no responsible landlord would risk his licence to sell to minors, though off-licence proprietors might take a calculated risk. But it is hardly a horror scenario.

However, we do have at least one case where the clean-up brigade felt justified by the fears. Tragic Graham Bailey and pals were celebrating a 15th birthday party, bought alcopops but also, let's emphasise, lager and spirits. They guzzled Hooch in a Lancashire hotel, before Graham was killed on a railway crossing on his way home. "Alcopops are a killer. Without them our boy would be alive," condemned his mother disingenuously. I heartily applaud and endorse the writer of the editorial in *The Sun* (26 June 1997) whose perspective is spot on:

> 'You can't blame alcopops for the death of Graham Bailey. You can blame the criminally stupid landlord who served a lad of 14 with Hooch. And irresponsible parents who watched underage kids drink. Who holds 15th birthday parties in pubs anyway?'

I would be being naïve, however, not to feel such names as Bliss, Squeal, Kinky and Bullshit are not aimed at an immature section of consumers, perhaps even underage alcotots. Merrydown bemoaned the fact that its hope of salvation, Two Dogs, had slumped in the face of no fewer than 90 rival alcopops. (*Daily Telegraph*, 12 July 1997). Nevertheless, alcopops have revitalised the drinks industry, becoming the fastest growing alcoholic beverage in retail history, worth an estimated £375m this year. With an average alcohol content of five per cent they are stronger than most beers. (*Sunday Times*, 22 June 1997). At one point it looked as if the Blair government was going to legislate on alcopops but it had lost its bottle. One M.P., Nigel Waterson, made news for the folklorists when he unwittingly swallowed an urban myth, hook, line and sinker. He called for a complete alcopops ban when a bottle of such was allegedly put in a schoolgirl's lunchbox by her grandma with dire consequences. Teachers sent the girl home from lessons when she began staggering and gulping down the alcoholic lemonade with her sandwiches.

> 'This poor woman saw only a brightly packaged lemonade bottle. She put it in her granddaughter's packed lunch... and the first she knew of her mistake was when the girl was sent home from school when she was staggering. The only answer is a total ban. Who other than children would want these drinks?' (*Daily Star*, 13 June 1997)

Who indeed would want to follow in the fictitious footsteps of the figment of this ludicrous parliamentarian's addled imagination, assuming with scant assurance that he himself had not been at Two Dogs and more? Well, my thirty-something son-in-law wants them and stacks our fridge with alcopops. I would reckon a fair proportion of the 90-odd variations have passed through his liver for analysis.

Age is also a prime factor in the TV *Teletubbies* debate. My grandson is 20 months old and loves them. Should fifty-somethings like me be involving ourselves in such a trivial matter because it has raised hackles in certain quarters? Basically the programme supposedly insults the intelligence of pre-nursery age kiddies. Is that why it has achieved cult status among undergraduates? Then there is the suggestion that its makers are on drugs and seducing youngsters into such a culture. Shades of the sexual innuendo supposedly in the earlier children's programme *Captain Pugwash*, with the alleged characters Seaman Stains, Master Bates and Roger the Cabin Boy.

For anyone just arrived from Mars, the Teletubbies are Tinky Winky, Laa-Laa, Dipsy and Po, who are targeted at those aged ten months to five years. The BBC has invested a staggering £8m of licence payers' money commissioning 260 programmes of toddler talk. The fiscal freakout has gone on their Tubbytronic Superdrome, a spaceship under Astroturf, and a virtual reality landscape with live rabbits and a sun made of a baby's face. (*You*, 6 July 1997). Creator Anne Wood describes them as 'technological babies' (*Hartlepool Mail*, 14 August 1997) but mothers have deluged the viewers' feedback programme *Points of View* with accusations that the BBC is turning children into morons. A Po-faced debate was carried out in *Radio Times* and one Sunday broadsheet into whether the characters were subversive symbols of exactly what parents fear their children will become if they watch too much TV, 'small zombies with pale faces and poor language skills who have ingested the television screen.' Crazy, isn't it, or as Teletubbies' spokesman Tinky Winky commented: "Biddle, biddle, boddle." (*Night and Day*, 3 August 1977).

Outraged mothers have three options it seems:

One: It holds no interest for adults preferring to watch *The Big Breakfast*, so TV reviewer Stephen Pile suggested *Teletubbies* could be much improved and popularised by the inclusion of a beefcake hunk in a skimpy G-string to divert the mothers' attention from the contentious babytalk. He added: 'Such a character would pass unnoticed [by children] in the already bizarre environment of the Teletubbies, but what would we call him? Tinky Winky has already been taken.' (*Daily Telegraph*, 5 May 1997). Despite parents, the combined audience for the two daily screenings has swelled to at least two million (ironically, under-fours are not counted in these surveys). (*The Sun*, 2 August 1997).

Two: It is uneducational because the Teletubbies do not speak properly, saying "Harro" and "Wossat?" But it is geared not to pre-school but pre-language children; the repetition harnessing their stage of development.

Three: It looks as if the creators are on drugs. That's par for the course. As Pile observed,

'Whoever thought up Andy Pandy was smashed out of his head.' Were drugs behind *The Wombles* and *The Magic Roundabout*? Dylan the hippie rabbit. I rest my case. Think of Bill and Ben's 'Blobalop.' Was the three-in-a-bed Little Weed a veiled reference even in the 1950s to a herbal high? And the Clangers chase the Soup Dragon...

The psychedelic rainbow shower of colour and light spurted by the windmill sets off gurgles of unseemly pleasure in the Teletubbies, observes 'Couch Potato,' the anonymous television critic of *Private Eye*. 'As they pick up the signal on their aerials, they grab their haunches, moan slightly and roll their eyes up into their foreheads; hard-hitting documentaries on heroin addiction are rarely this explicit... After awhile, of course, you are actively looking for evidence of pharmaceutical enhancement' (*Private Eye*, 15 May 1997). Couch Potato also suggested that the dog-cum vacuum cleaner, NuNu, had perhaps worked in advertising since its nose-nozzle suggested cocaine abuse. And just as you thought that the Teletubbies analysis could get no more absurd, along comes the Rev Alan Garrow, of Waltham Abbey, Essex, who sees their talk as having parallels with Charismatic Christian language: 'They have their own idiolect built around their name, 'tubbiecustard' for example. This reminds us of the religious jargon often used by Christians.' He also claimed that the programme demonstrated rituals to Church liturgical actions; the Teletubbies' group hugs being reminiscent of demonstrations of peace in Anglican services. (Daily Telegraph, 16 August 1977).

All we need now is for some subversive sexuality to be suggested. Po, apparently, is a girl, but the gender of the others remains a mystery.

MORAL INDIGNATION:
SNOWMEN, BUILDERS AND PUBES
(Letters to Ambrose Merton, No. 26, 2001)

Some time ago, I wrote here about moral panics, those featuring alcopops and Teletubbies. Here I want briefly to examine moral indignation: milder than panic because it is more individual and its resonances are focussed, specific and - to a degree - barmy.

Last Christmas, academic Dr Tricia Cusack published a 15-page paper on the image of snowmen on seasonal cards, 'The Christmas Snowman: Carnival and Patriarchy.' The University of Birmingham found the image a patriarchal anachronism or a 'reminder of masculine dominance, ordering and surveillance.' Put into plain language, 'the snowman's location in the semi-public space of the garden or field reinforces a spatial-social system marking women's sphere as the domestic-private and the men's as the commercial-public.' Powerful symbol of greed, nationalism and capitalism, the snowman is also a phallic symbol, though with the passing of the pipe as an accessory, he seems to have become non-smoking (*Daily Mail*, 21 December 2000). Jenny McCartney pointed out that you could change him into a snow-woman by simply putting a different hat on the icy sculpture (*Sunday Telegraph*, 24 December 2000). I think Dr Cusack is several Xmas crackers short of a box and so does author of the popular children's tale *The Snowman*. Raymond Briggs responded with the caustic putdown: "God Almighty, does this woman get paid to say this sort of thing?" However, Dr Cusack could point to the earliest historical reference to snowmen, when, in Brussels in 1511, snow figures of the aristocracy were made and then destroyed as a public statement. (*Sunday Telegraph*, 24 December 2000).

Another figure popular last Christmas, and who also came under fire, was television animation *Bob the Builder*. "Can we fix it?" goes the catchphrase. "Yes we can!" the response. So resolute is Bob's sense of purpose that some professional builders have complained about him in their trade press for giving customers 'unrealistic expectations.' His global dominance has also not gone without a problem. As a profile on him in the *Sunday Telegraph* (17th December 2000) noted: 'The Japanese noted with alarm and suspicion that Bob had only three fingers on each hand. Finger amputation being the speciality of the country's dreaded Yakuza gangsters, the television networks declared that Bob would be "too frightening" for early viewing. Not only that, but buildings in Japan never fell down anyway, so what's the novelty?'

Anything which might corrupt children is fair game for the morally outraged. Again last Christmas, telephone giant BT was under investigation for showing graphic pictures of pubic hair to youngsters. BT Cellnet division was the subject of a probe by the Advertising Standards Authority for the way it promoted mobile phones to youngsters. A controversial advert in *Playstation* magazine showed a girl on a beach wearing a tiny bikini sprouting pubic hair. The caption read: 'Life contains enough embarrassments without your mobile being one.' The authority confirmed that it had launched an investigation into the campaign after seventeen complaints from parents. (*Daily Sport*, 22 December 2000).

Just about anything to do with sex or the human (usually female) body stokes up the Mary Whitehouse gene in the prudish or sublimated, and I could give thousands of examples, but that one should suffice. From dotty dons to bikini lines, via builders' bum cleavages, the blessed outraged, like the poor, will always be with us.

THE RECYCLED BATTERED BEER MAT SAGA

(Letters to Ambrose Merton, No. 26, 2001)

Much in life has deteriorated over the years, even the humble beer mat. Today's examples do not have the same quality as yesteryear and tend not to lie flat. Notwithstanding, there's been a beer mat contemporary legend circulating and being recycled.

First off, chef Phillipe Maupas got fed up with a particular complaining customer, so he took a drip mat, marinated it in wine, coated it with batter and served it to the customer with vegetables as veal. The diner in Paris continued to complain, saying the veal as fine but the greens were below standard. (*Daily Sport*, 19 June 2000). Six days later, readers were told a nameless Parisian chef served a beer mat in batter to a man who moaned about the veal and similarly got roasted when the vegetables were poor. (*Sunday People*, 25 June 2000). The urban legend was picked up again in August where a battered beer mat was gains served as a veal cutlet to a Paris diner. Monsieur Maupas's Christian name had changed slightly to Philipe. (The Sun, 3 August 2000). The rag which published version two thought the story was so good it was worth repeating but, unlike *The Sun*, which spelled the customer's moan as 'whinging,' spelled it as 'whingeing.' (*Sunday People*, 27 August 2000). Perhaps the story also appeared elsewhere in one form or another. The moral of the story seems to be to order veal, but instead of vegetables a side salad.

I used to collect beermats – it's called tegestology – and one I retained shows Prime Minister Harold Wilson reclining on a deckchair in bathing trunks, while on the reverse was printed his famous broadcast statement of 1967 on devaluation: 'That doesn't mean of course that the pound here in Britain – in your pocket or purse or in your bank – has been devalued.' They disappeared very quickly, either through collectors, or withdrawn through political expediency. I heard there was a threatened legal action. Is anyone reading this able to tell me if my beermat is so rare it is going to make me rich – or should I marinate and batter it?

Obituaries of TV chef Keith Floyd reheated the veal/beermat tale and attributed its

genesis to the bibulous gastronome. But even before boozy 'UnPretty Boy Floyd' went to that great restaurant in the sky, I spotted a brief mention where he attributed this legend to himself: 'TV chef Keith Floyd has told how he took revenge on a moaning customer by disguising a beermat as 'escalope of veal' which the man ate. (The Sun, 21 February 2007). Also, remember the US hitmakers of *Yaketty Yak* and *Charlie Brown* fame; they were the Coasters, named after the American term for dripmats. Had they been a UK vocal group, might they have been known as The Beermats?

FREDDIE & AIDS

IDS is a modern-day epidemic whose folklore dates back to 1722 and Daniel Defoe's novel *Journal of the Plague Year*, where a fictional variant of the 'AIDS Mary' or 'Welcome to the World of Aids' highlighted the very real fear of deliberate infection revenge. Other aspects to be covered include origination and transmission, some experts' doubts as to a HIV/AIDS connection, denial in Africa and its seriousness, 'cure' claims and belief it is purely a 'gay plague' bypassing heterosexuals. Nor does it only affect druggies who share needles. Those celebrities who have succumbed to the virus include Rock Hudson, Kenny Everett, Bruce Chatwin ... and Freddie Mercury.

Several days before the official announcement that Queen pop group star Freddie Mercury had died of AIDS, I was told on seemingly good authority that he was actually already dead. Officially the flamboyant bisexual singer was announced dead on 24 November 1991. However, a colleague at the *Hartlepool Mail*, features editor Bernice Saltzer, had been checking a rumour that Mercury had earlier departed this Earth. Various showbiz insiders confirmed it to her, including a member of The Buggles, as I recall. [1] On 23 November a statement had been issued confirming the performer born Farrokh Bulsara was seriously ill. This was the announcement made to the press:

> 'Following the enormous conjecture in the press over the last two weeks, I wish to confirm that I have been tested HIV positive and have AIDS. I felt it correct to keep this information private to date to protect the privacy of those around me. However, the time has come now for my friends and fans around the world to know the truth and I hope that everyone will join with my doctors and all those worldwide in the fight against this terrible disease. My privacy had always been very special to me and I am famous for my lack of interviews. Please understand this policy will continue.'

Mercury had supposedly called Queen's manager, Jim Beach, to his Kensington home to discuss a public statement on 22 November. A little over 24 hours after making the announcement Mercury was declared dead, aged 45, with the official cause being bronchial pneumonia resulting from AIDS. There had been months of speculation after the pomp rock star's weight dropped dramatically and he became a virtual recluse in his west London home. Rumours at the time were fuelled by reports that he was suffering from pneumonia and bouts of blindness. He knew he was HIV positive five years previously but kept it secret. [2] Guitarist Brian May said the band members were told two months before his death of his condition. The 24 November death announcement prompted general speculation that Mercury's body may have been 'lying in state' for some time before the media was informed. [3] *NME* understood a memo was issued to managers of major record retailers before news of Mercury's illness, asking them to reserve space on their shelves for Queen material in the event of the singer's death. The various stories surrounding a possible 'sting' over the re-release of Queen's *Bohemian Rhapsody* make the 'lying in state' sound more plausible. Before his 'official' death big bets were being laid on *Bohemian Rhapsody* being the Christmas chart-topper.

According to writer Rick Sky, Mercury had spent weeks planning his funeral in meticulous detail, being 'a bewildering mixture of flamboyance and secrecy, witnessing the collision of two very different worlds – the modern world of rock music and the ancient world of Zoroastrian religion, in which Mercury had been brought up.' [4] Robed Zoroastrian priests chanted traditional prayers to their god Ahura Mazda for the salvation of the singer's soul; the body lying in an oak coffin, covered in a satin sheet, topped by a single red rose. Commands to stand and sit were uttered in English to the forty mourners, otherwise the 25-minute service was conducted in the ancient Avestars language. Those attending included the singer's parents, Bomi and Jer Bulsara, the remaining members of Queen, musician Elton John and Mary Austin, a long-time girlfriend with whom he lived for many years. His final journey was to Kensal Rise, where he was cremated; the whereabouts of his ashes being now unknown.

As with the 'lying in state' rumour, it is unclear when Mercury was diagnosed with HIV. In the 1970s he had regarded Mary Austin as 'my common-law wife. To me it was a marriage,' but by 1985 he began another long-term relationship with hairdresser Jim Hutton, who he referred to as his husband and who cared for him when he was ill. Hutton was at Freddie's bedside when the singer died, wearing a wedding band that his companion had given him. Hutton claimed Mercury was diagnosed with HIV in the spring of 1987, [5] while Freddie continued to deny this, despite his physical appearance and reports from former lovers in the tabloids. Despite the lack of touring, Queen was at the height of its commercial success. As mentioned, his bandmates had been informed, as for telling his family, Roger Cooke, husband of Freddie's sister Kashmira, told journalist Tim Teeman: "He didn't tell anybody in the family. We gradually became aware he had an illness but we had no idea what it was or how serious it was. Then in August 1990 Kash and I saw a mark on his foot. It was Kaposi's sarcoma (a malignant tumour of the connective tissue often associated with Aids) Kash asked what it was, whether it was getting better. Freddie said: 'You have to understand that what I have is terminal. I'm going to die.' That was it. He didn't say it was AIDS. It didn't register immediately. We were driving home and I put a cassette on, and of all things it was him singing *Who Wants to Live Forever?* That suddenly brought home the significance of what he said." Freddie changed his name to Mercury after his ruling astrological planet. Teeman adds that he held exotic parties 'featuring so one exotic rumour goes, dwarves serving cocaine.' [6] This was expanded by Cosmo Landesman to: 'Would he have thrown one of his infamous parties featuring (or so legend has it) leather-clad dwarfs serving trays of cocaine ...' [7]

Mercury was lauded for his showmanship, but criticised for aspects of his personal life, ranging from his Indian background (he was a Parsi – or Parsee – born in Zanzibar, who grew up there and in India until his mid-teens) to sexual orientation acknowledgement, promiscuity and reluctance to admit his HIV status and shame at contracting AIDS. [8]

References:

1. Paul Screeton, 'Was Freddie Mercury 'lying in state'?,' *Folklore Frontiers*, No. 15, 1992
2. *The Sun*, 4 December 1991
3. *New Musical Express*, 30 November 1991
4. Rick Sky, *The Show Must Go On: The Life of Freddie Mercury*, Citadel Press / Carol Publishing Group, USA, 1994
5. Jim Hutton, *Mercury and Me*, Bloomsbury, 1995
6. *The Knowledge (The Times)*, 2-8 September 2006
7. *The Sunday Times News Review*, 10 September 2006
8. En.wikipedia.org/wiki/Freddie-Mercury

This choice is of general interest to both those admirers of Freddie Mercury, celebrity gossip and folkloric ramifications. This extraordinary rumour has never been properly examined. It formed the introduction to my chapter covering AIDS and other bodily contaminations for my book *Mars Bar & Mushy Peas* (Heart of Albion, 2008). As the scene-setter for the original Chapter Five, it covered various aspects of AIDS, but I found myself both confused as to whether there was even an HIV and AIDS connection, plus how depressing the subject matter was. Hence I dropped it from the planned format, but feel this excerpt worthy of a wider audience. As for Freddie, despite massive media interest around the time of his death, no newspaper to my knowledge even hinted that he might have been dead premature to the official announcement. If true, its first airing was by me in *Folklore Frontiers* and would amount to a minor scoop.

INTERLUDE - THREE
FOLKLORISTS & FORTEANS: FRIENDS OR FOES?

(UnCon 2008, noon, 2 November 2008, Room 2, Fyvie Hall, University of Westminster)

This is the transcript of a talk where I switch briefly from this book's convention of using bold type for any additional commentary to an article, to use the darker type to highlight where I vocalised 'asides' to the audience. Emphases are underscored. I was tempted to put a 'P' in red letters - as I did in my notes – to denote moments where I paused, but desisted.

Good afternoon. This is the first time I have spoken in public for 25 years, so I hope you will forgive any rustiness – or nerves.

Firstly, the title, 'Folklorists and forteans: friends or foes?' Well, that came into my head when [chief organiser and *Fortean Times* editor] David Sutton asked for a title for the programme. Actually it sounds dramatic, but I don't really expect any violence in the hall. It's not as if folklorists and forteans can be compared to mods and rockers, or the British National Party and Anti-Nazi League! Yet it is a fact that there is a quite clear division – as I will demonstrate. That said, I would call myself a lifelong folklorist <u>and</u> an avowed fortean of many years' standing. At this point I would just like to offer my credentials as both folklorist and fortean. Many of you here will also be aware of my role in earth mysteries research, both as editor of *The Ley Hunter* magazine, between 1969 and 1976, and as author of the book *Quicksilver Heritage*. I have also published two books on dragon legends,a volume on the Hartlepool monkey-hanging legend (**I'm a local lad**), a history of ley hunting, and most recently a book on railway folklore, and in September one on urban legends and celebrity. Oh, and I edit and publish *Folklore Frontiers*, a miscellany of mostly contemporary legend. That's Paul Screeton – folklorist.

As Paul Screeton – fortean. Well, one of the reasons you are all sitting here is in some very,

very small part my responsibility – **I suppose**! After Bob Rickard began *Fortean Times* – then called *The News* – in 1973, he later went on record as saying he was encouraged to go ahead by four people: Steve Moore, the late Paul Willis, the late Tony Roberts, and my good self. (**It says so on Wikipedia – so it must be true!**) That said, I've only met Bob once before. Many, many years ago. Away from the mundane pen and paper – or rather word processor and floppy disk – I have had fortean experiences. I've seen ghosts – seen UFOs – even seen a black panther cross a road in Northumberland – but have yet to spontaneously combust! Still, at 62, there's time yet.

Right. Now, I want to get onto the meat of the argument; starting where forteans and folklorists share some small common ground. Although I cover in detail in *Mars Bar & Mushy Peas* what Charles Fort thought of scientists and how he was misunderstood as being anti-science, I was writing for an audience I thought unlikely to be familiar with forteana. But here I shall not go over ground I expect to be familiar to this audience. My point is that – with a few notable exceptions, such as Michael Persinger – people still ignore anomalous data. Yes, ignore – suppress – discredit – or explain away in inadequate fashion genuine events or phenomena which conflict with what orthodoxy has established. Fortean data is largely regarded by mainstream science as being pseudoscience. To be ignored. Even mocked. Also, I need hardly stress, that there is a large body of sceptics – even professional sceptics – ready to pounce upon anything remotely paranormal – or the faintest whiff of the supernatural.

Yet Fort himself urged scepticism. (I deal at length with this in my book, and feel no need to hammer on at the pathetic sceptics – spelt with or without a 'K'!). But before moving on to the folklorists, I want briefly to discuss public perception. Both as to urban myths and – quickly – fortean topics. Here I am going to quote someone else. In a 1997 essay primarily aimed at examining biologist Richard Dawkins' motives and methods, Richard Whittaker was equally harsh towards the fortean viewpoint and its public perception. He wrote:

> 'For all the leaps made in public understanding and professional acceptance, fortean research has a terrible reputation. Whereas the traditional scientific community is seen by many people in the general public as a cult of methodology, forteana is seen as a belief system. In reality, forteana is defined not by how the researcher defines a topic but instead by the topic covered. Researchers, no matter what their expertise, are seen as a legion of woolly-hatted nit-wits. Even debunkers run the risk of being seen as intelligent people, sidetracked into unwinnable debate with crackpots.'

And that's from an insider – a fortean supporter. So, have things changed?

Certainly contemporary legend research has come a long way in the past few decades. However, judging by submissions to the prestigious Katherine Briggs Award, the Folklore Society itself sees urban belief tales as something crude – nasty - - brutish – short – and above all to be marginalised or better still ignored. **Sound familiar?** If mainstream folklore research has the air of aristocratic, blueblood breeding and upstairs manners, urban myth has about it the dank downstairs atmosphere of a slavering, bastard child, chained to the walls of the cellar or dungeon. In popular perception, folklore is all about Robin Hood's derring-do, lowly Dick Whittington becoming Lord Mayor, modern folk in mediaeval costumes, harvest festival (**actually quite modern itself**) and so on. Folklore – in the public's eye – should not be about kidney thefts – masturbation and biscuits contests – or sparkling glitter welcoming the probing gynaecologist!

If I seem to have strayed somewhat, I have at least laid the foundations for my main point (**and got a few laughs**). The point being the relationship between folklorists and forteans: friends or foes?

I want now to give a second quote. It could just as easily come from Charles Fort himself – or the musings of a contemporary legends collector. This is the quote:

> 'When I come upon the unconventional repeating, in times and places far apart, I feel – even though I have no absolute standards to judge by – that I am outside the field of the ordinary liar.

In fact, it is Charles Fort, in *Wild Talents*, but my point is that such repetition, across a geographical distribution, could be of frog falls or equally reports of circus elephants crushing small cars. Or cases of spontaneous human combustion as opposed to philandering husbands' cars being sold for a song by aggrieved widows. (I record in my book how recently radio disc-jockey Tim Shaw told glamour model Jodie Marsh he wanted to marry her – **actually probably just wanted a quick shag**. Anyway, Tim's real wife was at home listening. This was the last straw for her. So she immediately put his beloved £100,000 sports car on eBay and sold it for a fiver (or 50p, versions differ)! **Serves him right!**

In reality, both folklorists and forteans are collecting material whose tellers are reporting what they believe to be true. That they are separate from Fort's 'hypothetical liar.' That is not to say that Fort took everyone's report at face value. He was not that naive. He was well aware of the dubious provenance of many entries in his collection – regarding certain assertions as unlikely. What Fort said about this was quite blunt. He simply stated – 'I offer the data. Suit yourself.' (**Can't speak plainer than that!**)

Similar collections of urban myths – particularly the more popular, non-academic ones – offer a similar take-it-or-leave-it view towards veracity. You either believe the allegedly authenticating names, places and dates – or not. Folklorists speak of 'migratory anecdotes' and see the greater the number – and wider the distribution – as evidence of falsity and narrative repetition. Conversely, forteans assume correlating data – separated over time and distance – to be indicative of genuine phenomena occurring. I must stress this. This is the crux of the difference between folklorists and forteans. Let's get this crystal clear. For folklorists repetition equals falsity. For forteans repetition equals veracity. I'll expand on this to make my case even more crystal clear.

Generally, fortean reports of events focus upon a human witness – someone who experiences something anomalous in a natural – let's say normal – setting. For forteans this may be an apeman, lake monster, UFO, weeping statue or just weird coincidence. In urban legend, the credible witness is generally replaced by the ubiquitous friend-of-a-friend (hence such stories are often called foaftales – that is, friend-of-a-friend tales). In these stories, the friend-of-a-friend might have brought back an exotic miniature dog from abroad, which upon being taken to the vet's is identified as a Mexican sewer rat. Or the foaf's grannie dies while the family is overseas on holiday, so they wrap her up in a carpet, tie it to the luggage rack, and while taking a café break, their camper van is stolen. Or the teller's uncle's cleaner's butcher goes to a brothel, only to be shown into a bedroom where he finds – to his surprise – his wife or daughter. (**Time permitting, I will return to this theme at the end of the talk**). Or there's the milkman's sister's nephew, waking up in a blood-stained bath in Bangkok, to see an instruction on the tiles – 'Dial 911. We've removed your kidney.' *Fortean Times* itself published an anatomy – **kidney ... anatomy** – of this unsavoury rumour in 2000. (**Issue 138, in fact**).

But should *Fortean Times* have printed this – **and as a cover story at that!** – and other contemporary legends? Should it not stick to ghosts - flying saucers – Blessed Virgin Mary encounters – rather than AIDS Mary lore? **I only ask**! I'm sure Messrs Sutton, Rickard and Sieveking can think of good reasons. They could easily, in fact, point to contemporary legend magazines themselves reporting fortean events! For instance, *Dear Mr Thoms*, between 1987 and 1994, covered such forteana as Crying Boy paintings, anomalous big cats, satanic child abuse, hauntings and contemporary horse-ripping. (**Ripping yarns, for sure!**) When *Dear Mr Thoms* morphed into *Letters to Ambrose Merton* in 1994 (**odd titles for magazines – too complicated to explain here**) it continued this procession of damned fortean data – Loch Ness Monster, moon landing conspiracy, Angel of Mons, UFOs, Turin Shroud, Rosslyn Chapel and dowsing. Oh, and even, penis snatching and penis-shrinking panics.

Chroniclers, in four books of urban myths, Phil Healey and Rick Glanvill, in their first paperback, also had a collection of real alien but naturalised wildlife examples as if they were imaginary – coypus in East Anglia, Peak District wallabies and my favourites, the scorpions at Ongar railway station – but spoiled it with escaped pet crocodiles near power station outlets on the River Trent and a two-headed sheep at Windscale. But not all contemporary legend collectors are as frivolous as Healey and Glanvill – or as popular – **or maybe as awash with dosh!** Anyway, back with the 'friend or foe?' question in my talk title, as well as my personally having a foot in both camps, so has Thomas Bullard – Eddie to his friends (**and maybe foes?**). I say foes, as he is controversial, and will doubtless have made enemies. Bullard is a folklorist at the University of Indiana at Bloomington; where he received his folklore doctorate. However, Bullard combines his professional study of contemporary folklore with research into UFO-related abductions. Here he has concluded that a lack of variation in structure, or content, of abductees' narratives, suggests an underlying core of real experience. Bullard compared his research and findings with those of another folklorist, David Hufford. Hufford, in his book *The Terror That Comes in the Night*, featured what are known as 'old hag' experiences. These being of 'supernatural assault.' Not urban myths, but supposedly true accounts of nighttime assailants.

Another academic, Bill Ellis, of Pennsylvania State University, has delved deeply into the cattle mutilation subject. Ellis, in *Contemporary Legend* magazine, even claimed folklorists –

and I quote – 'are perhaps best equipped to participate' in anomalous events research. **Well – are they?** It might be beneficial that folklore academics are aware of forteana, and actively pursuing research, but my examples certainly seem to suggest that the participants have blurred the categories. <u>**Perhaps I am the only one seeing things so black and white**</u>. To be packing urban myths in one box. Packing fortean events in another. Perhaps there is – or should be – genuine crossover.

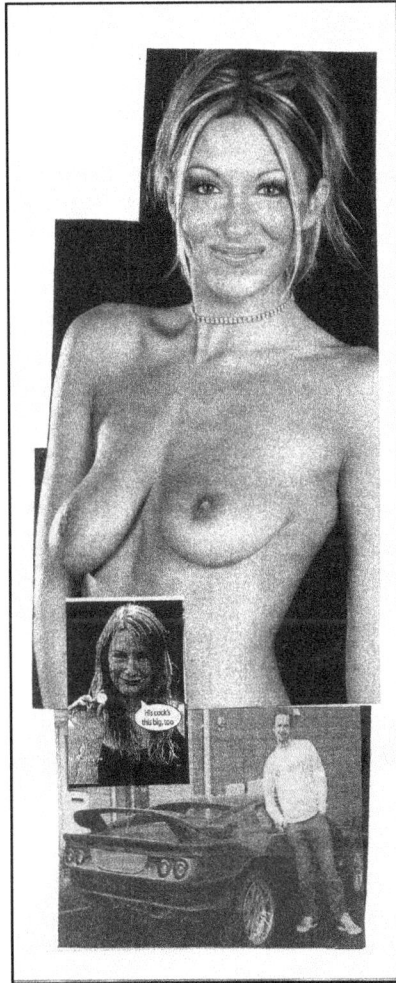

A TRIANGLE OF SORTS. Tim Shaw (lower) fancied Jodie Marsh (top) which did not please his wife (centre).

Remember Tim Shaw and Jodie Marsh? When Tim's wife sold his £100,000 car for a fiver/50p she was unwittingly enacting ostension. Ostension is a folklorists' tern whereby a well-known urban myth springs to life. (I have a whole chapter on this, so will be brief here). In this case the familiar belief tale is known as 'The Philanderer's Porsche' and has a long pedigree. Traditionally a rich husband runs off with his secretary and contacts his wife asking her to sell his posh car – and forward the proceeds. Some lucky buyer gets the car for a song. My point being that there can be a crossover from myth to truth – or rather actuality. So maybe it is false to see a great divide between fortean events and urban myths. Yet my personal feeling is to keep them separate. However, if everyone was like me, there would be no professional folklorists such as Bullard, Hufford and Ellis researching forteana. Or for that matter, if I had specialised only in either folklore or forteana, I would not be able to paint a coherent picture of the differences between urban myths and fortean events.

So, just to recap. Folklorists and forteans respond in diametrically-opposed directions to the same sort of source material. Forteans will grant that it may be true because there has been such a great accumulation of strange occurrences – **also known as 'weird shit happens!'** Folklorists will vote that it is unlikely to be true, because urban myths are – by definition – not true. Forteans stand accused of too much naïvety – credulity – concerning legend-like reports. Folklorists stand accused of too much obtuseness – **stubborn buggers** – as they have already decided stories are just that: stories. There again, what is it that constitutes valid evidence, or for that matter truth? **Oh, dear, I feel the leaden weight of philosophy coming on....**

Finally, I suggest that an understanding of contemporary legends, their nature, function, and meaning, should be a requisite part of the modern fortean's critical armoury. Equally, folklorists display scant familiarity with standard fortean texts or, for that matter, the essential *Fortean Times*.

Analysis is crucial for serious students of both anomalous data and those friend-of-a-friend tales of less than believable human behaviour. Also, that the caveats of tentative and temporary acceptance, and benign scepticism, should apply to both. Folklorists and forteans – friends or foes? – let the dialogue begin.

[Thunderous applause? Ten-minute standing ovation? Knickers thrown on stage? In my dreams...]

Actually, not quite finished yet. You may recall, I said earlier that if there was time I would return to the husband or father in the brothel finding wife or daughter. I seem to have that time. So, hands up who's been to a brothel? (No one) (Yes! Wife or daughter there?)

[To my astonishment a woman put her hand up. Flummoxed, I asked her to enlighten the audience with the circumstances, but she had misheard me, and I moved swiftly on...]

I wasn't too sure where to start here. But *Fortean Times* fortuitously catalogued four – yes, four – in a single 2002 issue. (No. 156). In fact, *Fortean Times* has covered this topic in seven issues. In issue 156 an anonymous commentator wrote, and I quote:

'The following tales sound like variations on an urban legend , but *F.T.* would like to point out, yet again, that this doesn't mean that some of them didn't actually happen … Folklorists use the term ostension, when such legends are acted out and become news.'

So, that's F.T.'s justification. .No doubt,at some point, some bloke has been mortified to find his little princess or loving spouse about to offer him her charms for £50 in a knocking-shop. Of course, this may all seem like going off at a tangent, but it's not really. I have raised this particular and familiar modern folklore motif because it has displayed an equally familiar fortean trait – cultural tracking. I'm sure most of you are aware of how this is probably best exemplified as to how UFOs have mimicked mankind's advances in science and technology **(let's leave out abductions, please!)**. And as for *belles de jour*, it similarly reflects our changes in society and relationships. What I mean is, how we enter into illicit relationships – **(not me personally, by the way)** – and how we use technology for unsavoury clandestine trysts.

The earliest versions are the simplest. From 1992, I have a randy businessman whose wife refused to make love, so he storms out and checks into a local hotel – in Tel Aviv, Israel – and orders a call girl for a steamy sex romp. However, the gorgeous hooker turns out to be his 27-year-old wife Rachel. **(She seems to have got to the hotel in double quick time, but urban myths were never designed for such doubting analysis)**. *The Sun* newspaper, also in 1992, mentioned a cheating Polish husband, visiting a German brothel, while his wife was suppos-edly 'staying with friends.' Yes, by a remarkable coincidence his wife was working there. Two weeks later, the *Daily Sport* named businessman Stanislaw Kania, a Pole visiting a brothel in Dresden – and, yes again, the alluring charms were those of his wife. Same Polish couple in both papers? Anyway, variation was beginning to creep in. The brothel became more exclusive, a call-girl agency was introduced, and husbands using lonely hearts columns – only to find replies from their respective **(though hardly respectable)** wives, such as Teresa and Rowland Charlesworth suing each other for divorce in Jacksonville, USA.

Meanwhile, the wife in the brothel kept turning up – but stories becoming more detailed. For instance, in 1993, although the punter was not named, we learn that while choosing from an album of vice girls, he spotted a photo of his missus, and a list of her specialities. He went berserk and smashed up the brothel. **(Ironic really – he was a bricklayer.).** Police in Torella de Lombardi, Italy, arrested him for damages. **No mention of what the cops thought of oper-ating a brothel**. And the *Daily Sport* must have thought the Stanislaw Kania tale from 1992 was so good that they reprinted it as new news in 2001. But it was not only the 'red tops' which were printing such tales. In 2002, the *Sunday Telegraph* wrote of an Israeli man who hired a prostitute. When she arrived at his Red Sea hotel he had a heart attack – the hooker was his daughter. *Fortean Times* also carried this urban legend presented as news in an Israeli newspaper. And that same Israeli paper was monitored in 2003 by *F.T.* with a story of a woman whose husband replied to her anonymous lonely hearts advert.

By 2005, *F.T.* was reporting a married couple flirting on an internet chatroom, with divorce following their Jordan bus station assignation. In that Jordan example, the man was named as

Adnan and the woman Sana. Surely it was more than coincidence that the next variation to appear in *Fortean Times* had the husband and wife also named as Adnan and Sana. However, this 2007 urban belief tale was set in central Bosnia, but – being acted out online – could have been anywhere... **I suppose**. Back with that 2002 *Fortean Times* round-up of four examples I mentioned earlier, it featured:

*   A man encountering his wife in a red-light district.
*   An ex-wife, of only a month, encountered through a computer dating agency.
*   And two internet chat website encounters.

The tale/motif had truly entered the Facebook era. The geography having moved from seedy hotels, whorehouses and red-light districts to street-walking in cyberspace. Forteana – or at least *Fortean Times* – seems to want this particular myth to evolve and still be believed. That old standby ostension being invoked. As for folklore, I have so far seen no analysis. Even that doyen of urban myths, the American professor Jan Harold Brunvand, seems to have hardly noticed it. The nearest he comes to discussion in this area is to relate a version of that old chestnut 'The Stuck Couple.' Teenagers, making out on the backseat of a car at a drive-in movie find they cannot get separated. To cut the story short – film is stopped, lights come on, cops summoned, sheriff arrives, recognises girl as his daughter. **Oh, dear!** Brunvand has another version where cops discover a girl having under-age sex in a tent. The boy bribes the police to keep quiet in exchange for the girl offering them sexual favours. When it's the second cop's turn, he discovers the little minx is ... his little princess. Yes, all rather sordid – and somewhat far-fetched. On that note – high – or low – I think we can safely close that topic.

It only leaves me to sum up. In essence, I have pointed to differences in approach by forteans and folklorists. Friends or foes? As I said, previous to this digression about the husband or father finding his wife or daughter in the house of ill repute, let the dialogue begin – or at least we can agree to disagree. Surely friends not foes?

RELAXING AFTER IT'S ALL OVER. Paul Screeton (foreground) outside a pub near the venue. Others present include *Fortean Times* editor David Sutton (left of Paul's right shoulder) and *F.T.* sub-editor Owen Whiteoak (in anorak).

This talk was based upon my chapter regarding the different approaches to data between folklorists and forteans, which I examined in my book *Mars Bar & Mushy Peas*. Respected author Nick Redfern, reviewing the book, singled out for special praise the chapter which formed the basis of my talk. He wrote: ' ...an excellent section on forteana and Charles Fort himself (this chapter, alone, should be firmly digested by anyone and everyone with an interest in urban-legend, the world of the unexplained and the development of stories, tales and mythology).'

A woman in the audience brought up the subject of ostension, with particular reference to 'Canoeman' John Darwin, who faked his own death by abandoning his kayak. She knew I also came from Seaton Carew. <u>Fort</u>uitously, her question gave me just the opportunity to launch into my prepared vindication of ostension, as brilliantly summarised by Bob Rickard. Bob stated:

'No matter how ancient these stories are, sooner or later the god of circumstance arranges for it to happen just so. Then it is recorded as a factoid or seemingly true incident. Orthodox folklorists will have none of this, preferring to believe that every reported occurrence is fictitious and any documentation is part of the necessary apparatus of making it seem factual. As forteans we are interested in these opposite currents; one making the imaginary real, balanced by another mythologising facts.'

Well, I couldn't have put it better myself. Friends or foes? I'll just shake hands with myself.

LAST WORDS

After publishing three books in six years my writing career has had something of a renaissance, so a retrospective such as this seemed timely. If nothing else, it proves I've been active for a long time and been around a few blocks – history, archaeology, natural history, geography, traditional folklore, earth mysteries, flying saucers, cryptozoology, ferroequinology, tavernology, breastology, contemporary legend, not to mention a few writing blocks. In making selections for this compilation, I was assisted by having compiled a database of my writings in 2005 and printed it on my birthday. It was for my own reference, but for a modest fee it has been available to the public. The title came quite quickly, *FLAGONS, DRAGONS and WAGONS*, to reflect my interests of pubs, folklore and railways. But here's the fortean bit:

> '... rocket scientist and ceremonial magician John Whiteside Parsons had also used these three capitalised words in one sentence. Writing in 1943, a poem printed in the *Oriflamme Journal of the O.T.O.*, notorious Jack Parsons included the prophetic line: *Each wagon a dragon, each beer mug a flagon that brims with ambrosial wine'* Weird or what!? (Douglas Chapman, 'Jack Parsons: Sorcereous Scientist,' *Strange Magazine*, No. 6, 1990); *Folklore Frontiers*, No. 55, 2007)'

At the risk of indulging my ego and boring the reader, my oeuvre as listed here has included four novels (all unpublished); a play (a reading of part was semi-public); humorous fiction (*Going Places, Newcastle Life*, etc.); children's stories (45 published); poem (in *Stardock*); articles in all the newspapers I worked for, plus regional glossies. My journalism has been prolific and ranges from garden show results to front page splashes, and I even 'went back to the shopfloor' 2000 to 2002 as a local correspondent, making the front page with my first and last copy filed! Nose for a good story and a consummate professional journalist.

Articles published have been across dozens of magazines (some pieces duplicated in more than one), including general folklore (31); contemporary legend (52); forteana (43); ufology (17); shamanism (5); dragonlore (8); earth mysteries (64, discounting columns); rock music

(13); railway enthusiasm (43); and modern art (6). There were columns: 'Strange Northumbria,' in *The Mail*, Hartlepool (26) with six duplicated in *The Echo*, Sunderland; 'The Long Man of Wilmington,' *The Ley Hunter* (46); 'Pub Spy,' *The Mail* (200); 'Countryside Concerns,' *The Mail* (43); natural history, general history and cycling; plus numerous travel pieces in *The Mail*, including a colour series on my mission to dig up potatoes planted on an Outer Hebrides island by Prince Charles!; and reams of book reviews, 19 of which formed articles; 'Discdate' in *The Mail*, from which I extracted 'Star Profile' pieces, photocopied them and these were compiled into three self-published booklets, which have been offered to and bought by the public – *The Ballad of Marianne Faithfull, Sizzling Cher and More Breast Sellers* and *Close Your Eyes and Think of* [Natasha] *England* – my 'Rock Trilogy.' There was material extracted from unpublished books: *The Living Stones* (17), *Rumours* (7), *Tits Out for the Lads* (1) and *Celebrity Tits Out for the Lads* (1). Miscellaneous writing has also included self-publicity pieces (13) and numerous letters to various publications (28). Apart from two book forewords and one appendix, my photographs have appeared in a rail enthusiasts' photo location guide and there is a railway reminiscence and an EM book foreword available on the internet. Some figures here are low approximations as I don't make recording my prolific output a fetish (nor count contributions to internet forums).

So thank you for reading my anthology. All writers ply their trade and craft essentially for self-satisfaction (even the hardest-headed hack will grudgingly accept that definition), but penmanship should be more than a vainglorious pursuit if the words are to be deemed worthy of publication and appreciated by a readership; hopefully there is the pleasure of reader response and the satisfaction of being enjoyed and educative, and if the writer is lucky even some small financial remuneration. So, raise your glass to that unsung hero, the toiling author.

Cheers!

THE WORLD'S WEIRDEST PUBLISHING COMPANY
ANIMALS & MEN
ISSUES 16-20
THE JOURNAL OF THE CENTRE FOR FORTEAN ZOOLOGY
NEW HORIZONS
Edited by Jon Downes
BIG CATS
LOOSE IN BRITAIN
PREDATOR DEATHMATCH
WITH ILLUSTRATIONS BY ANTHONY WALLIS
Jonathan Downes and Richard Freeman
FOREWORD BY Dr. KARL SHUKER
STRANGELYSTRANGE
Tales from Travels
CARL PORTMAN
THE COLLECTED POEMS
Dr Karl P.N. Shuker
an anthology of writings by
ANDY ROBERTS

HOW TO START A PUBLISHING EMPIRE

Unlike most mainstream publishers, we have a non-commercial remit, and our mission statement claims that "we publish books because they deserve to be published, not because we think that we can make money out of them". Our motto is the Latin Tag *Pro bona causa facimus* (we do it for good reason), a slogan taken from a children's book *The Case of the Silver Egg* by the late Desmond Skirrow.

WIKIPEDIA: "The first book published was in 1988. *Take this Brother may it Serve you Well* was a guide to Beatles bootlegs by Jonathan Downes. It sold quite well, but was hampered by very poor production values, being photocopied, and held together by a plastic clip binder. In 1988 A5 clip binders were hard to get hold of, so the publishers took A4 binders and cut them in half with a hacksaw. It now reaches surprisingly high prices second hand.

The production quality improved slightly over the years, and after 1999 all the books produced were ringbound with laminated colour covers. In 2004, however, they signed an agreement with Lightning Source, and all books are now produced perfect bound, with full colour covers."

Until 2010 all our books, the majority of which are/were on the subject of mystery animals and allied disciplines, were published by `CFZ Press`, the publishing arm of the Centre for Fortean Zoology (CFZ), and we urged our readers and followers to draw a discreet veil over the books that we published that were completely off topic to the CFZ.

However, in 2010 we decided that enough was enough and launched a second imprint, `Fortean Words` which aims to cover a wide range of non animal-related esoteric subjects. Other imprints will be launched as and when we feel like it, however the basic ethos of the company remains the same: Our job is to publish books and magazines that we feel are worth publishing, whether or not they are going to sell. Money is, after all - as my dear old Mama once told me - a rather vulgar subject, and she would be rolling in her grave if she thought that her eldest son was somehow in `trade`.

Luckily, so far our tastes have turned out not to be that rarified after all, and we have sold far more books than anyone ever thought that we would, so there is a moral in there somewhere...

Jon Downes,
Woolsery, North Devon
July 2010

Other Books in Print

CFZ Yearbook 2011 edited by Jonathan Downes
Karl Shuker's Alien Zoo by Shuker, Dr Karl P.N
Tetrapod Zoology Book One by Naish, Dr Darren
The Mystery Animals of Ireland by Gary Cunningham and Ronan Coghlan
Monsters of Texas by Gerhard, Ken
The Great Yokai Encyclopaedia by Freeman, Richard
NEW HORIZONS: Animals & Men *issues 16-20 Collected Editions Vol. 4* by Downes, Jonathan
A Daintree Diary -
Tales from Travels to the Daintree Rainforest in tropical north Queensland, Australia by Portman, Carl
Strangely Strange but Oddly Normal by Roberts, Andy
Centre for Fortean Zoology Yearbook 2010 by Downes, Jonathan
Predator Deathmatch by Molloy, Nick
Star Steeds and other Dreams by Shuker, Karl
CHINA: A Yellow Peril? by Muirhead, Richard
Mystery Animals of the British Isles: The Western Isles by Vaudrey, Glen
Giant Snakes - Unravelling the coils of mystery by Newton, Michael
Mystery Animals of the British Isles: Kent by Arnold, Neil
Centre for Fortean Zoology Yearbook 2009 by Downes, Jonathan
CFZ EXPEDITION REPORT: Russia 2008 by Richard Freeman *et al*, Shuker, Karl (fwd)
Dinosaurs and other Prehistoric Animals on Stamps - A Worldwide catalogue by Shuker, Karl P. N
Dr Shuker's Casebook by Shuker, Karl P.N
The Island of Paradise - chupacabra UFO crash retrievals,
and accelerated evolution on the island of Puerto Rico by Downes, Jonathan
The Mystery Animals of the British Isles: Northumberland and Tyneside by Hallowell, Michael J
Centre for Fortean Zoology Yearbook 1997 by Downes, Jonathan (Ed)
Centre for Fortean Zoology Yearbook 2002 by Downes, Jonathan (Ed)
Centre for Fortean Zoology Yearbook 2000/1 by Downes, Jonathan (Ed)
Centre for Fortean Zoology Yearbook 1998 by Downes, Jonathan (Ed)
Centre for Fortean Zoology Yearbook 2003 by Downes, Jonathan (Ed)

In the wake of Bernard Heuvelmans by Woodley, Michael A

CFZ EXPEDITION REPORT: Guyana 2007 by Richard Freeman *et al*, Shuker, Karl (fwd)

Centre for Fortean Zoology Yearbook 1999 by Downes, Jonathan (Ed)

Big Cats in Britain Yearbook 2008 by Fraser, Mark (Ed)

Centre for Fortean Zoology Yearbook 1996 by Downes, Jonathan (Ed)

THE CALL OF THE WILD - Animals & Men issues 11-15

Collected Editions Vol. 3 by Downes, Jonathan (ed)

Ethna's Journal by Downes, C N

Centre for Fortean Zoology Yearbook 2008 by Downes, J (Ed)

DARK DORSET -Calendar Custome by Newland, Robert J

Extraordinary Animals Revisited by Shuker, Karl

MAN-MONKEY - In Search of the British Bigfoot by Redfern, Nick

Dark Dorset Tales of Mystery, Wonder and Terror by Newland, Robert J and Mark North

Big Cats Loose in Britain by Matthews, Marcus

MONSTER! - The A-Z of Zooform Phenomena by Arnold, Neil

The Centre for Fortean Zoology 2004 Yearbook by Downes, Jonathan (Ed)

The Centre for Fortean Zoology 2007 Yearbook by Downes, Jonathan (Ed)

CAT FLAPS! Northern Mystery Cats by Roberts, Andy

Big Cats in Britain Yearbook 2007 by Fraser, Mark (Ed)

BIG BIRD! - Modern sightings of Flying Monsters by Gerhard, Ken

THE NUMBER OF THE BEAST - Animals & Men issues 6-10

Collected Editions Vol. 1 by Downes, Jonathan (Ed)

IN THE BEGINNING - Animals & Men *issues 1-5 Collected Editions Vol. 1* by Downes, Jonathan

STRENGTH THROUGH KOI - They saved Hitler's Koi and other stories by Downes, Jonathan

The Smaller Mystery Carnivores of the Westcountry by Downes, Jonathan

CFZ EXPEDITION REPORT: Gambia 2006 by Richard Freeman *et al*, Shuker, Karl (fwd)

The Owlman and Others by Jonathan Downes

The Blackdown Mystery by Downes, Jonathan

Big Cats in Britain Yearbook 2006 by Fraser, Mark (Ed)

Fragrant Harbours - Distant Rivers by Downes, John T

Only Fools and Goatsuckers by Downes, Jonathan

Monster of the Mere by Jonathan Downes

Dragons:More than a Myth by Freeman, Richard Alan

Granfer's Bible Stories by Downes, John Tweddell

Monster Hunter by Downes, Jonathan

Fortean Words

The Centre for Fortean Zoology has for several years led the field in Fortean publishing. CFZ Press is the only publishing company specialising in books on monsters and mystery animals. CFZ Press has published more books on this subject than any other company in history and has attracted such well known authors as Andy Roberts, Nick Redfern, Michael Newton, Dr Karl Shuker, Neil Arnold, Dr Darren Naish, Jon Downes, Ken Gerhard and Richard Freeman.

Now CFZ Press are launching a new imprint. Fortean Words is a new line of books dealing with Fortean subjects other than cryptozoology, which is - after all - the subject the CFZ are best known for. Fortean Words is being launched with a spectacular multi-volume series called *Haunted Skies* which covers British UFO sightings between 1940 and 2010. Former policeman John Hanson and his long-suffering partner Dawn Holloway have compiled a peerless library of sighting reports, many that have not been made public before.

Other forthcoming books include a look at the Berwyn Mountains UFO case by renowned Fortean Andy Roberts and a series of books by transatlantic researcher Nick Redfern.

CFZ Press are dedicated to maintaining the fine quality of their works with Fortean Words.. New authors tackling new subjects will always be encouraged, and we hope that our books will continue to be as ground breaking and popular as ever.